Cat (Burgess/Carp)

Burgess-Carpenter Library
406 Butler
Columbia University
New York, N. Y. 10027

D1571323

ARTHURIAN LITERATURE

II

Contents of previous volumes

I

Chrétien de Troyes and England
Constance Bullock-Davies

The *Vera Historia de Morte Arthuri* and
its place in Arthurian Tradition
Richard Barber

An Edition of the *Vera Historia de Morte Arthuri*
Michael Lapidge

Malory and the Archaic Mind
Derek Brewer

From Logres to Carbonek: the Arthuriad of
Charles Williams
Karl Heinz Göller

ISSN 0261-9946

WITHDRAWN

Title page of *Kairo-kō* (1906) by Hashiguchi Goyo

Arthurian Literature II

EDITED BY RICHARD BARBER

Advisory editors
Tony Hunt
Toshiyuki Takamiya

WITHDRAWN

D.S.BREWER · ROWMAN & LITTLEFIELD

Published by D. S. Brewer
240 Hills Road, Cambridge
an imprint of Boydell & Brewer Ltd
PO Box 9, Woodbridge, Suffolk IP12 3DF
and Rowman and Littlefield
81 Adams Drive, Totowa, NJ 07512, USA

ISBN 0 85991 095 4

US ISBN 0 8476 7196 8

British Library Cataloguing in Publication Data
Arthurian literature.
2
1. Arthur, King   2. English literature —
History and criticism
I. Barber, Richard
820.9'351   PR149.A79

Burgess

PN

685

.A68

2

Burgess/Carp

83- 68906

CONTENTS

List of plates   vii
Preface   viii

I   Geoffrey of Monmouth and Gildas   1
    Neil Wright

II The Round Table: Ideal, Fiction, Reality   41
    Beate Schmolke-Hasselmann

III The Tradition of the Troubadours and the Treatment of the
    Love Theme in Chrétien de Troyes' *Chevalier au Lion*   76
    Fanni Bogdanow

IV *Kairo-kō: A Dirge*   92
    Toshiyuka Takamiya and Andrew Armour

V   Twentieth-Century Arthurian Literature: an annotated
    bibliography   127
    Mary Wildman

VI *Update*: Additional Manuscript Evidence for the
    Vera Historia de Morte Arthuri   163
    Michael Lapidge

LIST OF PLATES

Title page of *Kairo-kō* (1906) by Hashiguchi Goyo   frontispiece

The Round Table: Ideal, Fiction, Reality   between pages 56 and 57

1   The Modena archivolt
    (photo Richard Barber)

2   The Last Supper from the 'Augustine Gospels'
    Corpus Christi College MS 286 f.125
    (Reproduced by permission of the Master and Fellows of Corpus
    Christi College, Cambridge)

3   Galahad comes to take his place at the Siege Perilous
    Bibliothèque Nationale MS F.fr 343, f.3

4   Arthur at table
    Bibliothéque Nationale MS F. fr 776. f.374

5   Arthur at table
    Universitäts bibliothek Bonn MS S, 526, f.406

6   A Plantagenet king at table
    Public Record Office MS E36/284 f.1v

7   World map
    Bibliothèque Ste Geneviève MS 782, f.374
    (Photographic Giraudon)

8   Arthur at the Round Table
    Leiden Universiteitsbibliotheek MS Ltk 573, f.1

9   Arthur at the Round Table
    Fresco from Schloss Runkelstein illustrating the romance *Garel*

10 Arthur on a dais, surrounded by knights
    Bayerischer Staatsbibliothek, Munich, MS Cgm 19 f.49v

11 The Winchester Round Table
    (photo British Tourist Authority)

12 The mysteries of the Grail
    Bibliothèque de l'Arsenal MS 5218, f.88

13 The Siege Perilous
    Woodcut from Vérard's *Lancelot*, Paris 1494

Kairo-kō: A Dirge

Illustration for *Kairo-kō* by Nakamura Fusetsu   facing p.125

vii

PREFACE

The first volume of *Arthurian Literature* gave some indication of the range of Arthurian studies, in that its timespan ran from Chrétien de Troyes to Charles Williams, but this second volume casts its net even wider, taking us from Gildas at the very roots of Arthurian tradition to one of its most exotic off-shoots, Sōseki's *Kairo-kō: A Dirge*, a remarkable Japanese version of the story of Elaine. And the liveliness of modern creative writing based on the Arthurian legend is reflected in a valuable bibliography of twentieth century original treatments of Arthurian themes.

At the end of each volume, when appropriate, a section called *Update* will be included. This will provide a forum for further comments on themes from earlier volumes: in the present case, a new and very useful manuscript text of the *Vera Historia de Morte Arthuri* has come to light and is described by Michael Lapidge. This section will also list important reviews (if any!) of earlier volumes.

The editor is most grateful to the advisory editors for their help and support, and to Mr P.J.C.Field for drawing his attention to Miss Wildman's bibliography.

RICHARD BARBER
June 1982

I

Geoffrey of Monmouth and Gildas

Neil Wright

The *De Excidio Britanniae*[1] of the sixth-century British ecclesiastic Gildas is a text of great importance. Although the Middle Ages bestowed the epithet *historicus* upon Gildas, his work is not primarily a history. His aim is to castigate the folly of his people and, in particular, the sins of the kings and clergy. As an introduction to his attacks on these two classes, he includes a narrative of British history from the Roman invasions down to his own day. His concerns, however, are as much literary as historical. The story is told impressionistically and with many vivid touches of language;[2] like Classical historians, Gildas believed that history could teach, and he paints a pessimistic picture of British history from which moral lessons could be drawn. As a consequence the *De Excidio Britanniae* is both the unique product of a sixth-century Briton and a powerful work of literature bearing the stamp of a forceful personality.

In the eighth century the value of the *De Excidio Britanniae* was fully realised by the Anglo-Saxon historian Bede. Large sections of Book I of Bede's *Historia Ecclesiastica*[3] are reworkings of passages from Gildas, who was Bede's only British source for the sub-Roman period.

Among the Anglo-Norman writers of the twelfth century the

---

1 Ed. M.Winterbottom, *Gildas: the Ruin of Britain and other documents* (Chichester, 1978); all quotations follow Winterbottom's text.
2 On Gildas's Latin style, see F.Kerlouégan, 'Le latin du *De Excidio Britanniae* de Gildas', in *Christianity in Britain 300-700*, edd. M.W.Barley and R.P.C. Hanson (Leicester, 1968), pp.151-76.
3 Ed. C.Plummer, *Baedae opera historica* (2 vols, Oxford, 1896); Plummer signals Bede's use of Gildas by the use of italic type. Bede's borrowings have been examined from an historical perspective by M.Miller, 'Bede's use of Gildas', *English Historical Review* 90 (1975), 241-61. A convenient, if incomplete, hand-list of references to Gildas in later writers is given by H. Williams, *Gildas*, Cymmrodorion Record Series 3, (two parts only, 1899, 1901), II, pp.415-20.

situation was different. Bede's great successor William of Malmesbury in the *Gesta Regum*[4] describes Gildas as '*neque insulsus neque infacetus historicus*'; William, however, nowhere quotes Gildas directly and only uses the *De Excidio Britanniae* at second-hand through Bede. Moreover, William was familiar with the *Historia Britonum*[5] which is most frequently attributed to Gildas by manuscripts of the period.[6] It may well be, therefore, that William knew Gildas only as the author of *Historia Britonum*.[7] Certainly, despite his avowed approval of Gildas's worth as an historian, William does not show the familiarity with the *De Excidio Britanniae* which was characteristic of his predecessor Bede.

Later in the same century Gerald of Wales also passes favourable judgement on Gildas, calling him *imitabilis* and his work *veram magis historiam quam ornatam*.[8] In Gerald's case, we can be sure that he is referring to the *De Excidio Britanniae*, since in the same passage he describes Gildas as *excidiumque gentis suae deplorans potius quam describens*; the phrase recalls the opening sentence of *De Excidio Britanniae* 1, *in hac epistula quicquid deflendo potius quam declamando*.

There was, however, another side to the coin. In his *Historia Anglicana* composed at the end of the twelfth century, William of Newburgh says this of Gildas:[9]

> habuit autem gens Britonum ante nostrum Bedam proprium historiographum Gildam, quod et Beda testatur, quaedam eius verba suis literis inserens: sicut ipse probavi, cum ante annos aliquot in eiusdem Gildae librum legendum incidissem. *cum enim sermone sit admodum impolitus atque insipidus, paucis eum vel transcribere vel habere curantibus, raro invenitur.*

Again it is clear that William is referring to the *De Excidio Britanniae* not the *Historia Britonum*, since he notes Bede's reliance on Gildas's work. William's comments make it clear that the idiosyncrasy of the

4   Ed. W.Stubbs, Rolls Series (2 vols, London, 1881-9), vol.I, p.24.
5   Ed. J.Morris, *Nennius* (Chichester, 1980); for a refutation of the attribution of the work to Nennius, see D.Dumville, ' "Nennius" and the *Historia Brittonum*', *Studia Celtica* 10-11 (1975-6), pp.78-95.
6   See F.Lot, *Nennius et l'Historia Brittonum* (Paris, 1934), p.2.
7   Note the cautious comment of R.Thomson, 'The reading of William of Malmesbury', *Revue bénédictine* 85 (1975), 362-94, at p.389: 'he knew Nennius and perhaps Gildas as well'.
8   *Descriptio Cambriae, praef*, ed. J.F.Dimock, *Giraldi Cambrensis Opera*, Rolls Series (London, 1868), vol.VI, p.158.
9   Ed. R.Howlett, *Chronicles of Steven, Henry II and Richard I*, Rolls Series (4 vols, London, 1884-9), vol.I, p.11.

De Excidio Britanniae and particularly the difficulty of its highly rhetorical style made it generally unattractive to his contemporaries. Hence the *De Excidio Britanniae* was, in the twelfth century, a rare work.[10]

For the twelfth-century scholar, then, the *De Excidio Britanniae* was not a familiar text. For many, Gildas was known only as the author of the *Historia Britonum*. Some, including perhaps William of Malmesbury, may have praised him for that work. In the case of Gerald of Wales, who certainly commends the *De Excidio Britanniae*, we may suspect that he was motivated by sympathy for a fellow Briton. Yet even Gerald does not quote extensively from the *De Excidio Britanniae*. For the majority, as William of Newburgh tells us, the work was either distasteful or unknown.

One author of the period, however, proves to be an important exception. Geoffrey of Monmouth's *Historia Regum Britanniae*,[11] probably published in 1139, was undoubtedly among the most influential literary achievements of the twelfth century, presenting, as it did, an allegedly authoritative account of previously unknown areas of early British history. For the modern critic it is, of course, impossible to view Geoffrey of Monmouth as a 'serious' historian, but on a purely literary level, and as a masterly synthesis of diverse sources, the *Historia Regum Britanniae* remains a *tour de force.*[12]

It has long been recognised that Gildas's *De Excidio Britanniae* was among Geoffrey's sources for the *Historia Regum Britanniae*. A number of parallel passages were noted in the edition of San Marte (A. Schulz),[13] and have been discussed, in greater or lesser detail, by E. Faral,[14] J.S.P. Tatlock,[15] and J. Hammer.[16] They have, however,

---

10 The text history of the *De Excidio Britanniae* is to be studied by D. Dumville, *Gildas in the Middle Ages: studies in textual history*, Studies in Celtic History (Woodbridge, forthcoming).

11 Ed. A. Griscom, *The Historia Regum Britanniae of Geoffrey of Monmouth* (London, 1929); and E. Faral, *La légende Arthurienne* (3 vols, Paris, 1929) III, pp. 64-303. Here all quotations are from Faral's edition, since the text printed is slightly superior to Griscom's, and the division into chapters more convenient.

12 See the discussion by C.N.L. Brooke, 'Geoffrey of Monmouth as a historian' in *Church and Government in the Middle Ages*, edd. C.N.L. Brooke, D.E. Luscombe, G.H. Martin and D.M. Owen (Cambridge, 1976), 77-91.

13 *Historia Regum Britanniae* (Halle, 1854).

14 *op. cit., passim.*

15 *The Legendary History of Britain* (Berkeley and Los Angeles, 1950), *passim.*

16 'Remarks on the sources and textual history of Geoffrey of Monmouth's *Historia Regum Britanniae*', *Bulletin of the Polish Institute of Arts and Sciences in America* 2 (1943-4), 501-64; at p. 520 Hammer remarks, 'he inserts passages from Gildas, Bede and Nennius without even acknowledging his indebtedness to them', but does not give any examples.

3

never been considered together with the extensive verbal reminiscences of the *De Excidio Britanniae* to be found in the *Historia
Regum Britanniae*, nor has the precise nature of Geoffrey's debt to
Gildas ever been established. The aim of the present study is to in-
vestigate Geoffrey's borrowings from Gildas in order to discover his
methods of literary variation of a source.

To this end my examination has been divided into a number of
subsections. In the first I discuss extended parallel passages between
the *De Excidio Britanniae* and the *Historia Regum Britanniae*, and
the manner in which Geoffrey integrates such material from Gildas's
work into his own. In the second section I examine a considerable
number of verbal borrowings by Geoffrey from the *De Excidio
Britanniae*, most of which are here presented for the first time. They
illustrate how intimate was Geoffrey's familiarity with his predecessor's work. The third section concentrates on passages in the
Historia Regum Britanniae in which Gildas is mentioned by name
and on the evidence thus provided for Geoffrey's attitude to his
source. In the fourth section I discuss the handling of Gildas-derived
passages in the so-called 'variant' version of Geoffrey's work[17] and
the implications they have for the authorship and date of that text.
The final, short section is devoted to Geoffrey's debt to Gildas in his
last work, the hexameter poem, *Vita Merlini*.[18]

I. Parallel passages between the *Historia Regum Britanniae* and *De
   Excidio Britanniae*

Much of the basic framework of the *Historia Regum Britanniae*
was provided by the *Historia Britonum*; from this heterogeneous
work Geoffrey drew the British origin legend of the exile Brutus, the
main points of the history of Roman Britain from Caesar to Maximianus, the raids of the Picti and Scoti, and the story of Vortigern and
the *adventus Saxonum*. He fleshed out this skeleton from other
sources, including Bede, and added extensive material on the pre-
Roman kings, the Arthur cycle, and traditions about Cadwallon and
Cadwaladr, the last kings of Britain. Much of the historical content

17 Ed. J.Hammer, *Geoffrey of Monmouth: Historia Regum Britanniae — a
   variant version* (Cambridge, Mass., 1951).
18 Ed. B.Clarke, *Life of Merlin* (Cardiff, 1973).

of the *De Excidio Britanniae*, therefore, merely duplicated in essence that already available to Geoffrey in the *Historia Britonum*. Thus the artistry with which he integrated extensive passages from Gildas's work into the *Historia Regum Britanniae* is indicative of Geoffrey's free, yet carefully considered, approach to the adaptation of his literary sources. Moreover, Geoffrey's reworking in these passages of Gildas's highly rhetorical Latin sheds light on his own stylistic preferences.

Geoffrey's extended borrowings from the *De Excidio Britanniae* occur in eight separate passages: the description of Britain; St Alban; Maximianus/Maximus; the attacks of the Picti and Scoti; Arthur's successors; Ceredig and the Africans; Cadwallon's speech; the plague. As in some cases these passages are lengthy, they have not here been included in the body of this study, but appear as an Appendix; there each passage of the *Historia Regum Britanniae* is followed by the corresponding section or sections of the *De Excidio Britanniae* with the close verbal parallels indicated by italic type. Here I shall discuss each passage separately.

1. Description of Britain

Like Bede and the compiler of the *Historia Britonum* before him, Geoffrey follows the precedent set by Gildas in beginning his work proper with a discursus on the island of Britain. As comparison quickly demonstrates, Geoffrey's description is heavily indebted to the *De Excidio Britanniae*.

Gildas is not, however, Geoffrey's only source. Two short phrases, *omni etenim genere metalli fecunda* and *atque piscosis fluviis*, are adapted from Bede, *Historia Ecclesiastica* I.1: *quae etiam venis metallorum, aeris, ferri, et plumbi et argenti, fecunda* and *fluviis quoque multum piscosis ac fontibus praeclara copiosis*. Further, Geoffrey appends to this description the following comment:

> postremo quinque inhabitatur populis, Normannis videlicet atque Britannis, Saxonibus, Pictis et Scotis. ex quibus Britones olim ante ceteros a mari usque ad mare insederunt.

This represents in effect a modernisation by Geoffrey of two sentences from the *Historia Britonum* 7 and 9 respectively: *et in ea habitant quattuor gentes: Scotti, Picti, Saxones atque Britones* and *Britones olim implentes eam a mari usque ad mare iudicaverunt*. Such combination of sources is a favourite trick of Geoffrey's; but, apart

5

from these minor borrowings from Bede and the *Historia Britonum*, Geoffrey here relies most heavily on the *De Excidio Britanniae*. Since he adapts this directly, rather than at second-hand from the reworkings of Gildas's description contained in the *Historia Ecclesiastica* and the *Historia Britonum*, it is clear that the *De Excidio Britanniae* provided the main inspiration for Geoffrey in this passage.

Let us begin with Geoffrey's method of recasting the basic material provided by the *De Excidio Britanniae*, since his procedure in this chapter is typical of his general approach throughout the *Historia Regum Britanniae*. Gildas's description consists of one long sentence, which lacks a main verb (supply *est*), is loosely anchored by a series of participles and adjectives dependant on *Britannia* (*librata, tenens, vallata, meliorata, decorata, ornata* and *irrigua*) and abounds with subordinate clauses. This was too complex for Geoffrey and he breaks it into six shorter, more evenly balanced sentences, while altering their emphasis. Gildas proceeds with a grand sweep. From the overall geographical position of Britain, he moves round the coasts, then inland via the rivers to the towns to end with ornate, poetic descriptions of the fields and waterways; from simple simile – rivers like arms – he progresses to the more elaborate – fields resemble the jewels of a bride's necklace – and finally to the full-blown poeticism of sweet slumber pledged on the banks of brilliant brooks.[19] In contrast, Geoffrey makes a much more logical journey. Like Gildas, he begins with a survey of the island's size and location. Next, however, he passes on to Gildas's third topic, Britain's fertility in general: its fields, pastures and streams. Only then does he return to Gildas's second section by giving more particular details of the main rivers, the twenty-eight cities and, finally, the inhabitants. In its effect his description is both more methodically conceived and less emotive than that contained in the *De Excidio Britanniae*.

The same is true of a comparison of the Latin style of the two authors. Gildas's rhetorical prose is difficult, disorderly and often bombastic; Geoffrey's narrative is smoother-flowing, although it too sometimes has a trace of epic tone, caused by frequent borrowing from hexameter poets, especially Vergil. In the chapter under discussion, for instance, the phrase *ubertate glebae* derives, with slight variation, from Aeneid I.531: *terra antiqua, potens armis et ubere glebae*.[20] Geoffrey, however, avoids Gildas's awkward transitions,

19 M.Winterbottom, 'The preface of Gildas' *De Excidio*', *Transactions of the Honourable Society of Cymmrodorion*, (1974-5), 277-87, at p.286 has noted the debt of this passage to the rhetorical topos of the *locus amoenus*.
20 *sub aeriis montibus* also has a poetic ring.

6

piling up of words and frequent separation and interlacing of adjectives and nouns. Patterns such as *exceptis diversorum prolixioribus promonteriorum tractibus, fontibus lucidis crebris undis* and *frigidum aquae torrentem vivae*, characteristic of Gildas's mannered prose,[21] are either omitted or much simplified by Geoffrey. Similarly, he simplifies Gildas's *absque meridianae freto plagae* to *absque meridianae plagae freto*. He also dispenses with Gildas's more violent similes and metaphors. In this passage, however, Geoffrey retains both the comparison of rivers to arms and the imagery of slumber on the banks of streams; probably he too enjoyed the poetic feel they lent to prose. In short, Geoffrey seems to have been attracted by some elements of Gildas's eccentric Latin, but felt the need generally to adapt it to his own more lucid, but not unornamented style. Yet, despite his revisions, Geoffrey's borrowings from Gildas often stand out from their surroundings in the *Historia Regum Britanniae* by virtue of their more rhetorical nature. This point need not be laboured; the remaining seven passages, reworked to a greater or lesser extent by Geoffrey, well serve to illustrate the differences between Gildas's style and his own.

This passage, then, demonstrates how Geoffrey reorganises his borrowings from the *De Excidio Britanniae* both in content and form. This careful process of literary adaptation is combined with a very thorough knowledge of his original. This may be seen in Geoffrey's description of the fate in his own day of some of the twenty-eight British cities enumerated by Gildas: *quaedam dirutis moeniis in desertis locis squalescunt*. This picture of desolation is drawn from another later chapter of Gildas's *De Excidio Britanniae* 26.2: *sed ne nunc quidem, ut antea, civitates patriae inhabitabantur; sed desertae dirutaeque squalent*. Clearly Geoffrey was a painstaking editor; aware of Gildas's comment on the eventual abandonment of the British civitates mentioned in *De Excidio Britanniae* 3, he transferred it to his own version of that chapter as a neat additional note.

2. St Alban

It is only after a long interval that Geoffrey returns to the *De Excidio Britanniae*, using it as the source for his account of the perse-

---

[21] See F.Kerlouégan, 'Une mode stylistique dans la prose latine des pays celtiques', *Études celtiques* 13 (1972-3), 275-97; and M.Winterbottom, 'A Celtic hyperbaton?', *Bulletin of the Board of Celtic Studies* 27 (1976-8), 207-12.

cutions of Diocletian and the story of St Alban. Typically he begins by following Bede,[22] but soon turns to Gildas, despite the fact that Bede devotes an extensive chapter to the passion of St Alban.[23] Probably Geoffrey thought it was a subject worthy of Gildas's more emotive style.

Geoffrey adapts Gildas's narrative in his usual way; he reorganises, conflating three chapters of the *De Excidio Britanniae* into one, and omitting some of his source's more high-flown language. It is, however, noteworthy that Geoffrey, unlike Gildas, is able to name Alban's confessor as Amphibalus. This is something of a *cause célèbre*, since, in so doing, Geoffrey elevates the unusual *amphibalus*, 'ecclesiastical robe', which is found at *De Excidio Britanniae* 28.1 (below, p.10), into a proper name. It might be suggested, as Faral has,[24] that Geoffrey simply misunderstood Gildas's difficult Latin; but this is to underestimate Geoffrey. We have already witnessed his careful reworking of his source. It is more likely that Geoffrey deliberately created Amphibalus, borrowing his name from a rare word of Gildas's. As we shall see, such wilful, even playful manipulation of the *De Excidio Britanniae* is a frequent keynote of Geoffrey's literary technique.

3. Maximianus/Maximus

Geoffrey's character Maximianus is better known to history as Maximus, the Spanish usurper who supposedly denuded Britain of her defenses in the 380s. He is so named by Gildas at *De Excidio Britanniae* 13. In the *Historia Britonum*, however, he is confused with Maximianus[25] and Geoffrey, remaining faithful to that text, also uses this name. Indeed, Geoffrey relies for the most part on Bede and the *Historia Britonum* for the events connected with Maximianus.[26] Yet he borrows one sentence from Gildas's highly rhetorical condemnation of Maximus. Perhaps Geoffrey was attracted by the pointed antithesis *duos imperatores legitimos, unum Roma, alterum religiosissima vita pelleret*; if so, however, his own version is less violent.

22 Faral, *op. cit.*, ii, p.181.
23 *Historia Ecclesiastica* I.7.
24 *op. cit.*, ii, p.183.
25 chapters 26, 27 and 29.
26 Faral, *op. cit.*, ii, pp.191-2.

4. Attacks of the Picti and Scoti

This passage contains the most extensive single group of borrowings made from the *De Excidio Britanniae* by Geoffrey. Up to the events of Maximianus's reign, Geoffrey's account of the Roman occupation is loosely modelled, with additional material, on the sparse notes contained in the *Historia Britonum*. For the period of barbarian attacks up to the *adventus Saxonum*, Gildas is Geoffrey's verbal source, though, under the influence of the *Historia Britonum*, he makes sweeping changes of content. It will, perhaps, be helpful to tabulate the narrative of *De Excidio Britanniae* 14-20 and *Historia Regum Britanniae* 89-91.

De Excidio Britanniae

Chapter 14: first attacks of Picti and Scoti.
Chapter 15: first Roman intervention; construction of turf wall.
Chapter 16: first return of the Picti and Scoti.
Chapter 17: second Roman intervention.
Chapter 18: final Roman departure; construction of stone wall.
Chapter 19: second return of the Picti and Scoti; rout of the British; civil war and famine.
Chapter 20: appeal to Agitius; plague and first British victory.

Historia Regum Britanniae

Chapter 89: attack by Picti, Scoti, and other barbarians; intervention of Roman legion; construction of (stone) wall.
Chapter 90: exhortations by departing Romans.
Chapter 91: final Roman departure; return of barbarians; rout of British; appeal to Agitius.

As can be readily seen, Geoffrey conflates episodes from the *De Excidio Britanniae* in order to streamline its narrative. Most obvious is his reduction of the Roman expeditions from two to one, in line with the version of the *Historia Britonum*.[27] Geoffrey's account of Roman intervention is closely based on *De Excidio Britanniae* 15. Thereafter, however, he omits the construction of the turf wall, substituting for it the stone wall of *De Excidio Britanniae* 18, quoting Gildas closely. Geoffrey entirely omits *De Excidio Britanniae* 16-17 and continues his narrative by selective editing of *De Excidio Britanniae* 18-20. His main interest in the *De Excidio Britanniae* was clearly

[27] chapter 30.

not in following its content faithfully, but, by excerpting rhetorical passages, to elevate the tone of his prose. In dealing with his next topic, the *adventus Saxonum*, he again abandons Gildas in favour of the *Historia Britonum*.

5. Arthur's successors

After the lengthy discursus on the reign of Arthur which forms the literary core of the *Historia Regum Britanniae*, Geoffrey returns once more to the *De Excidio Britanniae* as a source. In chapters 28-36 of that work Gildas savagely attacks the five kings who are apparently his contemporaries: Constantinus, *inmundae leaenae Damnoniae tyrannicus catulus*;[28] Aurelius Caninus (a pun on the Welsh Cynan?);[29] Vortiporius, *Demetarum tyrannus*;[30] Cuneglasus, *auriga currus receptaculi ursi*[31] (Din Eirth?);[32] Maglocunus (Maelgwn of Gwynedd).

From these kings Geoffrey, who cannot have misunderstood the *De Excidio Britanniae* at this point, manufactures a chronological list of four successors to Arthur, omitting only Cuneglasus. This represents another case of deliberate manipulation of his source on Geoffrey's part.

Moreover, Geoffrey replaces Gildas's treatment of these kings as monsters of depravity with a more sympathetic approach. Constantinus is condemned by Gildas for his cruel butchery of two princes at the altar; Geoffrey mitigates the savagery of the act by converting it into the legitimate revenge of Arthur's successor on the sons of Mordred. Gildas's single murder is also duplicated by Geoffrey to become two acts of sacrilege: one in a London monastery, the other in the church of St Amphibalus in Winchester. As we have already seen (p.8, above), Geoffrey created this saint from an unusual term for a clerical robe; it was in this passage that Gildas had employed the word.[33] This oblique reference by Geoffrey is, therefore, another ironic touch in his free adaptation of the *De Excidio Britanniae*.

Constantinus's 'successor' Aurelius Caninus is described by Gildas as

---

28 *De Excidio Britanniae* 28.1.
29 Winterbottom, *Gildas*, p.152 (notes by J.Morris).
30 *De Excidio Britanniae* 31.1.
31 *ibid.* 32.1.
32 Winterbottom, *Gildas*, p.152.
33 St Amphibalus's church at Winchester is also mentioned by Geoffrey in connection with Constans, Utherpendragon's brother at *Historia Regum Britanniae* 93.12.

civilia bella sitiens; Geoffrey concurs, echoing the phrase with *civilis belli amator*, but generously concedes that Conanus was a *mirae probitatis iuvenis*, worthy of rule if only he had not had that besetting sin. Geoffrey also transfers the detail of the deposition of an uncle from Maelgwn, the worst of the tyrants in Gildas's catalogue, to Conanus.

Vortiporius, accused by Gildas of incest among other sins, is transformed by Geoffrey into a good king, ruling *cum diligentia et pace*.

Finally Maelgwn, Gildas's *bête noir*, is represented in the *Historia Regum Britanniae* as a successful and powerful king, a worthy successor to Arthur, whose rule is marred only by his homosexuality. In the *De Excidio Britanniae* Maelgwn is attacked by a series of bitter antitheses, undercutting his positive qualities with contrasting vices. Geoffrey reforms the king by the emphasis on the former at the expense of the latter. He is further rehabilitated, as we have seen, by the reattribution by Geoffrey of his elimination of his uncle to Conanus.

6. Ceredig and the Africans

This passage provides a further excellent example of Geoffrey's ready familiarity with the *De Excidio Britanniae* and the freedom with which he adapted it. As we have seen, Geoffrey's account of the raids of the Picti and Scoti generally followed *De Excidio Britanniae* 14-20, though with the reduction of Roman interventions to one, as recorded in the *Historia Britonum*. Thereafter Geoffrey reverted to the *Historia Britonum* for its version of the *adventus Saxonum*. Geoffrey, therefore, was left with no place for Gildas's account of that event in *De Excidio Britanniae* 23-4, the latter chapter in particular containing a very highly-wrought rhetorical passage on the ruin of Britain. Geoffrey's solution was simple; he repositioned Gildas's description within an incident of his own confection: the defeat of the British king Ceredig by an African army summoned, while it was attacking Ireland, by the Saxons to become their allies.[34]

It may be tentatively suggested that the *De Excidio Britanniae* itself provided the inspiration for this episode. Geoffrey's phrase *ignem cumulavit*, 'heaped up a fire', represents Gildas's *ignis orientali sacrilegorum manu exaggeratus*, 'a fire piled up by the band of blas-

---

34 For Geoffrey's sources, see Faral, ii, p. 313 and Tatlock, p. 135.

phemers in the east'; presumably this latter is a reference to the original location of the Saxons in the south-east of Britain. Why does Geoffrey omit the words *orientali sacrilegorum manu*? Did he perhaps interpret them as 'by an eastern band of heathens' and conjure from this his African army allied to the Saxons?[35] This would represent not a misreading of the *De Excidio Britanniae*, but another example of the playful rewriting Geoffrey readily indulged in: such as the conversion of an abbot's robe into St Amphibalus and his complete reworking to his own ends of Gildas's diatribe against the British kings.

Gildas's vivid phrase, echoed in this passage, *crebris arietibus* 'repeated battering of rams' is also borrowed by Geoffrey in a description of an attack by the Greek Pandrasus on a castle of Brutus at *Historia Regum Britanniae* 10.11-13: *alii crebris arietibus ceterisque machinationibus murorum compaginem dissolverent.*[36]

7. Cadwallon's speech

In this speech Geoffrey was enabled to incorporate into the *Historia Regum Britanniae* another, later chapter from Gildas's narrative of the incursions of the Picti and Scoti. In *De Excidio Britanniae* 21 Gildas describes the recovery of Britain after their second attack and decries the subsequent moral decline of the British. Geoffrey transfers these vituperations to a setting in the seventh century and puts them into the mouth of Cadwallon, who laments the degeneration of his race to Salomon, king of the Armorican Britons. This passage is distinguished by unusually close quotation of the *De Excidio Britanniae*, and by the fact that here alone Geoffrey acknowledges his borrowing with the words *ut Gildas historicus testatur* (see Section III, below).

---

[35] It must be noted, however, that Avranches 162, a manuscript with which Geoffrey shares some minor, but no extensive, variants from Winterbottom's text, transfers *orientalis* from *manus* to *mare*; it gives: *ignis videlicet exaggeratus sacrilegorum manu de mari orientale usque ad mare occidentale finitimas quasque civitates agrosque depopulans, qui non quievit accensus donec cunctam paene exurens insulae superficiem supra occidentalem oceanum truci lingua delamberet.* If Geoffrey's copy of the *De Excidio Britanniae* read something similar — as his use of de*populans* may suggest — then it is unlikely to have suggested an army of Africans to him.

[36] Geoffrey's fondness for the phrase is doubtless explained by his recognition of its ultimate origin at *Aeneid* 2.492-3 *labat ariete crebro/ianua.*

8. The plague

Geoffrey places his 'ruin of Britain' in the reign of Cadwaladr, when famine and plague cause a mass exodus of the British population. This he recounts in a skilful integration of various, disparate elements drawn from Gildas. Thus, the *fames dira* belongs to the period of the failure of the appeal to Aetius, but is described in terms borrowed from *De Excidio Britanniae* 19 picturing the effects of civil strife. The *pestifera lues* belongs to *De Excidio Britanniae* 22, where it afflicts the decadent Britons before the final attack of the Picti and Scoti. Finally, the seaborne fight abroad is just one of the fates endured by the hapless Britons in *De Excidio Britanniae* 25, after the devastating assault of the Saxons and before their recovery under Ambrosius Aurelianus. Virtually everything in Geoffrey's description originates in the *De Excidio Britanniae*, yet he combines the ingredients of plague and depopulation to produce an original synthesis for his own literary ends.[37]

Examination of these eight common passages shared by the *Historia Regum Britanniae* and *De Excidio Britanniae* makes it immediately clear how Geoffrey reworked his borrowings in structure and style. Even more striking, however, is the great freedom with which he adapted the *De Excidio Britanniae* in order to integrate it with his other sources. In the eight passages Geoffrey includes materials from the following chapters of the *De Excidio Britanniae*: 3, 9, 10, 11, 15, 18, 19, 20, 21, 22, 25 and 28-36 (especially 28, 30 and 33); but he rarely simply copies the text of the *De Excidio Britanniae* closely, preferring an editorial policy of omission, combination and repositioning of his material. He is content merely to revise the construction of Gildas's description of Britain and his account of St Alban. The incursions of the Picti and Scoti and the condemnation of the five kings he also retains in approximately the chronological position assigned to them by Gildas; but the former are pared down to conform with the account of the *Historia Britonum*, while the latter are transformed, not without a certain whimsy, into successive rulers in the period immediately following Arthur's reign, who pad out the numbers of Geoffrey's British kings. Events, for which Geoffrey has no place in their original context, are imaginatively reallocated. The sack of the British cities inflicted by the Saxons is transferred to an errant African army of Geoffrey's own creation. Gildas's denunciation of British decadence is reallotted to Cadwallon, while plague

[37] Cf. Faral, ii, p.338.

and famine, which occur quite separately in the *De Excidio Britanniae*, are conflated to produce the catastrophe which finally ended British greatness. Obviously, Geoffrey was concerned not faithfully to reproduce the historical information contained in the *De Excidio Britanniae*, but to harmonise it with the literary demands of his own historical narrative.

Another aspect of Geoffrey's painstaking transformation of this source material is his variation of the tone of his borrowings from Gildas. Gildas was essentially a Christian author, concerned to draw a religious lesson from the past and to illustrate the terrible retribution visited by God on the previous sins of the British.[38] Hence he presents the reader with a grim catalogue of foolish and tyrannical leadership, impiety and heresy, and general moral decline. True, his few heroes, such as St Alban and Ambrosius Aurelianus, are praised; but more often he is concerned to denounce and condemn.

Geoffrey's view of British history is much broader, though it too has a tragic aspect. It runs from the early promise of the reigns of the founder of British kingship, Brutus and his successors, through the period of Roman occupation, to the culminating achievements of Arthur; only afterwards do the British decline and lose their greatness. It is noticeable that Geoffrey generally suppresses Gildas's criticisms until this later period. Geoffrey's treatment of the weakness of the British in the face of the raids of the Picti and Scoti is markedly more sympathetic than Gildas's. Similarly Arthur's successors, all bitterly attacked in the *De Excidio Britanniae*, receive a more favourable press from Geoffrey. It is not until the reign of Cadwallon that Geoffrey reproduces almost verbatim Gildas's tirade against the corrupt British, while under Cadwaladr British rule comes to a virtual end in a mood of gloom and despondency directly inspired by Gildas's 'ruin of Britain'.

II. Verbal reminiscences of the *De Excidio Britanniae* in the *Historia Regum Britanniae*

The previous section examined Geoffrey's major borrowings from Gildas; here, my concern is with those occasions on which Geoffrey echoes shorter phrases and motifs from the *De Excidio Britanniae*.

---

[38] Gildas's historical perspectives are lucidly discussed by R.W.Hanning, *The Vision of History in Early Britain* (New York, 1966), chapter 2.

14

These reveal a more subtle aspect of its influence upon him, and confirm his interest in the text as a literary as much as an historical model.

Geoffrey makes two such verbal borrowings in the course of his account of Britain before the Roman invasions. At *Historia Regum Britanniae* 44.19-21 he describes the great prosperity of Belinus's reign with the words: *in diebus igitur eius tanta copia divitiarum populum refecit quantam nec retro aetas habuisse testetur*; at *Historia Regum Britanniae* 49.7-9 he draws a very similar picture of the rule of the slightly later king Gorbonianus: *omnibus diebus vitae eius tanta divitiarum copia insula affluebat quantam nullae conlaterales provinciae habebant*. Although Geoffrey is careful to vary the vocabulary on each occasion, both passages clearly stem from *De Excidio Britanniae* 21.2: *quiescente autem vastitate tantis abundantiarum copiis insula affluebat ut nulla habere retro aetas meminisset*. Gildas assigns to this period of abundance, which in his narrative follows the first defeat of the Picti and Scoti by the unaided British, the seeds of subsequent moral decline. Geoffrey suppresses these sinister overtones and transfers this now harmless time of plenty to the reigns of two early British kings.

In his treatment of the raids of the Picti and Scoti Geoffrey, as we have seen, relies heavily on the *De Excidio Britanniae*. A number of Gildasian phrases also occur in this section of the *Historia Regum Britanniae*. In chapter 90 the Romans, who are about to leave Britain for good, call a council at London. There an emotive, Vergilian speech is delivered by archbishop Guithelinus, another character of Geoffrey's own invention.[39] This oration contains three borrowings from Gildas: *Historia Regum Britanniae* 90.15-6 *Maximianus regnum istud omni milite omnique iuventute spoliavit* from *De Excidio Britanniae* 14 *Britannia omni armato milite . . . ingenti iuventute spoliata*;[40] *Historia Regum Britanniae* 90.16-17 *plebs usus belli ignara* also from *De Excidio Britanniae* 14 *omnis belli usus ignara penitus*; *Historia Regum Britanniae* 90.22-4 *non instruetis manus vestras peltis ensibus hastis in latrones nequaquam vobis fortiores si segnitia et torpor abesset* from *De Excidio Britanniae* 18.1 *et gentibus nequaquam sibi fortioribus, nisi segnitia et torpore dissolveretur, inermes vinculis vinciendas nullo modo, sed instructas peltis ensibus hastis et*

39 For the origin of the name, see Tatlock, p. 241.
40 Geoffrey also echoes this phrase at *Historia Regum Britanniae* 88.31: *insulam Britanniae ab omni armato milite vacuatam*; again, Geoffrey would have been aware that the poetic collective singular 'armed soldiery' originates from *Aeneid* 2.20 *uterumque armato milite complent*.

ad caedem promptas protenderet manus, suadentes.

In addition to the frequent echoes of the *De Excidio Britanniae* which it contains, the speech with its condemnation of British sloth-fulness has a decidedly Gildasian feel. Indeed, it is hard not to see in the stern ecclesiastic Guithelinus a playful reflection on Geoffrey's part of Gildas himself. Guithelinus begins his address with the words (*Historia Regum Britanniae* 90.11-3): *cum vos iussu asstantium allo-qui debeam, magis in fletum prorumpere cogor quam in exclesum sermonem.* This is, in effect, a paraphrase of the opening words of *De Excidio Britanniae* 1.1: *in hac epistula quicquid deflendo potius quam declamando . . . fuero prosecutus.* Such casting of Guithelinus in a Gildasian role is a further example of Geoffrey's independent and sometimes whimsical approach to the *De Excidio Britanniae.*

After the failure of the British appeal for help from Aetius, Geoffrey has a further use for the oratory of Archbishop Guithelinus; he sends him on a mission to the Armorican Britons. Here, too, the speech which Geoffrey puts in his mouth contains a borrowing from Gildas. At *Historia Regum Britanniae* 92.14-16 Guithelinus laments: *et insulam nostram omni copia deliciarum repletam evacuaverunt ita ut universae eiusdem nationes totius cibi baculo excepto venatoriae artis solatio careant.* The same situation ensues after the British defeat by the Picti and Scoti at *De Excidio Britanniae* 19.4: *vacuaretur omnis regio totius cibi baculo excepto venatoriae artis solatio.* Further-more, Guithelinus's embassy is introduced at *Historia Regum Britan-niae* 92.1 by the phrase *inito itaque consilio* which may reflect *initur namque consilium* at *De Excidio Britanniae* 22.3.[41] For Geoffrey, then, Guithelinus's two speeches afford a convenient context for reminiscences of Gildasian passages which were extraneous to the main narrative framework of the *Historia Regum Britanniae.*

Historia Regum Britanniae 110-18 is devoted to retrospective political prophecies of a type which became increasingly popular in the course of the Middle Ages.[42] Geoffrey places these predictions, which are clothed in highly obscure metaphorical language, in the mouth of Merlin. It is interesting that several of the phrases they contain may also be found in the *De Excidio Britanniae*: *dira fames* (*Historia Regum Britanniae* 112.22 and *De Excidio Britanniae* 20.2); *catuli leonis* (*Historia Regum Britanniae* 113.23 and *De Excidio*

---

[41] Geoffrey may, however, have derived the words *inito consilio* direct from the Bible; see J. Hammer, 'Geoffrey of Monmouth's use of the Bible in the *Historia Regum Britanniae*', *Bulletin of the John Rylands Library* 30 (1946-7), 293-311, at p. 301.

[42] See R. Taylor, *The political prophecy in England* (New York, 1911).

Britanniae 33.4); *rupti foederis* (*Historia Regum Britanniae* 114.7 and *De Excidio Britanniae* 23.5); *stragem non minimam* (*Historia Regum Britanniae* 114.8-10 and *De Excidio Britanniae* 26.1).[43] Thus Gildas's grandiloquent style provided Geoffrey with a useful quarry for the rhetorical imagery necessary for the enigmatic language of these prophecies.

Before we move on to the account of the reign of Arthur, one further Gildasian borrowing in Geoffrey's narrative of the wars of his predecessors against the Saxons merits attention. At *Historia Regum Britanniae* 126.5-6 Geoffrey describes the Saxon leader Octa as *gestans catenam in manu et sablonem in capite*. The second of these tokens of submission stems from Gildas's depiction of British envoys to Rome at *De Excidio Britanniae* 17.1: *scissis ut dicitur vestibus opertisque sablone capitibus*. Moreover, the word *sablo*, 'gravel', is characteristically Gildasian.[44] Thus a further chapter of the *De Excidio Britanniae* for which Geoffrey had no place in the scheme of the *Historia Regum Britanniae*, since he suppresses the second appeal to the Romans, still provides him with a striking phrase in an entirely new context.

It might be expected that in the chapters of the *Historia Regum Britanniae* dealing with his chief hero, Arthur, Geoffrey would feel no need for borrowings from the *De Excidio Britanniae*, particularly as Gildas makes no mention of this shadowy British commander, not even in his account of the battle of Mount Badon; in fact, these chapters contain many Gildasian echoes.

The first of these occurs at *Historia Regum Britanniae* 144.3-5, when Geoffrey describes Arthur's planning for his Saxon war: *quaerit consilium quid optimum quidve saluberrimum contra paganorum irruptionem faceret*. This is a simplification of *De Excidio Britanniae* 22.3 *initur namque consilium quid optimum quidve saluberrimum ad repellendas tam ferales et tam crebras supra dictarum gentium irruptiones praedasque decerni deberet*. Gildas is here dealing with the council held by the *superbus tyrannus* (conventionally identified as Vortigern) at which the disastrous decision to call in the Saxons was

[43] The same phrase is also found, of the Picti and Scoti, in *Historia Regum Britanniae* 88.39.
[44] See F. Kerlouégan, 'Une liste des mots communs à Gildas et à Aldhelm', *Études celtiques* 15 (1975-8), 553-67, at p.555; this passage of the *De Excidio Britanniae* is also imitated by *Historia Britonum* 30 *et, dum legati mittebantur, cum magno luctu et cum sablonibus super capita sua intrabant*. Since, however, Geoffrey more often relies on the *Historia Britonum* as source of historical material rather than of striking vocabulary, he is more likely to have borrowed the word directly from the *De Excidio Britanniae*.

17

made. Geoffrey's transfer of the words to Arthur's policy-making, which proves entirely successful, is another ironic inversion of his source. After the defeat of the Saxons, Geoffrey at *Historia Regum Britanniae* 151.8 tells us that Arthur restored the war-torn churches: *ecclesias usque ad solum destructas renovat*. The phrase is virtually identical to that originally applied by Gildas (at *De Excidio Britanniae* 12.2) to the rebuilding of churches by the British after the nine-year persecution of Diocletian: *renovant ecclesias usque ad solum destructas*. Here, Geoffrey consigns to Arthur's reign one of the few happier moments of Gildas's version of British history.

At *Historia Regum Britanniae* 156 Geoffrey includes in his work a descriptive excursus on *Urbs Legionum* (Caerleon) in Arthur's time. In this chapter he repeats two phrases from *De Excidio Britanniae* 3 which he had already employed in his description of Britain (*Historia Regum Britanniae* 5): [i] *Historia Regum Britanniae* 156.10 *amoeno situ locata* (*De Excidio Britanniae* 3.3); [ii] *Historia Regum Britanniae* 156.12-14 *nobile flumen . . . per quod transmarini reges et principes qui venturi erant navigio advehi poterant* and *ostiis nobilium fluminum . . . per quae . . . transmarinae deliciae ratibus vehabantur* (*De Excidio Britanniae* 3.1). Similarly, Geoffrey at *Historia Regum Britanniae* 156.10-11 applies to the city the words *prae ceteris civitatibus divitiarium copiis abundans*; they may represent a paraphrase of another favourite passage of Geoffrey's, *De Excidio Britanniae* 21.2: *tantis abundantiarum copiis insula affluebat*. By means of these repetitions, Geoffrey characterises Arthur's capital as a prosperous microcosm of the island of Britain as a whole.

Arthur's campaign against the Romans, which provides the climax of the *Historia Regum Britanniae*, contains three further reminiscences. The first two of these reveal Geoffrey borrowing striking phrases and words from Gildas. At *Historia Regum Britanniae* 165.42-3 Arthur's reaction to a piteous tale is described as follows: *at ille, quantum humanae naturae possibile est, commotus*. Exactly the same phrase occurs at *De Excidio Britanniae* 17.2, where Gildas uses it of the response of the Romans to the second appeal for help from the British. Geoffrey's second Gildasian echo is found at *Historia Regum Britanniae* 167.26; a minor British victory is related in the words *vicem praedictae stragis impudentibus grassatoribus redidere*. The vivid expression 'impudent freebooters', which Geoffrey here applies to the Roman enemy, originally at *De Excidio Britanniae* 21.1 described the Scoti: *revertuntur ergo impudentes grassatores Hiberni domos*.

The final borrowing is at once more interesting and more complex. Geoffrey describes the surrender of the Romans after the complete

18

defeat of Lucius at *Historia Regum Britanniae* 175.12-14 in the following terms: *ita quod maxima pars eorum ultro protendebant manus suas muliebriter vinciendas ut pauxillum spatium vivendi haberent.* This represents a conflation of at least two Gildasian passages: *De Excidio Britanniae* 20.2, *quae multos eorum cruentis compulit praedonibus sine dilatione victas dare manus ut pauxillum ad refocillandam animam cibi caperent*; and, primarily, *De Excidio Britanniae* 6.2, *manusque vinciendae muliebriter protenduntur.* Furthermore, the expression *spatium vivendi haberent* is very probably a variation of Geoffrey's part of a similar phrase at *De Excidio Britanniae* 1.14, *spatium respirandi non habent.*

This combination of elements from three different passages of the *De Excidio Britanniae* illustrates how artful Geoffrey's literary imitation could be. Moreover, the borrowing from *De Excidio Britanniae* 6.2 constitutes a nice irony on Geoffrey's part. Gildas uses the words of the shameful defeat of the British, whom he characterises as cowardly and treacherous, at the hands of the invading Romans. Geoffrey transposes their meaning by employing them in a diametrically opposed context: Arthur's triumph over the Romans which forms the culmination of British success in the *Historia Regum Britanniae*.

There remains one further reminiscence of the *De Excidio Britanniae* in the Arthurian section of the *Historia Regum Britanniae*. At chapter 177.1-4 Geoffrey announces his intention to relate Arthur's final conflict with Mordred:[45]

ne hoc quidem, consul auguste, Galfridus Monemutensis tacebit, sed, ut in praefato Britannico sermone invenit et a Waltero Oxenofordensi, in multis historiis peritissimo viro, audivit, *vili licet stilo*, breviter *tamen*, propalabit.

Geoffrey here echoes his predecessor's preface; at *De Excidio Britanniae* 1.1 Gildas promises that he will write *vili licet stilo, tamen benigno*. The unusual verb *propalo* is, moreover, favoured by Gildas.[46] This reminiscence of the opening of the *De Excidio Britanniae*, so prominently positioned, can only be an indication of Geoffrey's admiration for Gildas, despite the great freedom he displays in adapting his work. It is, however, typical of Geoffrey's capricious approach that he should echo the *De Excidio Britanniae*, a text to which he almost never openly acknowledges his extensive debts, in connection

45 In most manuscripts this passage forms the preface to the final book of the *Historia Regum Britanniae*, though Faral does not follow this division of the work into books.
46 See Kerlouégan, 'Une liste', p.555.

19

with his alleged 'source': the British book supposedly in the possession of Archdeacon Walter of Oxford.

The remaining echoes of the *De Excidio Britanniae* in the *Historia Regum Britanniae* are all contained in Geoffrey's account of Britain's gradual decline under the successive kings, Ceredig, Cadwallon, and Cadwaladr. For this part of his history Geoffrey found in Gildas's pejorative judgements on his fellow Britons much suitable ammunition for his own version of the closing stages of British history.

After the sack of the British cities by the Saxons and their African allies, Geoffrey at *Historia Regum Britanniae* 185.1-6 gives vent to an uncharacteristically savage outburst against the Britons:

> quid odiosa gens, pondere immanium scelerum oppressa, quid semper *civilia* proelia *sitiens* tete *domesticis* in tantum debilitasti *motibus*, quae, cum prius longe posita regna potestati tuae subdidisses, nunc velut *bona vinea degenera*ta *in amaritudinem* versa, *patriam, coniuges, liberos* nequeas ab inimicis tueri?

The passage is a patchwork of Gildasian borrowings. The ultimately Biblical imagery of the spoiled vineyard is derived from *De Excidio Britanniae* 24.4: *ita enim degeneravit tunc vinea illa olim bona in amaritudinem*; *civilia proelia sitiens* is a variation upon Gildas's phrase *civilia bella . . . sitiens* applied at *De Excidio Britanniae* 30.1 to Aurelius Caninus; *domesticis motibus* originates from *De Excidio Britanniae* 19.4, where such civil strife follows the rout of the British by the Picti and Scoti; finally the emotive *tricolon, patriam, coniuges, liberos* stems from *De Excidio Britanniae* 18.1, a passage from which Geoffrey had also borrowed in one of the speeches he attributes to Guithelinus (above, p.15). This process of careful synthesis is, again, a keynote of Geoffrey's variation of his source material.

Further echoes occur in these later chapters of the *Historia Regum Britanniae*. At *Historia Regum Britanniae* 185.14 Geoffrey describes the Saxons metaphorically with the words *barbarae leaenae catulos*, 'whelps of a barbarian lioness', an epithet which had been applied to them by Gildas at *De Excidio Britanniae* 23.3. At chapter 186.7 the phrase *crebras et ferales irruptiones*, a variation on *tam ferales et tam crebras irruptiones* at *De Excidio Britanniae* 22.3, is employed by Geoffrey with another interesting change of context: while Gildas used it to refer to the attacks of the Picti and Scoti, Geoffrey transfers it to raids carried out by the British themselves against the Saxons. Another such transference can be found in Brian's address to Cadwallon at *Historia Regum Britanniae* 191.32; Geoffrey borrows the impressive phrase *post horribile . . . iuramentum*, 'after a tremendous oath', from *De Excidio Britanniae* 28.1, where Gildas uses it to describe an undertaking of the tyrant Constantinus. Geoffrey, however, uses the expression in the plural for the oath of fidelity given by the Saxons to Ambrosius Aurelianus.

Finally, in the penultimate chapter of the *Historia Regum Britanniae*, which deals with the irrevocable collapse of the British, Geoffrey repeats two Gildasian phrases which he has already previously quoted: *Historia Regum Britanniae* 207.6-7 *quod hostes longius arcere nequiverant* (cf. *De Excidio Britanniae* 15.1 and *Historia Regum Britanniae* 89.11) and *Historia Regum Britanniae* 207.17-18 *externas et domesticas clades incessanter agebant* (cf. *De Excidio Britanniae* 19.4 and *Historia Regum Britanniae* 185.2-3). It is only fitting that, in sounding the death-knell of the British, Geoffrey should incorporate reminiscences of Gildas's ruin of Britain.

This list of verbal echoes of the *De Excidio Britanniae* contained in the *Historia Regum Britanniae* is impressively long; it indicates how very intimate was Geoffrey's knowledge of Gildas's work. In addition to those chapters of the *De Excidio Britanniae* from which he made more substantial, extended borrowings (above, p.13), he also includes in his history elements of Chapters 1, 6, 12, 13, 17 and 26. In total, then, Geoffrey quotes or echoes the preface of the *De Excidio Britanniae*, a good part of the *historia* section (2-26) and the opening chapters of the denunciation of the kings. It is, therefore, most likely that he knew Gildas's book in its entirety, since the sections which he does not use – the attack on the clergy and the multitudes of Biblical quotations employed by Gildas to justify both it and its counterpart against the kings – were hardly suitable material for incorporation into the *Historia Regum Britanniae*. Geoffrey certainly had an excellent working knowledge of what was, as we have seen, a rare text in the twelfth century and was readily able to employ it with great effect as a literary and verbal model.

Of the reminiscences collected here, many bear witness to Geoffrey's admiration for Gildas as a writer, as he borrows effective or striking expressions or images directly from the *De Excidio Britanniae*. Others demonstrate how Geoffrey softened his predecessor's hostility to the decadence of the British or adapted it to the artistic needs of his own history. Very many of the echoes appear in contexts far removed – often pointedly so – from their Gildasian originals. Whatever the verdict on Geoffrey of Monmouth as an historian, this imaginative and skilful use of the *De Excidio Britanniae* throws valuable light on his talents as a creative artist reinterpreting a source for his own literary purposes.

III. Geoffrey of Monmouth's attitude to Gildas

Despite his wide-ranging use of the *De Excidio Britanniae* as a source for literary imitation and variation, Geoffrey only once acknowledges his debt to Gildas: in Cadwallon's speech at *Historia Regum Britanniae* 195 (above, p.12). Yet this direct recognition of Gildas as a source is only one of seven occasions when Geoffrey mentions him by name in the *Historia Regum Britanniae*. These references to Gildas present important evidence for Geoffrey's attitude to his source. They are, in order:

1. *Historia Regum Britanniae* 1.3-4 (Gildas and Bede as sources for British history): *mentionem quam de eis Gildas et Beda luculento tractatu fecerant.*

2. *Historia Regum Britanniae* 22.14-17 (dispute of Lud and Nennius): *quam contentionem quia Gildas historicus satis prolixe tractavit, eam praeterire praeelegi ne id quod tantus scriba tanto stylo paravit videor viliori dictamine maculare.*

3. *Historia Regum Britanniae* 34.29-31 (the Molmutine laws): *statuit etiam inter cetera, quae multo tempore post beatus Gildas scripsit, ut . . .*

4. *Historia Regum Britanniae* 39.20-22 (the Molmutine laws again): *legat Molmutinas leges, quas Gildas historicus de britannico in latinum, rex vero Alvredus de latino in anglicum sermonem transtulit.*

5. *Historia Regum Britanniae* 72.37-40 (Roman missionaries at the time of Lucius): *eorum nomina et actus in libro repperiuntur quem Gildas de victoria Aurelii Ambrosii inscripsit. quod autem ipse tam lucido tractatu peraraverat, nullatenus opus fuit ut inferiori stylo renovaretur.*

6. *Historia Regum Britanniae* 100.43-5 (Germanus and Lupus): *multa per eos miracula ostendebat Deus, quae Gildas in tractatu suo luculento dictamine peraravit.*

7. *Historia Regum Britanniae* 195.13 (Cadwallon's speech; Appendix, p.39): *et ut Gildas historicus testatur.*

It has long been recognised that Geoffrey's appeals to Gildas as an historical authority are, with the exception of the first and last, patently fraudulent.[47] Gildas nowhere describes a dispute of Lud and

---

[47] See Faral, ii, *ad loc.*

his brother Nennius over the naming of London; nor could he within the historical confines of the narrative section of the *De Excidio Britanniae*. Gildas no more translated the so-called Molmutine laws from British into Latin than did Alfred from Latin into English. Gildas does record the British success under Ambrosius Aurelianus (*De Excidio Britanniae* 25.3), but the *De Excidio Britanniae* could never be legitimately termed the book which Gildas devoted to that victory. Nor does it contain the names and deeds of missionaries dispatched to the British king Lucius. Furthermore, the miracles of St Germanus can be found, not in the *De Excidio Britanniae*, but the *Historia Britonum*.[48] Since the largest family of manuscripts of this work attributes it erroneously to Gildas, it might be maintained that here — but here, it must be stressed, alone — Geoffrey alludes to Gildas as the author of the *Historia Britonum*.[49] This argument, however, has been neatly countered by Faral,[50] who argues that Geoffrey would hardly have extended his verdict on the style of the *De Excidio Britanniae*, *luculentus*, 'brilliant', to that of the simpler *Historia Britonum*. Most probably the account of Germanus given by the *Historia Britonum* was in Geoffrey's mind, but he mischievously assigns it to Gildas. Thus, despite his extensive borrowings and imitation of the *De Excidio Britanniae*, Geoffrey on all but two occasions cites Gildas falsely as the source of material nowhere extent in that work.

Yet, in contrast to this flagrant abuse of Gildas's reputation as an historian, Geoffrey professes great admiration for his predecessor. Twice Gildas's tract is characterised as 'brilliant': *luculentus* (1) and *lucidus* (5). Its style too is so termed — *luculento dictamine* (6) — while Gildas himself is described as *tantus scriba* (2), 'so distinguished a writer'. With the conventional modesty of rhetoric Geoffrey claims that in comparison his own writing is 'homelier', *vilior* (2), and 'inferior' (5). All of this praise accords well with Geoffrey's frequent verbal echoing of the *De Excidio Britanniae*; but how can his intimate knowledge of that tract and his self-professed admiration for it be reconciled with his citations of it as an historical source in fraudulent circumstances?

Gildas, as we have seen, enjoyed a considerable reputation in the twelfth century; both William of Malmesbury and Gerald of Wales mention him with approval. But, as William of Newburgh tells us, its difficult style made the *De Excidio Britanniae* a far from common text. Many probably knew Gildas, if at all other than by reputation, as the author of the *Historia Britonum*.

48 Chapters 32-5, 39 and 47-50.
49 As, for instance, by Tatlock, *Legendary history*, p.401, n.22.
50 *op. cit.*, ii, p.223, n.1.

Geoffrey, who knew the *De Excidio Britanniae* so intimately, was able to exploit this situation. He incorporated large sections of Gildas's work into his own *Historia Regum Britanniae* and made extensive verbal borrowings from it; but this was done silently and a debt only once openly acknowledged. Instead, Geoffrey chose to attach Gildas's name to a series of fictions and so used his reputation as an historian to shore up more dubious elements in his narrative. At the same time, he included in these passages conventional compliments to Gildas's stature as a writer. It is an irony typical of Geoffrey: to adapt the *De Excidio Britanniae* almost without a word, while citing Gildas as an authority several times, almost always falsely. It is, perhaps, easy to imagine Geoffrey's wry smile when he penned the words (*Historia Regum Britanniae* 22.14-17): 'since Gildas the historian has dealt with this quarrel at sufficient length, I prefer to omit it, for I do not wish to appear to spoil with my homelier style what so distinguished a writer set out with so much eloquence'.

IV. The *De Excidio Britanniae* and the variant version of the *Historia Regum Britanniae*

Since the first publication of the variant text of the *Historia Regum Britanniae*,[51] a version which differs considerably from the vulgate, the question of its authorship and date has been the subject of scholarly debate: a debate which still has not been resolved. Hammer himself has suggested that the general characteristics of the variant are a tendency to omit or simplify speeches and rhetorical language and *a greater reliance on its sources*.[52] The following is an attempt to

---

51 ed. Hammer, *op. cit.* Hammer used four main manuscripts in his edition, but of these only two, D (Trinity College Library, Dublin, MS. 515 [E.S.12]) and E (Exeter Cathedral Chapter Library manuscript No.3514) are reliable witnesses to the variant version. H (London, British Library, MS. Harley 6358) is a hybrid, variant in its first half, vulgate thereafter. C (Cardiff, Central Library, manuscript 2.611) is a contaminated witness, heavily interpolated with the vulgate: see D.Dumville, 'The Origin of the C-Text of the Variant Version of the *Historia Regum Britanniae*', *Bulletin of the Board of Celtic Studies* 26 (1974-6), 315-22. It is unfortunate that Hammer used C extensively in his edition. For the purposes of this study, therefore, by the term variant version is meant only that given by D and E, as reconstructed from Hammer's apparatus.
52 *ibid.*, pp.10-12.

establish how far the latter is true of the variant text's use of the *De Excidio Britanniae* and assess the evidence for date and authorship afforded by its borrowings from Gildas. The variant does not, to my knowledge, contain any quotation of the *De Excidio Britanniae* independent of the vulgate text; this discussion has, therefore been limited to the eight passages of extended borrowings examined in section I.

In the first of these passages, the description of Britain (*Historia Regum Britanniae* 5 and Hammer, pp. 23-4[53]), the variant differs strikingly from the vulgate. All the Gildas-derived material from *quicquid mortalium usui congruit* to *traditionem praestant* is replaced by a shorter passage copied almost word for word from *Historia Ecclesiastica* I.1.[54] R.A.Caldwell[55] has used this close reliance on Bede to argue that the variant represents an early version of the *Historia Regum Britanniae* compiled by Geoffrey before he had access to a text of Gildas. He states that this 'looks like an early draft put together from original sources' and the vulgate 'like a deliberate revision'.[56] This is, however, highly illogical, since both versions are put together from original sources — the variant following Bede closely, the vulgate Gildas more independently — and it is impossible to establish priority on these grounds.

In fact, the variant version does contain in this chapter a phrase derived from Gildas. In common with the vulgate, it gives Britain's geographical extent as *octingenta milia passuum in longum, ducenta vero in latum continens*; this is not based on the Gildasian paraphrase of Bede and the compiler of the *Historia Britonum*,[57] but is far closer to Gildas's original at *De Excidio Britanniae* 3.1: *octingentorum in longo milium, ducentorum in lato spatium ... tenens.*[58] Thus, al-

---

[53] References to the variant are by page number in Hammer's edition, since Hammer divides the work into books. Although this follows the practice of Griscom's edition of the *Historia Regum Britanniae*, it is unfortunate, since the manuscripts are not consistent in their division and comparison with Faral's text is made more difficult.

[54] Both the variant and the vulgate versions are conveniently set out for comparison by Hammer, *op. cit.*, pp. 23-4.

[55] 'The use of sources in the variant and vulgate versions of the *Historia Regum Britanniae* and the question of the order of the versions', *Bulletin bibliographique de la Société Internationale Arthurienne* 9 (1957), 123-4.

[56] *ibid.*, p.124.

[57] *Historia Ecclesiastica* I.1, *per milia passum DCCC in Boream longa, latitudinis habet milia CC*; and *Historia Britonum* 7, *DCCC in longitudine milium, CC in latitudine spatium habet.*

[58] It should be noted, however, that the variant adds *passuum* to *milia*, an explanatory note drawn from Bede.

though it suppresses the majority of Gildasian borrowings in this chapter, the variant does here share one such borrowing with the vulgate; it cannot, therefore, be an early draft of the *Historia Regum Britanniae* assembled by Geoffrey *in ignorance* of the *De Excidio Britanniae*. It seems more likely to be a reworking of the vulgate (hence the common reminiscence of Gildas) in which the ornate rhetorical passage derived from the *De Excidio Britanniae* has been deliberately replaced by simpler material from Bede.

Such a suggestion can be supported by examination of the treatment by the variant of the remaining seven Gildasian passages. The fate of the description of Britain is shared by the account of St Alban (*Historia Regum Britanniae* 77) and the speech of Cadwallon (*Historia Regum Britanniae* 195), which are entirely omitted. The remaining five passages are found in both the vulgate and variant versions: Maximianus (*Historia Regum Britanniae* 86 and Hammer, p.98), the attacks of the Picti and Scoti (*Historia Regum Britanniae* 89-91 and Hammer, pp.100-103), Arthur's successors (*Historia Regum Britanniae* 180-3 and Hammer, pp.252-3), Ceredig and the Africans (*Historia Regum Britanniae* 184 and Hammer, p.253) and the plague (*Historia Regum Britanniae* 203 and Hammer, p.261). It is clear that the variant, despite omissions, retained the Gildas-based passages of the vulgate more often than it suppressed them.

In all the passages common to the vulgate and variant texts, however, the variant's treatment is very free; it omits much rhetorical writing and characteristic Gildasian imagery and vocabulary. Let us take as an example the account of the raids of the Picti and Scoti as remodelled by the variant version (Hammer, pp.100-103):[59]

V.13 ... *mittuntur* ergo *legati Romam cum epistolis* ad senatum, lacrimosis suspiriis *postulantes* auxilium, *vovent*es se *in perpetuum* servituros, *si* ab hac dira hostium immpressione liberarentur. *quibus mox committitur legio praeteriti mali* non *immemor*, quae, ut advenit in Britanniam, *cum hostibus congressa magnam multitudinem* stravit et reliquos usque ad Albaniam fugere coegit. sicque dei nutu *a tam atroci* oppressione exempti, vallum cum muro immensum *inter Albaniam et Deiram a mari usque ad mare* construxerunt, *arcendis hostibus* opportunum, indigenis vero magnum *tutamen* et defensionem facturum. *erat autem* tunc Albania penitus incursione *barbarorum vastata*, ita ut indigenis expulsis *receptaculum* esset omnium perditorum.

---

[59] Parallels between variant and vulgate text are indicated by italic type.

V.14 *Romani* igitur depulsis hostibus Romam reverti decreverunt, *denunti*antes Britonnibus *nequaquam se laboriosis expeditionibus posse* ulterius fatigari et *ob erraticos latrunculos* Romanam iuventutem ac potestatem *terra marique tam frequentibus* expeditionibus *vexari.* malle potius toto tributo fraudari quam tot laboriosis occursionibus subiacere. convocatis itaque in urbe Lundonia optimatibus terrae repedare se Romani profitentur.

V.15 atque ut se ab incursione erraticorum hostium tueantur, *turres, in litore quo* navigium piratarum applicare formidabant, struendas decernunt ut, sicut praefatus murus in terra ad munitionem erat, ita et turres sibi a mari pro munimento fierent. *armorum* quoque *instruendorum exemplaria* a Romanis habuerant, peltis et pilis suadentes ut se ipsos *coniuges, liberos,* opes *et, quod his maius* erat, *libertatem* vi propria atque armorum defensione *viriliter dimicando* tuerentur. sicque *vale dicto Romani, tamquam ultra non reversuri,* profecti sunt. quo audito Gwanius et Melga navibus, *quibus fuerant in Hiberniam vecti, emerg*entes cum Scotis et Norweiensibus, Dacis et Pictis, *omnem Albaniam murotenus capessunt.* contra hos constituuntur *in edito murorum* rudes *ad pugnam*, qui leviter prostrati atque telorum grandine territi, muris deiciuntur et fugam arripiunt. hostes itaque, deiecto ad solum muro, fugientes persequuntur, persequendo interimunt, quosdam mancipatos carceribus tradunt et fit tanta strages temporibus illis quanta antea numquam facta fuerat.

V.16 *igitur* rursum nihilominus *miserae* Britonum *reliquiae mittunt* Romam *epistolas ad Agitium*, summum *Romanae potestatis virum*, in hunc modum: *'Agitio ter consuli, gemitus Britonum.'* et post pauca *querentes adiciunt: 'nos mare ad barbaros, barbari ad mare repellunt. interea oriuntur duo genera funerum: aut enim submergimur aut iugulamur.'* verum Romani nulla commoti pietate, auxilium ferre recusant, praetendentes eorum saepissime laboriosam in Britanniam expeditionem et praeterea de tributis fraudationem. *Legati tristes redeunt* atque huiuscemodi repulsam denuntiant.

Examination of this passage reveals how unsatisfactory is the view that the variant version represents an early draft of the *Historia Regum Britanniae*. The variant does not rely more closely on the *De Excidio Britanniae* than the vulgate; though its account has its origins in Gildas's, it is completely rewritten and greatly abbreviated. If Geoffrey had produced such an initial version of the *Historia Regum Britanniae*, in which, although he knew the *De Excidio Britanniae*, he made only sparing use of it and altered its style extensively to produce a more unified, less rhetorical effect, was he likely at a later date to

27

incorporate further Gildasian passages into an expanded version and, moreover, rejecting his earlier complete rewriting, to allow more of Gildas's rhetoric to stand, although it was not entirely in keeping with the feel of his own Latin? Rather, the variant text, as examination of the above passage as transmitted by it reveals, is not a direct revision of the *De Excidio Britanniae* itself, but a remodelling of the vulgate, quite independent of the *De Excidio Britanniae*. The treatment of this and the remaining extracts of Gildas's work by the variant accords far better with the view that it is the work of a later redactor of the *Historia Regum Britanniae*: a view fully concomitant with its omission of speeches and rhetorical flourishes to produce a shortened, simplified version of Geoffrey's history.

Hammer has argued that an unknown, later redactor was indeed responsible for the variant text on the ground of its bold handling of the original vulgate.[60] Caldwell, despite his error in asserting that the variant was an early draft, has elsewhere maintained that it was used by Wace in the *Roman de Brut* and was, therefore, in circulation by the time of Geoffrey's death.[61] This naturally opens the possibility that Geoffrey himself revised the *Historia Regum Britanniae* and was, thus, the 'redactor' of the variant version.

The improbability of this supposition can be demonstrated by a comparison of the variant's narrative of the raids of the Picti and Scoti with its original in the vulgate. The redactor was not without skill; as has been noted he completes the process of integration of the style of Gildasian borrowings with that of the *Historia Regum Britanniae*, a process which Geoffrey had taken only half-way. A notable feature of the redactor's writing is, however, a certain artless repetitiousness. In his four short chapters some words recur with monotonous regularity. At V.14 the Romans are worn out not only by the *laboriosis expeditionibus* of the vulgate (and the *De Excidio Britanniae*), but also by *frequentibus expeditionibus* and *laboriosis occursibus*, while the complete phrase appears again in V.16 as *laboriosam in Britanniam expeditionem*. The enemy are called *erraticos latrunculos* in V.14 and the adjective repeated in V.15 in the phrase *ut se ab incursione erraticorum hostium tueantur*. Indeed, this whole phrase is a rehash, since *incursione barbarorum* appears in V.13 and the verb *tueor* later in *viriliter dimicando tuerentur* at V.15. In the

60 *Variant Version*, pp.19-20.
61 'Wace and the Variant Version of Geoffrey of Monmouth', *Speculum* 31 (1956), 675-82; Caldwell's arguments have, however, been vigorously countered by P.Gallais, 'La variant version de l'*Historia Regum Britanniae* et le *Brut* de Wace', *Romania* 87 (1966), 1-32.

same chapter *turres . . . collocari* of the vulgate becomes *turres . . . struendas* under the influence of *armorum quoque instruendorum exemplaria* three lines later and repeats both the verb *struo* and the gerundive form. Nothing could be further than these examples of heavy-handed and unimaginative repetition from the careful imitation and variation which, as we have seen characterised Geoffrey's treatment in the vulgate of passages borrowed from the *De Excidio Britanniae*. Whoever, then, was responsible for this revised version of the *Historia Regum Britanniae*, it was certainly not Geoffrey of Monmouth himself.

A final question: was the unknown redactor deliberately hostile to Gildas? Had he, like William of Newburgh, discovered a text of the *De Excidio Britanniae* and found it 'inelegant and tasteless in style'?[62] If so, his omission or comprehensive reworking of passages drawn from the *De Excidio Britanniae* could reflect an aversion to the peculiarities of Gildas's Latin. Conversely, much of the omitted material is contained in speeches which were themselves prime candidates for excision. The heavy rewriting of other passages may simply have resulted from the difficulty, *per se*, of Gildas-based borrowings, rather than a conscious attack on Gildasian *color*.

That the second hypothesis is the more probable is indicated by the variant version's treatment of allusions to Gildas by name. Of the seven discussed in section III, four are omitted; but in the case of at least two, context may be responsible, as one is to be found in Cadwallon's speech, the other in the highly-wrought preface. The remaining three appear as follows:

4. Molmutine laws (Hammer, p. 57)
   legat Molmontinas leges, quas Gildas historiographus de Britannico in Latinum (transtulit, *add.* E), rex vero Aluredus de Latino in Anglicum transtulit, et reperiet luculenter scripta quae optat.

5. Roman missionaries at the time of Lucius (Hammer, p. 85)
   quorum actus in libro quem Gildas historiographus composuit, lucide scripti reperiuntur.

6. Germanus and Lupus (Hammer, p. 116)
   multa per eos deus fecit miracula in regno Britanniae, quae Gildas in tractatu suo luculenter exposuit.

Of these, the first follows the vulgate exactly, the second is abbreviated and the third slightly altered; but in all three the references to Gildas are reproduced and also Geoffrey's assessment of him as a

---

62 Above, p. 2.

brilliant writer, *luculenter scripta, lucide scripti* and *luculenter exposuit*. If the redactor actively disliked the *De Excidio Britanniae* and worked through the *Historia Regum Britanniae* suppressing and simplifying passages borrowed from it, he was unlikely to allow this verdict to stand on three separate occasions. Rather, as the variant version demonstrates, he was the enemy of long speeches and rhetoric in general, and material from the *De Excidio Britanniae*, probably without being recognised for what it was, simply fell an innocent victim to his editorial policy.

It may be concluded that the treatment of passages derived from the *De Excidio Britanniae* in the variant version provides important evidence for the circumstances of its composition. The variant is not an early draft composed by Geoffrey before he had possession of Gildas's work, since it too contains Gildas-derived passages. Examination of these passages reveals that the variant is a later revision of the vulgate. Nor is Geoffrey of Monmouth likely to have been responsible for this slightly clumsy abbreviation of the *Historia Regum Britanniae* so inferior to his own literary methods. Whatever its precise date and place of origin, the variant is a simplified version of the vulgate, compiled by a later redactor.

V. The *De Excidio Britanniae* and the *Vita Merlini*

The *Vita Merlini*, Geoffrey's last work, probably composed between 1148 and 1155,[63] is of a very different character to that of the *Historia Regum Britanniae*. Its opening line announces its subject as: *fatidici vatis rabiem musamque iocosam*. It consists of an often light-hearted narrative of the madness of Merlin, interspersed with prophecies of the kind also to be found in the *Historia Regum Britanniae* (above, p.16). Although the work differs from Geoffrey's history in literary intent, it has much in common with it. Much of the alleged historical setting of the *Vita Merlini* is directly derived from the narrative of the *Historia Regum Britanniae*. The *Vita* also exhibits Geoffrey's characteristic freedom in adapting his sources, both Celtic and Latin.[64] As a postscript to my discussion of Geoffrey's borrowings from the *De Excidio Britanniae* in the *Historia Regum Britanniae*,

63 On authorship and date, see Clarke, *op. cit.*, pp.36-42.
64 See Clarke, pp.1-5 and 7-15.

I here append some further reminiscences in this, Geoffrey's final composition.

All the echoes occur in the context of a conversation between Merlin and Telgesinus (Taliesin) about the ills currently besetting their race. This leads to a long excursus from Merlin on the troubles he has witnessed in his lifetime. At *Vita Merlini* 954-59 Taliesin's expressed hope that, if Arthur were summoned to return, he might defeat the Saxons, draws a pessimistic reply from Merlin:

> 'ergo necesse foret populo transmittere quemdam
> et mandare duci festina nave reduci,
> si iam convaluit, solitis ut viribus *hostes*
> *arceat* et cives antiqua pace reformet.'
> 'non,' Merlinus ait, 'non sic gens illa recedet
> ut semel in nostris *ungues infixerit* ortis.'

The passage contains two reminiscences. *Hostes arceat* recalls *De Excidio Britanniae* 15.2, *si hostis longius arceretur*, already echoed in the *Historia Regum Britanniae* (above, p. 21). Here Geoffrey transfers the British hopes for a protector from the Romans, to whom Gildas applies the phrase, to their national saviour, Arthur. The second, vividly metaphorical image of the Saxons 'fixing their claws' into Britain is drawn from a passage of Gildas not previously quoted in the *Historia Regum Britanniae*: *De Excidio Britanniae* 23.4, *in orientali parte insulae iubente infausto tyranno terribiles infixit ungues.*[65] Moreover, Gildas's description at this point of the *tyrannus* (Vortigern) as *infaustus* is also picked up by Geoffrey, who uses the same adjective of his Vortigern at *Vita Merlini* 993: *ceperunt cunctas infausti principis urbes.*

The exchange between Taliesin and Merlin also contains two other slight echoes of the *De Excidio Britanniae*. At *Vita Merlini* 949-50 Merlin describes the Saxon destruction of British cities with the words: *et nostras iterum crudeliter urbes / subvertit.* The verb *subvertere* in this context was probably suggested to Geoffrey by a phrase of Gildas in what forms virtually a table of contents of his work; at *De Excidio Britanniae* 2 one of the subjects to be narrated is *de urbium subversione.* Later in his speech, at *Vita Merlini* 1053-5, Merlin relates a period of indecisive warfare between the British and Saxons:

> enses inde suos vertere recenter in Anglos
> congressique simul vincebant saepius illos
> et vice transverso devincebantur ab illis.

[65] This borrowing was first noted by Mrs A.J.Dempster, *apud* J.S.P.Tatlock, 'Geoffrey of Monmouth's *Vita Merlini*', *Speculum* 18 (1943), pp. 265-87 at p. 266, n. 2.

This is a poetic elaboration of a similar series of alternate victory and defeat at *De Excidio Britanniae* 26.1: *ex eo tempore nunc cives, nunc hostes, vincebant.*[66]

It may also be noted that the *Vita Merlini* provides some information about Geoffrey's knowledge of details of the life of his predecessor. At lines 687-88 Merlin describes Taliesin thus:

> venit enim noviter de partibus Armoricanis
> dulcia quo didicit sapientis dogmata Gildae.

The implication is that Taliesin had been taught by Gildas himself. The dramatic date of the *Vita Merlini* is fixed by lines 433-5 which relate the murder of Arthur's successor Constantinus by his nephew Conanus. As we have already seen (above, p.00), Geoffrey had manufactured the four immediate successors of Arthur named in the *Historia Regum Britanniae* from Gildas's condemnation of five kings contemporary to himself at *De Excidio Britanniae* 28-36. The inclusion of Gildas in the *Vita Merlini* is therefore fully concomitant with the chronology of the *De Excidio Britanniae* as adapted by Geoffrey.

It is interesting that Geoffrey here refers to Gildas not by the conventional epithet *historicus*, but by the more traditional *sapiens;*[67] he may have considered this more appropriate to Gildas's role as a teacher in this passage. Even more important is that Geoffrey, himself of Breton origin, here subscribes to the view that Gildas had spent at least some time in Armorica. This may indicate that Geoffrey was familiar with the *Vita Gildae* by the monk of Ruys,[68] or a similar work, but there is not enough evidence to be certain of his sources for this belief.

The *Vita Merlini* does not depend on Gildas's *De Excidio Britanniae* to the same extent as the *Historia Regum Britanniae*. It is, however, an offshoot of that work and it is not surprising that in it Geoffrey sometimes glances at phrases in the *De Excidio Britanniae* and includes them, with more or less modification, in the poem. It is a

---

66 This passage of the *De Excidio Britanniae* is also borrowed by the *Historia Britonum* at chapter 63: *in illo autem tempore aliquando hostes, nunc cives vincebantur.*

67 For the connotations of this term, see M. Deanesly and P. Grosjean, 'The implications of the term *sapiens* as applied to Gildas', in *Fritz Saxl, 1890-1948: a volume of memorial essays from his friends in England*, ed. D.J. Gordon (London, 1957), pp. 53-76.

68 Ed. T. Mommsen, *Chronica Minora*, III (Berlin, 1894-8), pp. 91-106; *cf.* F. Lot, 'Études sur Merlin. Les sources de la *Vita Merlini* de Gaufrei de Monmouth', *Annales de Bretagne* 15 (1899-1900), 325-47 and 505-37 at p. 535.

further indication of his extensive knowledge of Gildas's work that even ten years or more after the completion of his history Geoffrey returned to the *De Excidio Britanniae* as an occasional source for his last literary production.[69]

[69] I am deeply indebted to Dr M. Lapidge and Dr D. Dumville who read drafts of this paper, to N.G. Davies, and above all to K.C. Grabowski without whom this article would not have been possible.

APPENDIX

Parallel passages between
the *Historia Regum Britanniae* and *De Excidio Britanniae*

1. *Historia Regum Britanniae* 5.1-24: description of Britain.

Britannia, insularum optima, in *Occidentali Ocea*ni inter Galliam et Hiberniam sita, *octingenta milia in long*um, *ducenta* vero *in lat*um con*tinens*, quicquid mortalium usui congruit indeficienti fertilitate ministrat. omni etenim genere metalli foecunda *campos late pansos* habet, colles quoque *prepollenti culturae aptos*, in quibus frugum diversitates ubertate glebae temporibus suis proveniunt. habet et nemora diversis ferarum generibus repleta, quorum in saltibus et *alternandis animalium pastibus* gramina conveniunt et advolantibus apibus *flores diversorum colorum* mella distribuunt. habet etiam prata sub aeriis montibus *amoeno situ* virentia, in quibus *fontes lucidi per nitidos rivos leni murmure* manantes *pignus suavis soporis in ripis accubantibus* irritant. porro *lacubus* atque piscosis fluviis *irrigua* est et *absque meridianae plagae freto quo ad Gallias navigatur* tria *nobilium flumina*, *Tamesis* scilicet et *Sabrinae* necnon et Humbri, *velut* tria *brachia* extendit, quibus *transmarina* commercia ex universis nationibus *eidem* navigio feruntur. *bis denis*, etiam, *bisque quaternis civitatibus* olim *decorata* erat, *quarum* quaedam *dirutis* moeniis in *desertis* locis *squal*escunt, quaedam vero adhuc integrae templa sanctorum cum *turri*bus perpulchra *proceritate erecta* continent, in quibus religiosi coetus virorum et mulierum obsequium Deo iuxta Christianam traditionem praestant. . . .

De Excidio Britanniae 3

Britannia insula in extremo ferme orbis limite circium *occidente*mque versus divina, ut dicitur, statera terrae totius ponderatrice librata, ab africo boreali propensius tensa axi, *octingent*orum *in longo mili*um *ducent*orum *in lat*o spatium exceptis diversorum prolixioribus promontoriorum tractibus, quae arcuatis *Ocea*ni sinibus ambiuntur, *tenens*, cuius diffusione et, ut ita dicam, instransmeabili undique circulo *absque meridianae freto plagae, quo ad Galli*am Belgicam *navigatur*, vallata, duorum ostiis *nobilium fluminum Tamesis* ac *Sabrinae veluti brachi*is, per quae *eidem olim transmarina*e deliciae ratibus vehebantur, aliorumque minorum meliorata, *bis denis bisque quaternis civitatibus* ac nonnullis castellis murorum *turri*um serratarum portarum domorum, *quarum* culmina minaci *proceritate porrec*ta in edito forti compage pangebantur, munitionibus non improbabiliter instructis *decorata; campis late pansis* collibusque *amoeno situ* locatis *praepollenti culturae apt*is, montibus *alternandis animalium pastibus* maxime *conveni*entibus, quorum *diversorum colorum flores* humanis gressibus pulsati non indecentem ceu picturam eisdem imprimebant, electa veluti sponsa monilibus diversis *ornat*a, *fontibus lucid*is crebris undis niveas veluti glareas pellentibus, *pernitid*isque *riv*is *leni murmure* serpentibus ipsorumque *in ripis accubantibus suavis soporis pignus* praetendentibus, et *lacubus* frigidum aquae torrentem vivae exundantibus *irrigua*.

2. *Historia Regum Britanniae* 77.4-29: St Alban.

In diebus eius orta est *Diocletiani* imperatoris *persecutio*, qua fere deleta fuit christianitas in insula, quae a tempore Lucii regis *integra* et intemerata *permanserat*. supervenerat enim Maximianus Heraclius, princeps militiae praedicti *tyranni*, cuius imperio *omnes subversae sunt ecclesiae et cunctae sacrae scripturae, quae inveniri poter*ant, in mediis foris *exustae* atque *electi sacerdotes* cum fidelibus sibi subditis *trucidati ita ut agmine denso certatim ad amoena caelorum regna, quasi ad propriam sedem, festinare*nt. *magnificavit igitur misericordiam suam nobis Deus, qui gratuito munere persecutionis tempore ne penitus crassa atrae noctis caligi*ne populus *Brito*num *offuscaretur clarissimas lampades sanctorum martyrum* ei *accendit. quorum nunc sepulturae et passionum loca non minimum divinae caritatis ardorem intuentium mentibus incuterent, si non lugubri barbarorum divortio civibus ademp*ta fuissent. inter *ceteros utriusque sexus summa magnanimitate in acie Christi perstantes* passus est *Albanus Verolami*us *Julius* quoque et *Aaron Urbis Legionum cives: quorum* Albanus, *caritatis gratia* fervens, *confessorem* suum Amphibalum, a *persecutoribus insectatum et iam iamque comprehendendum*, primum in *domo* sua *occuluit* et *deinde, mutatis vestibus, se*se *discrimine* obtulit, *imitans in hoc Christum animam pro ovibus ponentem. ceteri* autem duo, *inaudita membrorum discerptione lacerati* ad *egregia*s *Ierusalem port*as *absque cunctamine* cum *martyrii trophae*o convolaverunt.

De Excidio Britanniae 9-11

9.   quae licet ab incolis tepide suscepta sunt, apud quosdam tamen *integre* et alios minus usque ad *persecutio*nem *Diocletiani tyranni* novennem, in qua *subversae* per totum mundum *sunt ecclesiae et cunctae sacrae scripturae quae inveniri potu*erunt, in plateis *exustae* et *electi sacerdotes* gregis domini cum innocentibus ovibus *trucidati, ita ut* ne vestigium quidem, si fieri potuisset, in nonnullis provinciis christianae religionis appararet, *permansere*. ... ecclesiastica historia narrat, ita ut *agmine denso certatim* relictis post tergum mundialibus tenebris *ad amoena caelorum regna quasi ad propriam sedem* tota *festinaret* ecclesia.

10.   *magnificavit igitur misericordiam suam nobis*cum *deus* volens omnes homines salvos fieri et vocans non minus peccatores quam eos qui se putant iustos. *qui gratuito munere*, supra dicto ut conicimus *persecutionis tempore, ne penitus crassa atrae noctis caligine* Brittannia *obfuscare*tur, *clarissimos lampades sanctorum martyrum* nobis *accendit, quorum nunc* corporum *sepulturae et*

passionum loca, si non lugubri divortio barbarorum quam plurima ob scelera nostra *civibus adim*erentur, *non minimum intuentium mentibus ardorem divinae caritatis incuterent*: sanctum *Albanum Verolami*ensem, *Aaron* et *Iulium Legionum urbis cives ceterosq*ue *utriusque sexus* dive:sis in locis *summa magnanimitate in acie Christi perstantes* dico.

11. *quorum* prior postquam *caritatis gratia confessorem persecutoribus insectatum et iam iamque comprehendendum, imitans* et *in hoc Christum animam pro ovibus ponentem, domo* primum et *mutatis dein* mutuo *vestibus occuluit* et *se discrimi*ni in fratris supra dicti vestimentis libenter persequendum dedit ... *ceteri* vero sic diversis cruciatibus torti sunt et *inaudita membrorum discerptione lacerati* ut *absque cunctamine* gloriosi in *egregï*is *Ierusalem* veluti *porti*s *martyrii* sui *trophae*a defigerent.

3. *Historia Regum Britanniae* 86.14-16: Maximianus/Maximus

thronum autem *imperii* sui *apud Treveros statuens*, ita *debacchatus est in duos imperatores* Gratianum et Valentinianum quod, *uno* interempto, *alterum* ex *Roma* fugavit.

De Excidio Britanniae 13.2

... et *thronum* iniquissimi *imperii apud Treveros statuens* tanta insania *in* dominos *debacchatus est* ut *duos imperatores* legitimos, *un*um *Roma, alterum* religiosissima vita pelleret.

4. *Historia Regum Britanniae* 89-91: attacks of the Picti and Scoti.

89.7-22   *ob* hanc *infestationem ac dirissimam oppressionem legati Rom*am *cum epistolis mitt*untur, *militarem manum ad se vindicandam lacrimosis postulationibus posc*entes *et subiectionem sui* in perpetuum *vov*entes *si hostis longius arceretur*. quibus *mox* committitur *legio, praeteriti mali immemor, quae, ratibus trans Oceanum vecta, cominus cum hostibus congressa* est. *magnam* denique *ex* his *multitudinem sternens omnes e finibus depulit* atque oppressam plebem a *tam atroci dilaceratione liberavit*. ad *quos iussit construere murum* inter Albaniam et Deiram, *a mari usque ad mare, ut esset arcendis hostibus* a *turba instructus terrori, civibus* vero *tutamini*. erat autem Albania penitus barbarorum frequentatione vastata et quicumque hostes superveniebant oportunum infra illam habebant receptaculum. collecto igitur *privato* et *publico sumptu*, incumbunt *indige*nae operi, et murum perficiunt.

90.1-7   *Romani, ergo patriae denuntiantes nequaquam se tam laboriosis expeditionibus posse frequentius vexari et ob inbelles et erraticos latrunculos Romana stegmata, tantum talemque exercitum, terra et mari fatigari, sed ut potius sol*is *consuescendo armis et viriliter dimicando terram, substanti*am, *coniuges, liberos et, quod his maius est, libertatem vitamque totis viribus* defenderent . . .

91.1-5, 8-23 and 29-40   Post haec Romani *fortia monita formioloso populo tradunt. exemplaria instruendorum armorum relinquunt. in litore quoque Oceani, quo naves eorum habebantur, ad meridianam plagam, quia* exinde *barbar*i *timebantur, turres per intervalla ad prospectum maris colloc*ari praecipiunt. . . .
. . . Nam, ut *vale dict*o Romani *tamquam ultra non reversuri* abscesserunt, *emergunt* interum praedicti hostes Guanius et Melga ex navibus, *quibus* in Hiberniam *vecti* fuerunt, cum *taetris cune*is *Scotorum et Pictorum* et cum Norvegiensibus, Dacis et ceteris, quos conduxerant, et omnem Albaniam *murotenus capessunt. cognita* etiam *condebitorum reversione et reditus denegatione confidentiores solito* destructioni insulae eminent. *ad haec in edito* murorum *statu*untur rustici *segnes ad pugnam, inhabiles ad fugam trementibus precordiis inept*i, qui *diebus ac noctibus stupido sedili* marceba*nt. interea non cessant uncinata* hostium *tela, quibus miserrim*um vulgus *de muris tr*ahebatur et *solo allidebatur. hoc scilicet eis proficiebat immaturae mortis supplicium, qui tali funere rapiebantur quo fratrum pignorumque suorum miserandas imminentesque poenas cito exitu divitarent. . . . . . . quid plura? relictis civitatibus muroque celso iterum civibus fugae, iterum dispersiones, desperabiliores solito, iterum ab hoste insectationes, iterum crudeliores strages accelerant. et sicut agni a lupis ita deflenda* plebs *ab inimicis decerp*itur. *Igitur rursum miserae reliquiae mittu*nt *epistolas ad Agitium Romanae potestatis virum hoc modo loquentes:* "*Agitio, ter consuli, gemitus Brit*onum." *et post pauca querentes* adiciunt. "*nos mare ad barbaros, barbari ad mare repellunt.* interea oriuntur *duo genera funerum: aut* enim sub*mergimur, aut iugulamur.*" *nec pro eis quicquam adiutorii habent*es tristes redeunt.

De Excidio Britanniae 15, 18, 19, 20

15.   *ob* quarum *infestationem et dirissimam* de*pressionem legat*os *Romam cum epistolis mitt*it, *militarem manum ad se vindicandam lacrimosis postulationibus poscen*s *et subiectionem sui* Romano imperio continue tota animi virtute, *si hostis longius arceretur, vovens.* cui *mox* destinatur *legio praeteriti mali immemor,* sufficienter armis instructa, *quae ratibus trans Oceanum* in patriam ad*vecta* et *cominus cum* gravibus *hostibus congressa magnam*que *ex* eis *multitudinem sternens* et *omnes e finibus depulit* et subiectos cives *tam atroci dilaceratione* ex imminente captivitate *liberavit.* quos *iussit construere* inter duo maria trans insulam *murum ut esset arcendis hostibus turba instructus terrori civibus*que *tutamini* . . .

18.2   . . . murum non ut alterum, *sumptu publico privato*que adiunctis secum miserabilibus *indigen*is, solito constructurae more, tramite *a mari usque ad mare* inter urbes, quae ibidem forte ob metum hostium collocatae fuerant, directo librant.

18.1   igitur *Romani, patriae denuntiantes nequaquam se tam laboriosis expeditionibus posse frequentius vexari et ob imbelles erraticosque latrunculos Romana stigmata, tantum talemque exercitum, terra ac mari fatigari, sed ut potius sol*a *consuescendo armis ac viriliter dimicando terram substanti*olam *coniuges liberos et, quod his maius est, libertatem vitamque totis viribus* vindicaret.

18.2-3 ... *fortia formiduloso populo monita tradunt, exemplaria instituendorum armorum relinquunt. in litore quoque Oceani ad meridianam plagam, quo naves eorum habebantur, quia* et *inde barbari*cae ferae bestiae *timebantur, turres per intervalla ad prospectum maris colloc*ant et *valedicu*nt *tamquam ultra non reversuri.*

19.1-3 ... *emergunt* certatim de curucis, *quibus* sunt trans Tithicam vallem *evecti*, quasi ... vermiculorum *cunei, tetri Scottorum Pictorum*que greges, ... *cognita*que *condebitorum reversione et reditus denegatione solito confidentiores* omnem aquilonalem extremamque terrae partem pro indigenis *muro tenus capessunt. statuitur ad haec in edito* arcis acies, *segnis ad pugnam, inhabilis ad fugam, trementibus praecordiis inepta,* quae *diebus ac noctibus stupido sedili marceb*at. *interea non cessant uncinata* nudorum *tela, quibus miserrimi* cives *de muris tracti solo allidebantur. hoc scilicet eis proficiebat immaturae mortis supplicium, qui tali funere rapiebantur, quo fratrum pignorumque suorum miserandas imminentes poenas cito exitu devita*bant.

*quid plura? relictis civitatibus muroque celso iterum civibus fugae, iterum dispersiones solito desperabiliores, iterum ab hoste insectationes, iterum strages accelerant*ur *crudeliores; et sicut agni a* lanionibus *ita deflend*i cives *ab inimicis* discerpuntur ...

20.1 *igitur rursum miserae mitten*tes *epistolas reliquiae ad Agitium Romanae potestatis virum, hoc modo loquentes: "Agitio ter consuli gemitus Britannorum." et post pauca querentes: "repellunt barbari ad mare,* repellit *mare ad barbaros*; inter haec *duo genera funerum aut iugulamur aut mergimur." nec pro eis quicquam adiutorii habent.*

5. *Historia Regum Britanniae* 180-3: Arthur's successors

180.2-6 alterum iuvenem Wuintoniae, in ecclesia *sancti Amphibal*i diffugientem, *ante altare* trucidavit, alterum vero Lundoniis, in quorundam fratrum coenobio absconditum atque *iuxta altare* tandem inventum, crudeli morte affecit.

181.3-6 eiusdem diademate dignus esset si non foret *civilis belli* amator. *avunculum* enim alium, qui post Constantinum regnare debuit, inquietavit et in carcerem posuit, eiusque duobus filiis peremptis obtinuit regnum.

183.1-4 cui successit Malgo, *omnium* fere *ducum Britanniae* pulcherrimus, *multorum tyrannorum depulsor, robus*tus *armis, largior* ceteris, et ultra modum probitate preclarus, nisi sodomitana peste *voluta*tus sese Deo invisum exhibuisset.

De Excidio Britanniae 28, 30, 33.

28.1-2 ... sub *sancti* abbatis *amphibal*o latera regiorum tenerrima puerorum ... *inter* ipsa, ut dixi, sacrosancta *altar*ia nefano ense hastaque pro dentibus laceravit ...

30.1   Aureli Canine . . . *civiliaque bella* et crebras iniuste praedas *sitiens*

33.4   . . . *avunculum* regem cum fortissimis propemodum militibus . . . acerrime ense hasta igne *oppressisti* . . .

33.1-2   quid tu enim, insularis draco, *multorum tyrannorum depulsor* tam regno quam etiam vita supradictorum, novissime stilo, prime in malo, maior multis potentia simulque malitia, *largior* in dando, profusior in peccato, *robuste armis*, sed animae fortior excidiis, Maglocune, in tam vetusto scelerum atramento, veluti madidus vino de *Sodomitana* vite expresso, stolide *volutaris*? . . . quid te non ei omnium regum regi, qui te *cunctis paene Britanniae ducibus* tam regno fecit quam status liniamento editiorem, exhibes ceteris moribus meliorem, sed versa vice deteriorem?

6. *Historia Regum Britanniae* 184.18-23: Ceredig and the Africans

mox, de*populans agros*, ignem cumulavit in *finitimas quasque civitates. qui non quievit accensus, donec cunctam paene superficiem insulae a mari usque ad mare exussit, ita ut cunctae coloniae crebris arietibus omnesque coloni cum sacerdotibus ecclesiae, mucronibus undique micantibus ac flammis crepitantibus, simul* humi *sternerentur.*

De Excidio Britanniae 24.1-2.

. . . *de mari usque ad mare ign*is orientali sacrilegorum manu *exaggeratus*, et *finitimas quasque civitates agrosque populans non quievit accensus donec cunctam paene exur*ens *insulae superficiem* rubra occidentalem trucique oceanum lingua delamberet. . . . . . *ita ut cunctae coloniae crebris arietibus omnesque coloni cum* praepositis *ecclesiae*, cum *sacerdotibus* et populo, *mucronibus undique micantibus et flammis crepitantibus, simul* solo *sternerentur* . . .

7. *Historia Regum Britanniae* 195.11-19: Cadwallon's speech.

. . . et, ob *afflu*entiam divitiarum superbi, ceperunt *tali* et tantae *fornicationi* indulgere, *qualis nec inter gentes audi*ta est. et, ut Gildas historicus testatur, *non solum hoc vitium sed omnia quiae humanae naturae accidere solent et precipue, quod totius boni evertit statum, odium veritatis cum assertoribus* suis, *amorque mendacii cum fabricatoribus suis, susceptio mali pro bono, veneratio nequitiae pro benignitate, exceptio Sathanae pro angelo lucis. unguebantur reges non propter Deum, sed qui ceteris crudeliores exstarent, et paulo post ab unctoribus, non pro veri examinatione, trucidabantur, aliis electis trucioribus. si quis vero eorum mitior et veritati aliquatenus propior videretur, in hunc quasi Britannie subversorem omnium odia telaque torquebantur. denique omnia quae Deo placebant et displicebant, aequali lance* inter eos *penderent, si non graviora essent displicentia. itaque agebant*ur *cuncta quae saluti contraria* fuerant *ac si*

39

nihil medicinae a vero omnium medico largiretur. et non solum hoc *saeculares viri sed et ipse grex domini eiusque pastores* sine discretione faciebant.

De Excidio Britanniae 21.2-6

quiescente autem vastitate tantis *abundantiarum* copiis insula *affluebat . . . . . .* ita ut competenter eodem tempore diceretur: "omnino *talis* auditur *fornicatio qualis nec inter gentes.*" *. . . non solum* vero *hoc vitium, sed et omnia quae humanae naturae accidere solent, et praecipue, quod* et nunc quoque in ea *totius boni evertit statum, odium veritatis cum assertoribus amorque mendacii cum suis fabricatoribus, susceptio mali pro bono, veneratio nequitiae pro benignitate,* cupido tenebrarum pro sole, *exceptio Satanae pro angelo lucis. ungebantur reges non per deum sed qui ceteris crudeliores exstarent, et paulo post ab unctoribus non pro veri examinatione trucidabantur aliis electis trucioribus. si quis eorum vero mitior et veritati aliquatenus propior videretur, in hunc quasi Britanniae subversorem omnium odia telaque* sine respectu *contorquebantur, et omnia quae displicuerunt deo et quae placuerunt aequali* saltem *lance pendebantur, si non gratiora* fuissent *displicentia; . . . . . .* sicque *agebant cuncta quae saluti contraria* fuerint, *ac si nihil* mundo *medicinae a vero omnium medico largiretur. et non solum* haec *saeculares viri sed ipse grex domini eiusque pastores . . . indiscreto* boni malique iudicio carpebantur *. . .*

8. *Historia Regum Britanniae* 203.4-12: plague.

quia *fames dira ac famosissima insipienti populo* ahaesit ita ut *totius cibi sustentaculo vacaretur* provincia, *excepto venatoriae artis solatio.* quam etiam famem *pestifera* mortis *lues* consecuta est, *quae in brevi tantam* populi *multitudinem stravit quantam non* poterant *vivi humare.* unde miserae *reliquiae* patriam, factis agminibus, diffugientes *transmarinas petebant regiones, cum ululatu magno sub velorum sinibus hoc modo cantantes, 'dedisti nos deus tamquam oves escarum et in gentibus dispersisti nos.'*

De Excidio Britanniae 19, 20, 22, 25

20.2   interea *famis dira ac famosissima* vagis et nutabundis *haeret . . .*

19.4   . . . nam et ipsos mutuo, perexigui victus brevi *sustentaculo* miserrimorum civium, latrocinando temperabant: et augebantur externae clades domesticis motibus, quod huiusquemodi tam crebris direptionibus *vacuaretur* omnis regio *totius cibi* baculo, *excepto venatoriae artis solatio.*

22.2   . . . *pestifera* namque *lues* feraliter *insipienti populo* incumbit *quae in brevi tantam* eius *multitudinem* remoto mucrone *sternit quantam* ne possint *vivi humare.*

25.1   alii *transmarinas petebant regiones cum ululato magno* ceu celeumatis vice *hoc modo sub velorum sinibus cantantes: 'dedisti nos tamquam oves escarum et in gentibus dispersisti nos.'*

II

THE ROUND TABLE: IDEAL, FICTION, REALITY

Beate Schmolke-Hasselmann

'The rounde table at Wynchester beganne, and there it endeth, and there it hangeth yet.'[1] About the year 1450, when John Hardyng wrote these lines in chapter 83 of his *Chronicles*, King Arthur's Round Table was already as universally known as it is today. Many people in different countries seem to be agreed about what this table is or was, the Round Table being one of the most popular 'literary objects' that ever existed. Most of them would give a description of it very similar to the following: 'It is a circular dining table where King Arthur used to sit with his knights; an egalitarian institution where the seats were all alike and there was no difference in rank. The number of the knights was 12, or perhaps 24.'[2]

That is the general image of this venerable institution; of a sym-

---

[1] This table has recently been taken down and examined by Professor Martin Biddle and a team of experts. Their tentative conclusions were as follows: carpentry, 1250-1350; dendrochronology, c.1230; painting, 1518-1522 (with later restorations). A book on the Winchester Table will soon be published by Professor Biddle.

[2] An inquiry among students of medieval literature in Göttingen, professors of various historical disciplines and a representative number of participants at the XIIth Arthurian Congress in Glasgow 1981 gave the same results. A paper on the subject was first given at the congress. *Le Grand Littré* of 1961 gives the following definition: 'Chevaliers de la Table Ronde — les douze chevaliers que les vieux romans en langue d'oïl font compagnons d'Artus, roi des Bretons.' The 'blurb' of a popular student edition of Hartmann von Aue's *Erec* speaks of twelve knights, although Hartmann gives a long list of vassals and later in the text says that they are 140 in all. Film productions like the recent *Excalibur* have a tendency to fix a vision of King Arthur sitting at the Round Table in the minds of millions of spectators. Robert Mannyng de Brunne says that it was in order to see the Round Table that foreign barons came to Arthur's feasts (cf. Fletcher 1973, p. 207). A list of publications on the Round Table is to be found at the end of this contribution. They are referred to in the footnotes by the name of the author, the year of publication and the page number.

bolic, mystical, mythical object so practical and yet so strange, the history of which will be charted in the following pages.

Phenomena that appear simple and transparent at first sight often reveal themselves to be frustratingly contradictory and obscure when more thoroughly examined; and so it is with the Round Table. The first problem is that our modern vision of it openly contradicts the medieval concept as it is reflected by almost all French and English Arthurian poetry: in the medieval texts, King Arthur never had a seat at the Round Table. Secondly, its institution was never intended as a democratic device *avant la lettre*; on the contrary, it seems to have been an instrument of political repression. Thirdly, the membership of the Round Table fellowship was at no time limited to twelve or twenty-four.

Nor does the late thirteenth century confusion between the Round Table, a truly secular institution, and the Grail Table, a sacred symbol, help us to understand what the first of these two illustrious Arthurian tables was meant to signify at the time of its origin.[3] The main purpose of this contribution is in fact to give an answer to that basic question: what were the significance and function of the Round Table when it was first mentioned in the middle of the twelfth century?

In the European Middle Ages, dining tables were customarily rectangular.[4] They were made of simple wooden boards resting on trestles and covered by a linen cloth. These collapsible tables were set up in the great hall just before meals were served, and were removed by the servants immediately after.

> Quant on mangié, si font oster
> Napes et tables vistement.
>
> (*Le Conte del Graal*, ed. Roach, v.4080f.)

The word 'table', derived from the Latin *tabula* meaning 'board', has replaced the ancient *mensa* and *orbis* in Italy, France and Spain. In French, the word *table* is first attested in *La Vie de Saint Alexis*.

In medieval French, another word for *table*, the synonym *dais* or *dois* was frequently employed. It is rare in modern French and means *baldaquin, trône* or *estrade* today. The same word *dais* was taken over in English, and both the word and the object with its original function are still very common, and, as we shall see, not perhaps

---

3 For details on the relationship between Round Table and Grail Table see two articles in Micha 1976.
4 See Eames 1977 and Schultz 1879/80 *passim*.

without good reason. *Dais* is derived from *discus, δίσκος,* in late Roman times a wooden or marble disc on a pedestal serving as an individual dining table for one to three persons. But in the Middle Ages a dais is a large square dining table where the lord and his most honoured guests have their places. Although roundness is implicit in *discus*, and although the Romans dined almost exclusively at circular tables (also called *orbis*), old French *dais/dois* and English *dais* evoke no notion of circularity.

The medieval lord used to dine sitting at his *haut dais*, a rectangular table erected normally on an elevated platform (ME. hiȝe table). His most important guests were placed to his right and to his left, according to their rank. Rules of etiquette and precedence were extremely complicated. On feast days, when the hall was filled with a great crowd of knights, ladies, squires, and commoners, many other trestle tables were placed at right angles to the dais, a plan familiar from Oxford and Cambridge colleges.

In the medieval period, a circular table was an extraordinary object, not merely uncommon in every day life, but practically unknown. For this reason, it seems that such a table was not readily imagined in the twelfth and thirteenth centuries. Miniatures in Arthurian manuscripts show that King Arthur's Round Table was represented in a great variety of shapes — like a disc or a half-circle (sigma), like a ring (with a large or a small hole in the centre) or like a broken ring with an opening for servants to enter.

Like Tatlock and Delbouille,[5] I do not believe that any Round Table was ever associated with King Arthur before Wace, a chronicler patronised by Henry II Plantagenet, first mentioned it in his *Roman de Brut*[6] and proceeded to tell the story of its institution. Not one of the numerous references to the Arthurian legend before the middle of the twelfth century mentions the Round Table.[7] Nor is it present in the earliest iconographic material — the famous Modena archivolt and the mosaics in Southern Italy.[8] But immediately after Wace's

---

5 See Delbouille 1953, p.187; the author believes that King Arthur as owner of the Round Table was the result of a substitution; that it had before been ascribed to an Asian king, Herla; he finds a source in Walter Map's *De nugis curialium*. Tatlock 1950, pp.471ff. ('I find no sound argument for Welsh origin', p.473).

6 Ed. I. Arnold (SATF), 2 vols, Paris 1938/1940 and *La partie arthurienne du Roman de Brut* (Extrait du manuscrit B.N. fr. 794), ed. I. Arnold and M. Pelan, Paris 1962; the quotations are taken from the 1962 edition.

7 See Fletcher 1973 and Schirmer 1962 *passim*.

8 See Loomis/Loomis 1938, pp.15ff. and illus. 3-9a; as a twelfth century portal archivolt at the Abbey of Charlieu (where a Last Supper scene at a sigma-

painstaking elaboration of the Arthurian part of Geoffrey of Monmouth's *Historia Regum Britanniae*, into which he introduced only a small amount of other new material, practically all the extant Arthurian vernacular texts and some Latin writings refer to the Round Table as an object or, more often, as a fellowship, as if it were perfectly normal to do so.[9]

In addition to the famous passage where Wace speaks of the foundation of the Round Table, he mentions it twice a little later in the text.[10] Chrétien de Troyes, for whose romances Wace is the most important single source, only refers to it three times — twice in *Erec* and once in *Le Conte del Graal* — although his five Arthurian romances together total more than thirty thousand lines:

> uns chevaliers, Erec a non;
> de la Table Reonde estoit,
> an la cort grant los avoit.   (*Erec*, ed. Roques, vv. 82 ff.)

> Mes d'auques des meilleurs barons
> vos sai bien a dire les nons,
> de ces de la Table Reonde,
> qui furent li meillor del monde.   (*Erec*, ed. Roques, vv. 1669 ff.)

> Et estes vos, dites le moi,
> De cels de la Table Roonde,
> Qui sont li plus proisié del monde?
>   (*Conte del Graal*, ed. Roach, vv. 8125 ff.)

shaped table is represented) shows, it would have been easy to copy such a scene in Modena if the Round Table had been a famous attribute of King Arthur at the beginning of the twelfth century; see Fig. 5 in Loomis 1926, *PMLA*.

9 Vernacular texts from 1170 (the presumed date of Chrétien's *Erec*) onwards regularly mention the Round Table in the prologue or exposition, see Schmolke-Hasselmann 1981; it is curious, though, that even after 1155 Arthurian fiction in the Latin language omits references to the Round Table altogether. Neither of the two extant Latin romances mention it. Possibly it was so unfamiliar a motif to a conservative clerk deeply immersed in learned Arthurian texts like chronicles and genealogies, that he was unable to integrate the recent invention. The Table does not figure in the long list of Arthur's precious objects given by Andreas Capellanus; it is only Johannes de Hauvilla in his *Architrenius*, written 1183/84 who, drawing on Geoffrey of Monmouth and Wace as a source, speaks of 'Arturus, teretis mense genitiva venustas', ed. Schmidt, p. 214 (Liber Sextus, Cap. I, v. 2.) As usual, Arthur's name is mentioned in a political context, as a means to flatter the poet's patron, the archbishop of Rouen. *Historia Meriadoci* and *De Ortu Walwanii* were written in the twelfth century according to the recent research of Mrs Mildred C. Day (paper presented at the Glasgow congress); Mrs Day was able to point to several allusions to Henry II of England (cf. abstracts in *BBSIA* 31 and 33).

10 See quotations p. 46.

It is not difficult to see that these passages go back to Wace's *Brut* as a source. Like Wace, Chrétien, too, speaks of the Round Table as of something very familiar to his readers; on the other hand, these three quotations show that the Round Table evidently holds no important place in the poet's narrative plan — it is a negligible item mentioned *en passant*, never described in detail. This observation might serve as another argument against those scholars who believe that the table belongs to the most ancient Arthurian tradition.[11] Two inconspicuous couplets from Chrétien's *Perceval* assume their correct meaning only when viewed in the light of an apposition between *Table Ronde* and *dois*:

> Et li rois Artus ert assis
> *Au chief de la table* pensis.   (ed. Roach, v. 913 f.)

> La roïne sist dejoste
> Le roi Artu *al chief del dois*.   (*ibid.*, v. 2786 f.)

The King sits 'al chief de la table, al chief del dois'. Not even Chrétien would have dreamed of placing Arthur together with his knights at the Round Table. A monarch cannot be the equal of his barons; that would be against nature.

A survey of the two other very early authors who mention the *Table Reonde* confirms this view. Marie de France speaks of it in her Arthurian lay *Lanval*:

> A ceus de la Table Rounde —
> N'ot tant de teus en tut le munde —
> Femmes et teres departi.   (ed. Rychner, vv. 15 ff.)

Even more revealing are the references in Béroul's *Tristran*:

> A un pastor qui chalemele
> A demandé: 'Ou est li rois?'
> 'Sire', fet il, 'Il sit au dois;
> Ja verroiz la Table Reonde,
> Qui tornoie conme le monde;
> Sa mesnie sit environ.'   (ed. Ewert, vv. 3376 ff.)

Dais and Round Table are here for the first time neatly distinguished: the king sits at his rectangular table, while his *mesnie* is assembled around (*environ*) the *Table Reonde*. They all sit on a sort of stage, apart from the crowd of common knights, as we learn from two other passages in *Tristran*:

---

[11] See Brown 1900 and Loomis 1949.

> Devant le roi vint a l'estage
> Ou s[e] oient tuit li barnage. (vv. 3395 f.)

> Li rois se lieve sus des tables: (v. 3401)

These *tables* are probably those on the stage (see p. 56). Another line in Béroul's *Tristran* reflects the habit among authors of talking of 'those of the Round Table' as a fellowship:

> Tuit cil de la Table Reonde
> Furent venu sor le Mal Pas. (vv. 3706 f.)

Here *reonde* rhymes with *fonde* (v. 3705), but such a case is extremely rare.[12] In general, only two rhyming words are admitted or 'possible' – *ronde : monde* and *table : fable*; these are the rhymes introduced by Wace and imitated ever since, another fact pointing to this chronicler as an innovator where the Round Table is concerned. The classic models from the *Brut* are:

> Et cil de la Table Reonde
> Dont tel los ert par tot le monde ... (vv. 4699 f.)

and

> Qui sont de la Reonde Table,
> Ne vuel je mie fere fable. (vv. 1741 f.)

Nearly all the rhymes in the earliest testimonies from Béroul's *Tristran*, Chrétien's *Erec* and *Perceval* and Marie de France's *Lanval* belong to the *monde* type. As we shall see below, this may have a special significance. But it is now time for a close reading of Wace's often-quoted lines. They contain a great deal of precious information, but their traditional interpretation has too long been taken for granted; it might even be said that the passage is so famous that its

---

12 There are a few other instances in French Arthurian verse romances: *Le Bel Inconnu*, ed. Williams, v. 227 f. Reonde : responde; v. 249 Reonde : esponde; *1. Cont.*, ed. Roach/Ivy, MS MQ, v. 12625 Reonde : seconde; Robert de Blois, *Enseignement des Princes*, ed. Ulrich, v. 1654 tauble : erauble. It is evident that from the point of view of vocabulary there would have been an ample choice. But the poets go out of their way to find new meanings and phrases with 'monde' or 'fable' like the author of the *1. Cont.*: 'Que lever durent de la table. / Bien sai, e si n'est mie fable ...' This text contains 7 rhymes on 'monde'. There are some more in Robert de Blois, *Enseignement* v. 1646 f. and *2. Cont.*, ed. Roach, MSS EKLMPQSTUV, v. 28543. All these are reminiscent of Wace and follow his pattern 'dont tel los ert par tot le monde' semantically. But there are also verses like 'Dehé ait la T.R. / et cil qui sient a l'esponde' (*Bel Inc.*, v. 249 f.). Middle English texts also have fable/table rhymes: cf. *Of Arthour and Of Merlin*, ed. O. D. Macrae-Gibson, EETS, Oxford 1973, v. 2195 f. and 6517 f.

exact meaning has remained unrecognised.[13] A literal translation, however, reveals some misunderstandings which have hitherto vitiated the views of scholarship.

> N'ooit parler de chevalier
> Qui auques feïst a prisier,
> Qui de sa mesniee ne fust,
> Por ce qu'il avoir le peüst;
> S'il por avoir servir volsist
> Ja por avoir ne s'an partist.
> *Por les nobles barons qu'il ot,*
> *Don chascuns miaudre estre cuidot,*
> *Chascuns se tenoit au meillor,*
> *Ne nus ne savoit le peior,*
> *Fist Artus la Reonde Table,*
> *Dont Breton dient mainte fable.*
> *Iluec seoient li vasal,*
> *Tuit chevelmant et tuit igal;*
> *A la table igalmant seoient,*
> *E igalmant servi estoient;*
> *Nus d'aus ne se pooit vanter*
> *Qu'il seïst plus haut de son per;*
> *Tuit estoient asis mayen*
> *Ne n'i avoit nul de forien.*
> N'estoit pas tenus por cortois
> Escoz ne Bretons ne François,
> Normanz, Angevins ne Flamens
> Ne Bergoignons ne Loherens
> De cui que il tenist son feu,
> Des ocidant jusqu'a Mongeu,
> Qui a la cort Artu n'aloit . . .
> (ed. Pelan, vv.1201-1227 = ed. Arnold, vv.9741-9767)

This quotation from the *Brut* is deliberately longer than usual. If the lines concerning the Round Table had not been too often isolated from the rest of the text and the lines immediately preceding and following, one misunderstanding might have been avoided from the start: that the number of the knights of the Round Table had always

---

13 Eg. Foulon 1959, p.99: 'The poet added an important detail: "all were seated within the circle (assis meain), and no one was placed outside (de forain)". Whence Wace derived this concept cannot be determined precisely, but he did credit the Bretons with many tales about it.' Tatlock speaks of 'democratic equality', while Mergell 1949 says: 'In der Sitzordnung der Runde, die die Würde des Königs nicht eigens betont, spiegelt sich das Wesen der Gemeinschaftsidee des Artuskreises.' (p.96, n.45). Daube 1975, p.204: 'Somewhere at the table sat the King.'

been twelve. It is here said explicitly that all good knights from the occident to Mongolia (i.e. the whole world and especially those from King Henry II's dominions and his allies — Britain, Normandy, Anjou, and Scotland, France, Flanders, Burgundy and Lorraine) were to come to Arthur's court and join his household if they wanted to be considered as courtly.[14]

> Never did one hear of a knight who was in any way considered to be praiseworthy, who would not belong to his household, if it were possible to have him. If he wished to serve for recompense, he yet never left for recompense. For the noble barons he had, of whom each felt that he was superior [to his companions] — each one believed himself to be the best, and nobody could tell the worst — King Arthur, of whom the Britons tell many stories, established the Round Table. There sat the vassals, all of them at the table-head,[15] and all equal. They were placed at the table as equals. None of them could boast that he was seated higher than his peer. All were seated *in medio*,[16] and nobody was at the far end.[17]

[14] Here Alixandre, Cligés' father, comes to mind. He asks his father, the emperor of Constantinople, for leave to go to Arthur's court: 'Car issir vuel de vostre anpire, / S'irai presanter mon servise / Au roi qui Bretaigne justice, / Por ce que chevalier me face.' (ed. Foerster, vv.112ff.).

[15] The word 'chevelmant' (Loomis: 'in knightly wise') is rare and seems difficult to translate. Arnold proposes 'en chevalier', Keller in his *Étude descriptive sur le vocabulaire de Wace*, Berlin 1953, translates 'en qualité de vassal immédiat'. I do not believe that the word derives from chevalier, but rather from chief, chef (as in *chief de la table*, cf. Chrétien de Troyes, *Li contes del Graal*, vv. 914 and 2787); chevelment thus signifies 'as if they were placed at the table-head'.

[16] *In medio* is an expression used in Latin texts for the description of seating arrangements in lordly or royal households. It means 'on the middle seat of the board, on the seat of honour'. Houck 1941, pp.333-4 is on the right track when she proposes *mayen* to mean 'approaching the place of honor'. But *mayen is* the seat in the centre, and at a circular table all seats are *mayen*, and none is *forien*. The expressions derive from *medianus* and *foranus*; Lecoy 1956 thinks that *mayen* means 'in the middle of two', but this is unnecessary if we accept *in medio* as meaning 'not alone at the table', but surrounded by other eaters of high rank. The anonymous author of a Middle English romance uses the expression 'midest': 'King Arthour sat withouten fable / Midest at þe heiȝe table.' (*Arthour and Merlin*, ed. O.D.Macrae-Gibson, EETS 268, Oxford 1973, vv.6511-2).

[17] For comparison see Loomis' translation in Loomis 1948, p.61: 'For his noble barons, of whom each thought himself the best and each regarded himself as superior, and none would admit inferiority, Arthur made the Round Table, of which Bretons tell many tales. There the vassals sat all in knightly wise and all equal; at the table they sat on an equality and were equally served. None of them could vaunt that he sat higher than his peer; all were seated within, and there was none outside.'

In the celebrated passage which we have translated, the notion of equality is heavily stressed. In so many words, Wace expresses the same idea over and over again, no less than eight times in fourteen lines. But 'equality' by no means implies a new relationship between the king and his vassals. The word applies exclusively to the barons. At the Round Table 'seoient li vasal', while the king continues to dine at his dais, as will be shown below. This is so natural for Wace that he does not need to mention it here. Again, it is nowhere said that these knights were all objectively the best in the world and therefore all equal in rank, but rather, that they all wanted to believe this, and that in reality there was a strong sense of rivalry among them. It is clear that they are *not* equals, either in rank or in valour; each baron cherishes the illusion that he is a better knight and/or of a higher rank in the courtly hierarchy than his companion. In order to show his position in this hierarchy, he desires a place as near as possible to the king at table, but others continually contest his right to do so. The object of these jealousies, King Arthur, decides to stop the daily quarrels by establishing a new seating order. He has a circular table made, and withdraws from the rivalries among the company of his knights; at his dais, he choses his *privez amis* (Wace: *les privez le roi, Brut* v.1740). Far from blurring the fundamental distinction between monarch and vassals, the new order is apt to emphasize it.

As the quotations from Chrétien show, twenty or thirty years after Wace's lines were written, the quality of the knights belonging to the Round Table fellowship was no longer subject to discussion: it was by now a well established fact that they were indeed the best in the world. But the internal rivalry went on even in the last Arthurian romances; who is the better knight — Perceval or Gauvain, Lancelot or Galaad? This fundamental question provided a constant theme for all Arthurian literature.

The *Bretons* mentioned in the text are not the Armoricans in particular, but the *Britones* in general, the Celtic inhabitants of Great and Little Britain. They are known for telling many stories (or lies) of King Arthur, a cliché familiar from many Latin and vernacular sources before (and after) 1155.[18] M. Delbouille and others have

---

[18] *Brut*, v.1247ff. Wace says: 'En cele grant pes que je di, / Ne sai se vos l'avez oï, / Furent les mervoilles provees, / Et les aventures trovees / Qui *d'Artur* sont tant recontees / Que a *fables* sont atornees.' He presents a longish digression on *fableors* and *fabler*. This passage most probably derives from William of Malmesbury's words: 'Hic est Artur de quo Britonum nugae hodieque delirant; dignus plane quem non fallaces somniarent fabulae, sed veraces

assumed that the word *fable* referred back to *table*, a conclusion that engendered many problems, as the statement contradicted the complete silence of the sources. Viewed in this light — that the fables are told about *Arthur* — a light which conforms to the most ancient Arthurian tradition, line 1212 from Wace's *Brut* can no longer be quoted in favour of the popularity of the Round Table among the Bretons before its first explicit mention in 1155.

As far as one can judge, before the making of the Winchester table, the Arthurian Round Table had never been a real object. If it had been, it would probably have presented a more uniform shape in iconography and popular tradition, it would have been mentioned in Latin chronicles (at least in Geoffrey's *Historia*); it would have been described in more detail by one of the many vernacular romances; or it would have been preserved in the twelfth and thirteenth centuries as a (fake) relic, like Arthur's bones at Glastonbury or his crown at Nefyn, or his sword Excalibur, donated to Tancred of Sicily by Richard I. But it would appear that the Round Table as an object was 're-invented' only in the thirteenth century, 'and there it hangeth yet'. Nevertheless, the concept of a Round Table must have its origin somewhere; several explanatory theories have been proposed so far.

The first of these identifies the Round Table as a Celtic myth or tradition. Breton warriors apparently used to sit down in a circle around the hero of the day to honour him.[19] This habit is said to have led to the invention of the Round Table. But as far as actual tables are concerned, it is well known from ancient sources that the Celts had a reputation for not being familiar with tables at all, either

predicarent historiae' (*Gesta Regum*, I, 8). Delbouille 1953, p.177f: 'Nous ne croyons pas qu'il soit légitime de nier l'existence de récits légendaires sur Arthur avant Geoffrey de Monmouth ... et l'on sait aussi qu'il [Wace] avait entre les mains, en tout cas, à défaut du texte de Herman de Tournai où il est question de la chaire et du four "famosi secundum fabulas Britannorum regis Arthuri", les Gesta Regum Anglorum de Guillaume de Malmesbury.' Tatlock 1950 thinks *fable* is a mere rhyme word.

19 Cf. the works of Brown, Bruce, Loomis and Marx. Their argumentation is based on Laȝamon's description of the founding of the Round Table and on a passage from Posidonius: 'When several dine together, they sit in a circle; but the mightiest among them, distinguished above the others for skill in war, or family connexions, or wealth, sits in the middle, like a chorus leader.' (Athenaeus, *The Deipnosophists*, transl. Ch.B. Gulick, vol. 4, p.191). The custom is mentioned also in *Bricriu's Feast*. Bruce writes: 'This passage [from Laȝamon's *Brut*] must be accepted as undoubtedly derived ultimately from Celtic tradition.' (Bruce 1923, vol. I, p.87). Brown 1900 believed that the Round Table derived from the round houses of the Celts.

round or square.[20] They apparently used small individual stools to put the dishes on. Moreover, theirs was a highly hierarchical society where rank and precedence played an overwhelming rôle in everyday life.[21] All this seems to exclude any idea of equality between the chief and the others on the one hand, and also among the warriors themselves on the other. The very fact that sitting in a circle had the effect of symbolizing the superiority of the one in the centre of the ring shows that this seating arrangement is quite the contrary of what Wace stresses as the function of King Arthur's Round Table. The old Celtic custom of sitting in a circle survives only as a vague and inconclusive memory and has little or nothing to do with the origin of the Arthurian table; no strict comparison is possible. Divested of its objective nature as a *table* and of its function as an instrument of *equality*, the Round Table is no longer what it was meant to be — it has lost its two essential characteristics.

At this point another interesting passage from Wace's *Brut*, referring to Arthur's solemn crown wearing on Whitsunday, must be discussed. It might be quoted to corroborate the *théorie celtisante*; but a close reading soon reveals that the contrary can be proved:

> Quant li rois fu au dois assis,
> A la costume del païs
> Assis sont li Breton antor,
> Chascuns an l'ordre de s'enor. (vv.1913 ff.)

Although these lines occur several hundred lines after the first description of the Round Table, Wace already seems to have quite forgotten what he had said of the new institution. Arthur is sitting at a *dois*, according to the custom of the country (a comma ought to be placed after *païs*, as Wace does not yet apply the *brisure du couplet*, and the sense of the words becomes clearer). At this rectangular table he is surrounded by his Breton knights, each of them seated 'an l'ordre de s'enor'. Of course, this is a profoundly different arrangement from the one narrated in vv.1213 ff., and it conforms perfectly to the habitual hierarchical structure of medieval society in general.

[20] Posidonius, *loc. cit.*, explains: 'The Celts place hay on the ground when they serve their meals, which they take on wooden tables raised only slightly from the ground.' For a discussion of Celtic scholarship on the Table Ronde see Eberlein-Westhues 1979, pp.186-193.

[21] Binchy 1954, pp.56 f.: 'When I speak of a hierarchical order I mean one in which society was more or less rigidly stratified, and in which the inequality of man — based on differences in birth and calling — had been erected into a legal principle ... the differences in status were the corner-stone of Irish law. ... After the king came what the jurists call "the grades of nobility".'

On coronation day, Arthur is said to remember various ancient customs. This feature (recalling Chrétien's words in *Erec* vv.1749ff.) is here introduced by Wace in order to stress the genealogical link between Arthur and his Trojan ancestors; it is an ideologically coloured statement:

> Costume soloit estre a Troie,
> Et Breton encor la tenoient,
> Quant ansanble feste feisoient,
> Li home o les homes manjoient,
> Que nule fame n'i menoient. (vv.1906ff.)

Whatever Wace says serves the purpose of the moment. At this point of the narrative, his overriding consideration is to celebrate the ancient link with Troy; therefore contradictions of other passages are unimportant. The same is true for Arthur's seating at the dais without the ladies. The entire ceremony is a conscious act in memory of his father Utherpendragon and of other ancient ceremonial customs in the realm. Uther's crown-wearing is narrated in much the same words as Arthur's:

> E li jorz de Pasques venoit
> Que il coroner se voloit.
> . . .
> Et quant la messe fu finee,
> Au mangier est assis li rois
> Au chief de la sale, a un dois.
> Li baron s'assistrent antor,
> Chascuns en l'ordre de s'enor.
> Devant lui s'est, anmi son vis,
> Li cuens de Cornoaille asis,
> Lez lui sist Yguerne, sa fenme . . . (vv.13ff.)

Unlike Arthur, Uther seems to know nothing of the 'old' custom of dining without the ladies. But such an argument would entail a misunderstanding of the ways of medieval narrative. Yguerne is here present at table only to give Uther the opportunity of admiring her beauty and falling in love with her. Such is the contextual function of the words. But certainly this passage, like vv.1913ff., reflects the normal seating arrangement. On feast days like these the barons would not sit at the egalitarian Round Table, not even in King Arthur's reign. Therefore Wace, without bothering about contradictions, reestablishes the traditional hierarchy. And from vv.31f. it also becomes evident what *antor* means: the barons sit next to the king and in front of him (*anmi son vis*[22]) at the rectangular dais (more or

[22] The normal seating, however, was only on one side of the table, cf. Eames.

less *forien*), and he himself sits *in medio* (*mayen*). *In medio* means 'not apart from the barons at another table', 'in the centre of the company', 'on the seat of honour'. It has nothing to do with any concept of equality between the king and his vassals or with sitting in a circle. Therefore, Wace uses *antor* in a much more general sense than Béroul's *environ*. From this we can conclude that the line 'asis sont li Breton antor' in no way refers to the Round Table or to any circular seating arrangement.

Another theory advocates a Christian origin. It establishes a link between the Round Table and the twelve apostles of the Last Supper. The Arthurian table is thought to be an imitation of a *tabula marmorea* exhibited to pilgrims in Jerusalem until the twelfth century as the table of the Eucharist.[23] L.H.Loomis argued that in Christian iconography the table of the Last Supper had nearly always been round or sigma-shaped up to the middle of the twelfth century. And the divine fellowship of the apostles is said to have first inspired the group of Charlemagne's twelve peers and then, a century later, the secular fellowship of King Arthur's twelve knights.

Although this theory was admirably presented in three consecutive articles, it never found broad acceptance among Arthurian scholars; however, nobody had ever tried to refute it with sound data until quite recently a young art historian in a brilliant essay[24] undertook to prove that L.H.Loomis had been wrong in principle and in detail. In fact, none of the sources she used says anything about the table in Jerusalem having been round; on the contrary, the word *tabula* (instead of *orbis, discus* or the more neutral *mensa*) points to the squareness of the object. In all probability, it was shaped like an altar. Only secular tables have a tendency towards roundness.[25] Moreover, it is not true that most of the Eucharist scenes in Christian icon-

23 Cf. L.H.Loomis 1926, 1927, 1929.
24 Eberlein-Westhues 1979; this important contribution was listed only in the *BBSIA* 1981. Independently (and at the same time) I had examined the same material and worked out an almost identical corpus of passages in Old French literature referring to the Table Ronde as that published by Mrs Eberlein-Westhues on pp.209-230. My conclusions were tentatively published in Schmolke-Hasselmann 1980, pp.50f.: Arthur has no seat at the Round Table, the companions are not twelve. The quotations from the romances referring to his sitting at the dais were overlooked by traditional scholarship.
25 Cf. Eberlein-Westhues, pp.193ff. Saewulf, a pilgrim to the Holy Land, wrote in his *Relatio de Peregrinatione*: 'Illic est adhuc tabula marmorea supra quam cenavit' [i.e. Christ] (Palest. Pilgr. Text Soc. 4, 44). Cf. n.34 in Eberlein-Westhues 1979: a twelfth century stone relief in the Sepulchre Church of Jerusalem shows Christ sitting at a rectangular table.

ography before 1150 show round supper tables; the shape depends on the concept of the Last Supper as either a sacred or a secular meal. Last but not least, the erroneous analogy of the number twelve alone would suffice to prove that there is indeed no genetic relationship between the Last Supper and the Arthurian Round Table: before the very end of the thirteenth century — when the Grail Table, whose model is in fact an altar or *mensa sacra* ('et tot fust quaree', Huth-Merlin, ed. Paris/Ulrich, vol.I, p.95), being an explicit imitation of the Last Supper table, started to be confused with the secular Round Table — the number of King Arthur's *compaignie* was never limited to that holy, symbolical number.[26]

We have already seen what the situation is in Béroul's *Tristran*: there the King is sitting at his dais while his *mesnie* sits 'environ la Table Reonde'. But the King does not usually sit alone; he dines in company of other crowned monarchs,[27] of his Queen and sometimes

---

[26] Chrétien, in *Erec*, gives a list of 34 knights; they are 50 in *Suite du Merlin*, 140 in Hartmann's *Erec*, 150 in *Mort Artu* and *Queste*, 240 in the *Second Cont.*, 250 in the Vulgate *Suite du Merlin*, 366 in *Chevalier as Deus Espees*, and 1600 in Laʒamon. This is no exhaustive enumeration. The most characteristic feature of the Round Table community is its unlimited extension and its power of integration, cf. Schmolke-Hasselmann 1980, pp. 51-57.

[27] Other descriptions of seating arrangements are to be found in *L'Atre Perilleux*, ed. Woledge, v.134-9:

> Les le roi seoit la roïne,
> Et li rois de Wales aprés;
> Gauvains et Tors, li fix Arés,
> Et Erec sist de l'autre part,
> Et Carados Briesbras li quart;
> Apres sont tuit li autre assis.

This is a strictly hierarchical order. In *Li Chevalier as Deus Espees* only crowned kings sit with Arthur on the dais:

> Puis s'assissent pres a pres
> Au maistre dois du grant pales.
> Corones portent hautement
> Si comme a si haut ior apent.
> Pour la hautece et pour l'onnor
> De la fieste de cel haut ior
> porterent corone .x. roi
> Ke bien tous nomer vos doi
> . . .
> Tuit cil .x. coronnes portoient,
> A la table le roi seoient,
> Tuit issi con ie vous devis.   (vv.69-113)

A similar arrangement can be observed in *Lai du Cor*, vv.415ff. In *Hunbaut* (ed. Stürzinger/Breuer, vv.3607-3618) Arthur asks Gorvain to join his household:

even Gauvain, his nephew, because the latter is not only the most valiant of knights but he is also of the king's lineage. Normally, following the twelfth-century courtly custom, the ladies, too, are admitted at the dais as well as at the Round Table (cf. *Erec* vv. 50 ff.) instead of being sent to another hall as 'a Troie'. All this is not explicitly narrated in the famous passage from Wace's *Brut*, but it is probably implicit, because those authors who have adopted that first account of the founding of the Round Table, while being obviously familiar with Wace's wording, are much more explicit on these points. Robert de Blois says in his *Enseignement des Princes*:

> Molt fu li rois bien apansés
> Et de grant sens enluminez,
> Quant fit faire la tauble ronde;
> Ce fut uns des beau sans du monde,
> Car quant li moillors chevalier
> Durent esseor au maingier,
> Chescuns voloit seor adés
> Par prouesce du roi plus pres.
> Li rois ne vout, que par envie
> Feïst nuls de ces vilonie,
> Si fist faire la ronde tauble,
>
> . . .
>
> La fist li rois par grant savoir
> Les moillors chevaliers seoir,

> Or os pri je, par cortoisie,
> Que vos soiez de ma mainnie,
> Des pers de la Tavle Reonde,
> Qui sont prisié par tot le monde.
> — Mout volentiers, ce dist Gorvains,
> Adont n'i ot ne plus ne mains.
> Li rois est as tables assis,
> Avuec lui li barons de pris.
> Des mes ne vos ferai pas fable;
> Mais ains qu'il lievent de la table . . .

(Note the two rhyme-types and the King sitting with the 'barons de pris'.) An interesting parallel can be found in *Sir Gawain and the Green Knight*, v. 107 ff., where Arthur sits at the 'hiȝe table' with Gauvain, Guenevere, Agravain, Bishop Baudewyn and Ywain: 'þise were diȝt on þe des and derworþly serued, / And siþen mony siker segge at þe sidbordez.' (vv. 114 f.). On the Bayeux tapestry Bishop Odo and five others are seen sitting at a sigma-shaped table clearly deriving from a Eucharist scene (possibly from the sixth century St Augustine Gospels). Odo sits in the centre in the place of honour, but in Byzantine tradition this place could also be on the extreme left. This example shows that normally a Round Table would not automatically exclude precedence or imply parity; the idea expressed in Wace's lines is indeed rather unusual for the period.

Et quant il furent essis
Ne seüst nul per droit avis
Dire, li queus fust premerains
Ne li queus fust li derreains.
Li riches rois, qui tant valoit,
D'autre part richement seoit,
Avec lui sui privé ami.   (ed. Ulrich, vv.1643-1673)

The *Second Continuation* (ed. Roach, MSS EKLMPQSTUV), vv. 28523ff. relates that the King sits at his *mestre dois* in company of the Queen, Gauvain, seven other kings, five archbishops and fourteen bishops. 'D'autre part iert la baronie' (v.28542) – they are three hundred in this early thirteenth century text, each knight being accompanied by his damsel. And 'aval la sale' sit the knights not belonging to the Round Table: 'sus chapes, sus mantiaux manjoient . . .' This hierarchy of three distinct groups at King Arthur's court is the same as in Béroul's *Tristran* (vv.3395f. and 3401, cf. supra p.46; the meaning of those lines becomes still clearer with the help of a passage from the *First Continuation* (MSS EMQU):

Si lava touz premiers li rois.
Et en aprés au mestre dois
S'en est alez en haut seoir,
Si que tuit le porent veoir
Cil qui leanz sont au mengier,
Et li doze vins chevalier,
Trois moins, a la Table Reonde.
Et en apres a la seconde
Resont assis li trente per.
Li ranc n'estoient mie cler
Des autres chevaliers qui furent
Assis au dois si com il durent,
A banc, a table et a terre.   (ed. Roach/Ivy, vv.12619ff.)

Here, as it seems, are to be found even two Round Tables (one for the thirty peers and another for the other companions, two hundred and thirty-seven in number), then the *mestre dois* and many other *dois* for the 'autres chevaliers', sitting on benches and on the floor – four different groups in all.[28]

---

[28] In two of the three texts quoted the concept of equality among the Round Table companions is expressed in words recalling those of Wace:

Ne seüst nul per droit avis
Dire, li queus fu premerains
Ne li queus fust li derreains . . . (Robert de Blois, vv.1668ff.)

Ainsint ne pooit l'en eslire
Qui ert li miaudres ne li pire . . . (*Second Cont.*, v.28555f.)

1. The Modena archivolt (Porta della Pescheria), ca.1125-30. (Photo Richard Barber).

2. The Last Supper from the 'Augustine Gospels' (6th cent.) Corpus Christi College MS 286 f.125. (Reproduced by permission of the Master and Fellows of Corpus Christi College, Cambridge).

3. The Round Table, Galahad and the Siege Perilous from 'La Queste del Saint
Graal', Bibliothéque Nationale MS F. fr.343, f.3 (14th cent.).

4. Arthur at table from 'La Queste del Saint Graal', Bibliothèque Nationale MS F. fr.776, f.374 (13th cent.).

5. Arthur at table from 'La Queste del Saint Graal', Universitätsbibliothek Bonn MS S 526, f.406 (ca.1285).

6. A Plantagenet king at table, Public Record Office MS E36/284 f.1.

7. World map, Bibliothèque Ste-Geneviève MS 782, f.374 (13th cent.).
(Photographie Giraudon).

8. Arthur at the Round Table from 'Wigalois', Leiden UBL, MS Ltk 573, f.1 (1372).

9. Arthur at the Round Table, Fresco from Schloss Runkelstein, Tyrol, illustrating the romance 'Garel' (ca. 1400).

10. Arthur at table from 'Parzival', MS Bayerische Staatsbibliothek München MS Cgm 19, f. 49 (ca. 1250).

11. The Winchester Round Table (carpentry, 13th cent., painting, 16th cent.). (Photo British Tourist Authority).

12. The Grail Table from 'La Queste del Saint Graal', Bibliothèque de l'Arsenal MS 5218, f. 88 (1351).

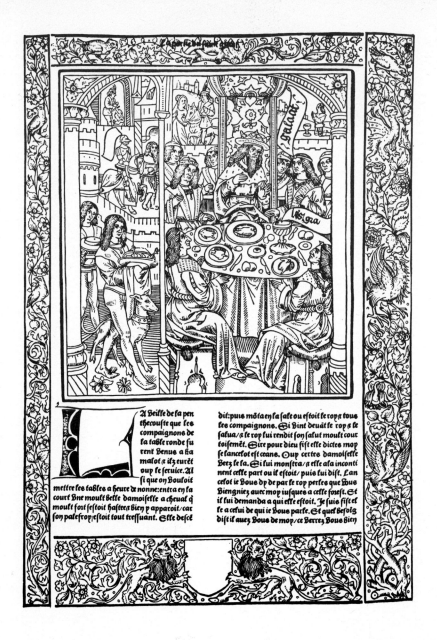

13. The Round Table with King Arthur, Galahad and the Grail from 'La Queste del Saint Graal'. (Woodcut from Vérard's 'Lancelot', Paris 1494).

The Arthurian prose romances explicitly distinguish between *haut dois* and Table Ronde:

> Et li rois fet l'eve corner; si s'asiet en son haut dois, et li compaignon de la Table Reonde s'assieent chascuns en son leu.
>
> (*La Queste del Saint Graal*, ed. Pauphilet, p.7)

> . . . les tables furent mises et s'assistrent li un et li autre; et servirent cel jor a la Table Reonde et a la table le roi Artu set roi . . .
>
> (*La Mort le Roi Artu*, ed. Frappier, p.138)

> [Artus] est si a malaise en son cuer qu'il ne pot mengier, ains sist a son haut dois en tel maniere que onques ne but ne ne menja tant com les tables sistrent.   (*Lancelot en Prose*, ed. Micha, II, p.316)

But the *Queste* also contains another passage where the institution of the Grail Table is described; it is Jesus Christ who speaks the words:

> . . . vos estes assis a ma table, ou onques mes chevaliers ne menja puis le tens Joseph d'Arimacie . . . le fais en semblance de mes apostres. Car tout autresi com il menjerent o moi le jor de la Cene, tout autresi mengiez vos ore a moi a la table dou Saint Graal. Et *si estes doze ausi come il furent doze apostres*. Et je sui li treziemes par desuz vos, qui doi estre vostre mestres et vostre pastres.   (pp.270f.)

Here for the first time the number twelve is to be found. But the knights who are admitted at the Grail Table are mostly not identical with those who were secular companions of the Round Table. It is a new group where spiritual purity counts more than chivalric prowess. In the *Queste*, Round Table and Grail Table are still neatly distinguished, although the former no longer appears as a place of merry-making; it has become a ritual object where all the seats bear the names of the owners (as on the Winchester Table) and the *siege perilleus* is covered with awe-inspiring words announcing the coming of its *mestre* (p.4). But several decades later, in the *Didot-Perceval*, a tendency the beginnings of which are to be found in the *Queste* is fully developed, and a new legend concerning the origin of the Round Table has arisen: not Arthur, but Uther and Merlin founded it; it has thirteen seats (the thirteenth is the *siege perilleus* in remembrance of Judas), and Arthur himself is but a humble servant at this sacred table which is no longer 'la Table le roi Artu': 'meismes le rois Artus servi' (p.146). The peers, once secular, have all become Grail seekers, they are now equals at last, equal before God:

> . . . je volrai molt onerer le Table Reonde, que Merlins estora au trans Uterpandragon, mon pere. Et si i volrai asseoir *es doze lius les doze pers de ma cort*. Si saciés que tot cil qui a ma feste seront et avuec moi volront de-

mourer seront a tous jours de la Table Reonde. (ed. Roach, p.141) ... Lors
commanda li rois que tout cil qui estoient a sa feste venu fussent tout
revesti *d'unes reubes et d'unes counissances* ... Et tant i ot de cevaliers et
de demisiaus que li rois en dona a cinc (sis) mil et quatre cens reubes et re-
counissances de la Table Reonde ... Et saciés que *Artus servi le corone el
chief en une reube d'or*.   (ed. Roach, p.143)

The Round Table community has changed to a chivalric order; all the
members wear the same garments and the same blazon. They are 'de
la Table Ronde', but have no seats 'a la Table Ronde'; these are
reserved for the Twelve Peers.

This slowly changing tradition goes back to Robert de Boron's
works, especially the *Estoire dou Graal*. But as a conception it is a
phenomenon secondary to Wace's Round Table; it is an explanation
a posteriori, serving the new religious spirit of the age which finds its
finest expression in the great prose romances. Other prose works like
the *Suite du Merlin* and *Tristan en Prose* start counting the king himself among the *compainz de la Table Reonde*, 'car Merlins l'i aveit
mis por la bonté de chevalerie qu'il sentoit en lui'. There, one of the
roots of the modern vision may be detected.

Like the *First* and *Second Continuations*, these latter prose
romances distinguish between three different *manieres de tables*: one
for the Peers including Arthur, a second for the 'compaignons erranz',
and a third for the 'chevalier mains prisié' (called 'chevalier mamelot'
in the *Second Cont.*).[29] Paradoxically, they establish a new hierarchy
where the traditional values like lineage, wealth and power are no
longer to be taken into consideration; but the differences in rank are
conserved. Arthur has now given up his separate seat at the *haut dois*
which had marked his superior position as a monarch; his new quality
as a distinguished member of the fellowship he (or Merlin) had
founded enhances his valour, because now be belongs to the sacred
brotherhood of those who will save the world. Although not their
equal by political standards, he is their peer from an ethical point of
view. And yet, for the anonymous author of the *Suite du Merlin* it
remains unthinkable that a crowned monarch like the mighty Arthur
should not have a seat at the Round Table different from all the
others. He therefore places him 'dreit el commencement de la table'.
(ed. Bogdanow, p.236).

The fact that the limitation to the number of twelve comes late in
the evolution of the Arthurian legend excludes a genetic link with
the epic Charlemagne and his Twelve Peers of France (although a
later mutual influence may be admitted). In any case, none of the

---

[29] Cf. J.Blanchard, ed., *Les deux captivités de Tristan*, Paris 1976, p.198.

chansons de geste ever mention any table in connection with the emperor, not even in the famous passage from *Le Pèlerinage de Charlemagne à Jerusalem et à Constantinople*. There the emperor and his peers during their tourist visit to the churches of the Holy City sit down unknowingly on the seats of Christ and his Apostles to have a rest; but the text mentions only *chaieres* (chairs). Seen from another point of view, however, the 'Charlemagne theory' could be regarded as the most plausible of all, because it considers literary influence as well as the ancient rivalry between the two head figures of French and British policy (according to Geoffrey of Monmouth, Arthur had been Charlemagne's overlord)[30] and other political necessities of the age simultaneously. It is indeed highly probable that more than one reason was to lead to the *inventio* of the Round Table towards 1154.

Some other theories concerning the origin of the Round Table must be mentioned here. Could its model be found in a passage from the Seven Sages of Rome[31] or in a quarrel about precedence that arose at the council of Rheims in 1049?[32] Was the altar of St Carantog in Wales the prototype of King Arthur's Table?[33] Did the Templars influence its making by their meetings in the round churches of their order?[34] It would be hazardous to exclude such possibilities categorically. Perhaps they all contributed to the evolution of the Round Table concept. But these theories do not attempt to explain the manifest function of the Round Table at King Arthur's court. Why should that monarch be driven to put such an imperious stop to the quarrels of his barons, an initiative resembling a social revolution? What were the true reasons for their envy and rivalry? Why would they not accept that 'natural' hierarchy and that structure of society which was proclaimed by religion and philosophy as God's holy will, at least in literature, if not in reality?

It was to King Arthur that Wace ascribed a round table. In later

---

[30] Also Gervase of Tilbury, speaking of Arthur's solemn and incomparable court at Caerlion has it that there were present the Twelve Peers of France whose company was instituted when Arthur was at Paris (cf. Fletcher 1973, pp. 186f.). The court of peers first became an official institution in France under Philippe II Auguste, cf. Köhler 1970, p. 20 and n.1.

[31] See Daube 1975.

[32] See Denomy 1951.

[33] See Kelly 1976.

[34] The Templars had a close relationship with the English royal house which fostered their interests. They settled in London before 1130 and built their 'New Temple' in 1161. During their meetings, they used to sit in a circle. As an order, their ideals are very similar in spirit to those of the Round Table brotherhood.

texts it is frequently called 'la table le roi Artu'. Arthur and his table are virtually inseparable. This object is the symbol of his power. The number of *compaignons* is unlimited. It is Arthur's pride to have at his table all the best knights in the world. Their integration in his realm and their increasing number enhance his reputation and make his court the centre of the world of *corteisie*. Paris and Constantinople cannot rival the glory of Caerleon/Camelot. All the mighty kings pay him homage. If anyone refuses to be his liegeman, Arthur becomes angry and aggressive.[35] Voluntary integration (submission) or annexation by treaty, marriage and war of all enemies are his foremost political aims. His ambition is to be an *imperator mundi*, a claim made legitimately by his supremacy in courtliness. He wants to follow in the footsteps of Alexander the Great, Solomon, Constantine and Charlemagne. And like all his ideal predecessors, he, too, is the owner of a round table.[36]

The hypothesis that the Arthurian Round Table might stand for a cosmic table ('Herrschertisch' or 'Weltentisch') as a symbol of Arthur's domination of the world was first developed by Mrs Eberlein-Westhues.[37] It is not difficult to prove that it is indeed a cosmic table or, to say the least, was intended as such in the second half of the twelfth century. I have already mentioned that *ronde*, during this period, rhymes almost exclusively with *monde*; this fact is highly significant. Wace, Marie de France and Béroul, all intimately connected with Henry II's court, obviously chose this rhyme intentionally. If it is said in *Tristran* that Arthur's table 'tornoie conme le monde', *monde* must be interpreted as the universe or cosmos, because in the twelfth century the *orbis terrae*, being the centre of the *mundus*, did not turn. The Round Table is a symbol, not an object in the world of reality; therefore the fact that it is said to turn is not a contradiction which would have to be explained by aid of mysterious Celtic myths. Another thirteenth century Arthurian verse romance, *Li Chevaliers as Deus Espees*, says that the number of seats at the Round Table is 366 (ed. Foerster, vv.114f.). What is intended by Béroul is fully explained by a passage from *La Queste del Saint Graal*:

[35] See Schmolke-Hasselmann 1980, pp.51-7 and Göller 1963 *passim*.
[36] For interesting details concerning the cosmic table tradition and the description of Charlemagne's table(s) see Eberlein-Westhues 1979, pp.230-247. Napoleon I seems to have been the last autocrat to order such a table (at Sèvres in 1806, see p.237, n.97).
[37] She describes the main difference between the Table Ronde and the 'Herrschertisch' as follows: 'Die Hauptabweichung im Konzept der "table ronde" stellt also die quasi-rationalistische Begründung durch Wace dar' (p.248). I shall try to elucidate in the following pages why Wace added his explanation which seems to me more realistic than rationalistic.

Aprés cele table fu la Table Reonde par le conseil Merlin, qui ne fu pas establie sanz grant senefiance. Car en ce qu'ele est apelee Table Reonde est entendue la reondece del monde et la circonstance des planetes et des elemenz el firmament; et es circonstances dou firmament voit l'en les estoiles et mainte autre chose; dont l'en puet dire que en la Table Reonde est li mondes senefiez a droit. Car vos poez veoir que de toutes terres ou chevalerie repere, soit de crestienté ou de paiennie, viennent a la Table Reonde li chevalier. (p.76)

Now Merlin, who in later tradition is said to have had the idea of the secular Round Table, is one of the shrewdest and greatest inventions of British political propaganda.[38] And perhaps the same may be said of the Round Table itself. The cosmic table theory is extremely convincing; it implies a political motivation for its invention and as such it constitutes the point of departure for a fresh approach to the problem. Mrs Eberlein-Westhues has not yet linked the re-appearance of a cosmic table in connexion with King Arthur, the ruler over the world, with the historical circumstances of the moment of its *inventio*, the beginning of Henry II Plantagenet's reign, the year 1154. I shall try to do this here.

Arthurian literature is ideological literature. Wace's *Roman de Brut* was deliberately planned as an instrument of political propaganda, just as his model, Geoffrey's *Historia*, had been some fifteen years before, if not even more so. And the *Brut*, especially its Arthurian part, was in all probability written mainly to promote young Henry Plantagenet's succession to the throne of England. The uncle of the king-to-be, Robert of Gloucester, a great magnate on the Welsh Borders, was a patron of several important chroniclers in the reign of Stephen.[39] It was no accident that Arthurian material held an important place in these documents of written tradition. Again and again, stories about King Arthur were repeated and amplified, and the results of this procedure were encouraging. Robert was a man of high literary culture. He well knew how to influence public opinion by the written word, be it Latin or French; and his nephew, Henry of Anjou, was his diligent pupil in these matters.[40]

[38] Cf. R. Taylor, *The Political Prophecy in England*, New York 1911.
[39] William of Malmesbury dedicated to him *Gesta Regum* and *Historia Novella*. He was also the patron of Geoffrey's second and third versions of *Historia Regum Britanniae*. The *Historia Novella* was apparently commissioned by Earl Robert.
[40] Pains had been taken with his education. Gerald of Wales describes him as remarkably polished in letters. He had a complete knowledge of history, a good memory and a great store of practical wisdom; he understood several foreign languages, but customarily spoke French and Latin (cf. Warren 1973,

The history and evolution of the Arthurian legend from William of Malmesbury to Jean Froissart is an impressive instance of slow, tenacious and much refined psychological propaganda, the aim of which was to further the interests of the English Crown and the royal family. In Wace's time it seemed politically wise to prove that the reigning monarch was the legitimate heir of the greatest of all rulers over Britain, King Arthur. In this ideological context, 'King Arthur', soon after the middle of the twelfth century, became a literary name for Henry II of England.[41]

It is well known that this youthful king was highly ambitious and had a true passion for power.[42] Enthroned at the age of 22 (a few months before the publication of the *Brut*), he had already been for some time the designated successor of Stephen. Thus Henry had had ample time to organise his own personal legend according to the spirit of the age, a national talent that was to flourish in Britain a few decades later and was to produce the courtly sub-genre of 'ancestral romances'.[43] Whether as *rex designatus* or as newly crowned king, probably counselled by his prudent uncle, Henry may have given precise instructions to the chronicler of his party how to write and amplify the Arthurian section of his work. This (pseudo-)historical study in the vernacular was to attain an enormous success not only immediately after its publication but over many centuries to come. It was re-written, recast, translated, modernized and imitated over and over again. And the part dealing with the great British ruler very likely was meant to have a well defined political and ideological function when it became for the first time accessible to a French-speaking courtly public: King Arthur's court and the customs he was said to have introduced in ancient times were to provide a model from the past for the court of King Henry II.

p. 208). The following digressions are heavily indebted to Warren's excellent book on Henry II. Henry was also a patron of learning and poetic activities. His court was the centre of courtly literature in the second half of the twelfth century. Chrétien, Béroul, Marie de France, Benoît de Sainte-Maure and many other outstanding French poets of the time worked in his entourage; he also used this same literature for a subtle and very elegant personal and political propaganda. William of Malmesbury reports of Henry's mother Matilda that she spent so much money on minstrels that she had to oppress her tenants to produce new revenues (ed. Hardy, vol. 2, pp. 650f.).

41 See G. J. Brault, *Early Blazon*, Oxford 1972, who demonstrates that in many Arthurian texts King Arthur wears the colours and the heraldic signs of Henry II and his successors.

42 See Boussard 1957, p. 394.

43 A useful phrase coined by Professor Legge in her 'Anglo-Norman Literature . . .' cf. Legge 1963.

Henry, married to one of the richest heiresses on the Continent, the former Queen of France, was conscious that he might become the most powerful monarch of his age before long. He planned to subdue the Welsh, the Irish, the Scottish and the Bretons with the help of King Arthur's authority.[44] But at the very beginning of his reign he encountered strong resistance among the barons and magnates, who had greatly profited from the disorderly political situation under Stephen's reign. The new king wished to reestablish without delay the original conception of an autocratic monarchy, which, since 1066, had given the supreme power to the king. The feudal structure in Britain was different from that on the continent; there the barons' power and their governmental influence had steadily increased over the centuries, and the French King, for example, had a much weaker position than Henry I, whose form of government his grandson was ruthlessly determined to restore.[45] Henry II was ready to use all the means available, including literary propaganda; his professed intention to cling to the lore of his forefathers makes his ideological orientation towards King Arthur, right from the beginning of his reign, all the more plausible.

But Henry was prudent and a man of great secrecy.[46] Although highly conscious of the dignity of kingship, he avoided showing it openly; he was simple in bearing and in manner. He often took solitary decisions of great moment but never explained his motives in public. He always took great pains to let his actions against his political opponents appear in a light of strict legality, and he also had a gift of making promises and breaking them when it suited him. In his coronation oath he had sworn to revoke all those evil customs which had arisen since his grandfather's day.[47] But naturally this revocation implied the firm restoration of all the Crown's rights, against the interests of a powerful barony. Henry's first effort was to demolish the many hundreds of unlicenced castles built under Stephen.[48] But while this had been agreed upon in the treaty with Stephen, his son William and his followers, only controversial political reasons could justify also the surrender of castles held by some loyal barons as custodians of the Crown. The military importance of the country's magnates was soon reduced. Another move in Henry's firm intention to reestablish an autocratic form of monarchy was his

[44] See Poole 1955 *passim.*
[45] See Boussard 1957, p. 589; Warren 1973, p. 219.
[46] See Warren 1973, p. 215.
[47] See Warren 1973, pp. 219f. and Richardson 1960, p. 163.
[48] Warren 1973, pp. 39, 364; they were estimated in 1153 to exceed 1,115.

refusal to recognise those earldoms which had been created by his own mother Mathilda and his predecessor during the civil war, or to let them die out. Since he himself created no new earls, their number steadily declined. By the end of his reign, there were only twelve earls left, while there had been twenty-four in 1154.[49] And even the remaining earldoms were trimmed of power and influence. Not a single earl was to be found in the king's inner counsels after the great war.

> It cannot be denied that the importance of the feudatories and of the feudal organization of society was considerably diminished in the course of Henry II's reign, nor that certain of his policies, if not specifically anti-feudal, were markedly non-feudal.[50]

The king succeeded in disciplining the barons and in trimming their feudal power while insisting on his feudal authority as their overlord. 'Paradox was implicit in Henry II himself, for he was a conservative who made a revolution.'[51] Of course, this proceeding caused bitter feelings of resentment and hatred among a party of the once powerful barons. Ralph Niger, spokesman of Henry's enemies, described the king as a seducer and a tyrant who hated men of dignity and noble birth as if they were vipers.[52] This particular point of criticism was equally stressed by Ralph of Diceto:

> The king . . . , with a view to enhancing the royal dignity, was trampling upon the necks of the proud and haughty . . . he was firmly insisting that those who were occupying properties which were known from old to pertain to his table [quae suam ad mensam quasi ad fiscum pertinere noscuntur] should be content with their own patrimony, and was even compelling them to do so.[53]

'He trampled on the necks of the proud and haughty . . . because he hated men of dignity and noble birth' — could there be any causal relationship between this attitude of the king and the institution of the Round Table under King Arthur (for whom read Henry II)? This question has to be asked because the value of the table as a symbol of the cosmos and of world supremacy does not sufficiently explain why King Arthur, discontented by the continuous quarrels of his

---

49 See Warren 1973, pp. 365, 366; perhaps this historical limitation later influenced the identification of Grail and Round Table companions.
50 Warren 1973, p. 378.
51 Warren 1973, p. 380.
52 Ed. R. Anstruther, London 1851, pp. 92f., 167f.
53 Warren 1973, p. 368 has the interesting metaphor 'mensa' in connection with the king's private as opposed to public revenue. The metaphor also appears in some French texts of the period.

barons over precedence, commanded them to sit around that cosmic table 'tuit igal', an unheard-of idea in the twelfth century. Equality among the peers (earls?) is brought about by an act of royal authority, and to their detriment. From Wace's description, these vassals seem haughty and arrogant, a storm centre in the legendary twelve-year peace, just like King Henry's barons in the year 1154. But the strong-willed young monarch, with Wace's help, decides to give them a pattern of conduct: a Round Table is invented for King Arthur by drawing on the cosmic table concept. In doing this, Henry conformed to the spirit of his age; he did not however, follow the example of his cousin, Roger II of Sicily, who, equally ambitious, had a round table of pure silver made for himself on the surface of which the cosmography of Edris was represented. That table was to be a symbolic expression of his wish for hegemonial power in the south of Italy in a period when he continually attacked both the Roman Emperor and the Emperor of Constantinople. It was made in 1154.[54] The fact that a real cosmic table existed in those years (and was probably much talked about) may serve to show how much more subtle Henry of England's way of demonstrating his worldly power was. Instead of exhibiting such an ostentatious token of his ambition, he, as the true patron of courtliness that he was, preferred to ascribe a cosmic table to his ancestor, King Arthur, whose inheritance he held. In the eyes of his contemporaries, this table was as precious as the cosmic tables of Charlemagne or Constantine:

> Si fist faire la ronde tauble,
> Non pas de sapin ne d'erauble,
> Mais de cristaul a l'or bendee,
> Et si fut tot entor orlee
> Espés de preciouses pierres,
> Des muez vaillanz et des plus chieres.
> (Robert de Blois, *Enseignement*, vv.1653ff.)

In this passage from a non-Arthurian work which has never before been quoted à propos, the first and only description in French literature of the Table as an object is to be found; it is evidently a product of Robert de Blois' literary fantasy. If such a table of crystal and gold had existed towards 1200, Laȝamon would not have maintained at about the same time that it was made of wood (a fact specifically denied by Robert) and could seat 1600.[55] But if the French author had in mind the Round Table's cosmic significance, it

---

[54] See Eberlein-Westhues 1979, p.236.
[55] See Layamon's *Brut*, ed. Madden, vv.22736ff. (ii, 534).

seems normal that he should describe it as resembling the extremely precious (real and legendary) objects of other historical rulers.

Relegated to the realm of political history, King Arthur's cosmic table served much the same purpose as Roger of Sicily's and, in addition, symbolized Henry's home policy of divesting his haughty and quarrelsome barons of much of their power by demonstrating by way of a literary and historical analogy that they were all equals in his eyes, that none of them had more rights than another and that he, being the king, was different from all of them. Like King Arthur, Henry II Plantagenet sits at his *haut dois*, surrounded exclusively by his *privé ami*, civil servants he has chosen from all levels of society and who serve him in loyalty.[56]

In my opinion, the institution of the Round Table reflects the well recorded serious conflicts between Henry II and his barons at the time when the *Roman de Brut* was written. The enforced equality of the barons in literature, apart from introducing a notion of peerage new in the English feudal system, has the function of rendering the vassals more obedient and docile, in a word: weaker. The Round Table in Wace's *Brut* constitutes a symbol, but not of harmony and union as we were all wont to believe; on the contrary, it stands for the separation of royal power and baronial power, for a deep schism between the monarch and his earls.

Since the Round Table, according to Wace's wording, was instituted by the monarch with the intention of disciplining his vassals, the institution of the Round Table can no longer be seen as a poetic expression of the wishful thinking of the nobility. The late Erich Köhler's famous sociological approach to Arthurian literature, so profoundly justified as a method in general,[57] is based on a lamentable misunderstanding in the particular case of the Round Table. Köhler, like so many others, firmly believed that King Arthur himself had a seat at the table, and that it was not invented by Wace but by Chrétien de Troyes; consequently, he interpreted the relationship between king and barons in literature as 'ein ideales Verhältnis', mirroring the aspirations of France's barony:[58]

> Jedenfalls erscheint die Einrichtung der Tafelrunde, die den König als primus inter pares hinstellt und eine ständige Mahnung an die Grenzen seiner Macht und an seine rein feudalrechtliche Stellung einbegreift, als

---

56 Like Philippe Auguste, Henry preferred as his friends and counsellors men who did not belong to the ancient aristocracy.

57 It has since become one of the pillars of our discipline. The methods applied in this paper owe a great deal to Köhler and his school.

58 Köhler 1970, pp.18, 21.

eine Erfindung des französischen höfischen Romans wahrscheinlicher denn als eine solche der im Dienste des angevinischen Königshauses stehenden Chronik.[59]

To support his theory, it was necessary to postulate that the three Table-Ronde passages in the *Brut* were interpolations.[60] Köhler himself felt that the Plantagenet governmental principles and the political reality of Henry II's reign were irreconcilable with the way he understood the significance of the Round Table; he therefore saw the Round Table as an object symbolizing the political aspirations of France's (petty) nobility under Philippe II Auguste:

> Die Bestimmung der Tafelrunde kann nach dem Gesagten kaum zweifelhaft sein. Sie bezeichnet die Möglichkeit eines idealen Verhältnisses zwischen König und Grossvasallen im Sinne der feudalen Gesellschaft und der vorbildhaften — wenn auch nicht einmal im Roman völlig herstellbaren — Ranggleichheit dieser hohen Vasallen untereinander. Indem sie sich einen primus pares [sic], einen in seiner Machtausübung feudalrechtlich eng eingeschränkten und den gleichen moralischen und politischen Kategorien unterworfenen Lehnsherrn gibt, verschafft sich diese Gemeinschaft der Grossen zugleich den ideellen Mittelpunkt, dessen sie als höfischritterliche, ästhetisch-sittliche Korrektur ihrer eigenen anarchisch-partikularistischen Kräfte bedarf.[61]

I hope to have been able to show that even if the lines in Wace's *Brut* were indeed an interpolation, they express exactly the opposite of what is maintained here. Arthur as the autocratic founder of the Round Table is by no means a 'feudalrechtlich eingeschränkter Lehnsherr'. If he were a *primus inter pares* (a concept totally inadmissible in the twelfth and thirteenth centuries, even in literary fantasy), he would give up all his rights as a monarch. If Wace had intended to express this, he would have contradicted and denied the whole purpose of his work.

Being treated as 'tuit igal' is against the interests of the barons and serves exclusively to fortify royal power. The institution of a literary Round Table might on the one hand be interpreted as an attempt at psychological preparation for hard times to come;[62] the historical Arthurian model might serve to appease the rebellious spirit of the

59 Köhler 1970, p.19.
60 An opinion held by Ph.A.Becker and St.Hofer, *Chrétien de Troyes*, Wien 1954, pp.38, 59. The interpolation-theory, however, finds no support in the manuscript tradition.
61 Köhler 1970, p. 21.
62 It could help to delude the barons into thinking that the new order was the restoration of a golden age.

discontented barony. On the other hand, it also points towards a higher ideal in political ethics. The pretended antiquity of the Round Table community where fraternal feelings and communal impulses are of great import makes it a custom in the legal sense. Most members of Wace's public must have accepted the narrative of the French chronicle as a historical authority. Both functions help to sublimate the general aggression against the new monarch, and to channel the rebellious military power of the barony in the direction of a fraternal or even spiritual *prouesse* in the service of an ideal and noble knighthood. The 'verray gentil parfit knight', following the sublime *exemplum* of Arthurian chivalry, would not fight against the king, his overlord, but always for him; and such an attitude was certainly more appropriate and desirable for any monarch than the conduct of the barony in Stephen's reign where the realm had suffered so badly from the civil war. If Henry II wanted to reestablish peace and order, an excellent method was to show the earls that it was mean and senseless to dissipate all their energies in fighting each other and to make them realize that they were all in the same situation! Beginning with the institution of the Round Table towards 1154, the Arthurian ideal was to be for many centuries the driving force of British politics.[63]

By the first half of the thirteenth century at the latest, the Round Table was envisaged as a kind of chivalric order by the Plantagenet court. Members could be elected or relegated. They had to promise that they would fulfill the ideals of Christian chivalry. This point in the evolution is reflected by some lines from *La mort le Roi Artu*:

> Gauvains ... dist au roi: 'Sire ..., vos loieroie ge que de ceste baronnie qui ci est eslisiez autant de bons chevaliers comme l'en ocist avant ier a rescorre la reine; si les meissiez a la Table Reonde en leu de ceus qui sont trespassé, si que nos aions autel nombre de chevaliers comme nos estions, si que nos soions cent et cinquante ...' (ed. Frappier, pp.137f.)

We have seen that they were supposed to wear the same robes and the same blazon (conuissance), that they might be recognized as 'cels de la Table Reonde' (cf. above, p.58). Later, the Order of the Garter followed the model of King Arthur's Round Table under Edward III: 'mensam rotundam inciperet eodem modu et statu quo eam dimisit dominus Arthurus'.[64] Far and wide, the celebrated ideal of the Round Table and its fraternal community made an impact on life. Throughout Europe, tournaments called 'tables rondes' were held

63 See Schmolke-Hasselmann 1980, part II.
64 See Loomis 1949, p.68.

68

from 1223 to 1345. Even Saint Francis of Assisi thought of King Arthur's table when he sought for a metaphor describing the spirit of his first followers: 'Isti sunt mei fratres milites tabulae rotundae'.[65]

Naturally, the head of these ideal fellowships, whether king or religious reformer, was not excluded from the company. The spiritual orientation of the noble chivalric order rendered integration possible where the feudal structure had been an insurmountable obstacle to it. Thus the oldest roots of our modern vision of a Round Table company including both King Arthur himself and a definite number of knights may be found soon after 1200. Another reason was the influence of iconography.

From the point of view of pictorial representation, the iconography of the Last Supper has had a strong influence on the minds of medieval illuminators who drew the Round Table and, consequently, on those who saw their miniatures. In many instances, the way of representing the Round Table is almost identical with one of the standard types of Eucharist representations. But the parallelism is only to be noticed towards the middle of the thirteenth century, that is, at a late stage in the evolution of the Round Table; before this period, miniatures in Arthurian manuscripts are extremely rare. But the great vogue of the Prose romances, especially the *Queste del Saint Graal*, resulted in richly illustrated codices; and it is here, in miniatures illustrating the famous opening scene ('A la veille de la Pentecoste. . .') where Galaad first comes to King Arthur's court, that the confusion between Grail Table and Round Table is first made by the illuminators. At the beginning, some of them continued with the traditional and exact representation of King Arthur at his *dois* (see illus. 4, 5); others tried to reconcile the rectangular form of the dais with the circular form of the Round Table, with an interesting, if clumsy, result. But only a few decades later, the initial illumination on the first page of the manuscript most often represents exactly the contrary of what the text expresses.[66] It shows a large round table where Galaad sits at the *siege perilleus*, exactly at the place of Christ in the Last Supper iconography, and he is even surrounded by a kind of halo like the Saviour. Usually the Grail is placed in the centre (see illus. 3). Then, a little later, Galaad's place is usurped again by King Arthur; the saintly knight sits at his side. Thus the original hierarchical order is reestablished through

---

[65] Quoted from GRMLA IV 'Le Roman', Heidelberg 1978, p.669: Boncompagno da Signa in his *Cedrus* (1194-1203) also refers to a fellowship of young men as 'de tabula rotunda societas' at this relatively early date. (*Ibid.*)
[66] Namely that Arthur dines at the *haut dois*.

the naive conservatism of manuscript illuminators and wood-engravers (see illus. 12, 13). It is natural that these pictures should have profoundly influenced the visual impression of the Round Table in the minds of the general public until the present day. And the same is true for the spectacular Winchester Table. Over a period of six centuries it has been exhibited to the easily impressionable visitors as the authentic Round Table of King Arthur. Since it was repainted in the second half of the fifteenth century according to the celebrated romance of Malory, it has been admired by innumerable crowds. It comes as no surprise, then, that all those who have seen this table remember the 24 seats of the knights on the one hand, and the conspicuous throne-like seat of King Arthur in the middle, on the other. Of course, these people, if asked, would reply that 24 companions belong to the Round Table and that Arthur himself has a place of honour there.

It is equally logical that the view of philologists does not differ very much from that of the general public. It is no secret that the history of medieval philology, French philology in particular, was deeply influenced by German scholars who, as a rule, had received their training from the great Germanists of the nineteenth century. Now, a significant factor that has hitherto escaped notice is to be observed in the literary representation of the *Tafelrunde* in German Arthurian poetry: in the works of Hartmann von Aue, Wolfram von Eschenbach and in the later Arthurian romances like *Wigalois* and *Garel*, King Arthur always, and from the very start of German Arthurian tradition, is a companion of the *Tafelrunde* (see illus. 9). This astonishing difference can, in my opinion, only be explained by the fundamental differences between the political systems of England and France on the one side, and Germany on the other. While it was a very rare incident in history to see the King of France dine with his barons at one table,[67] this was the normal situation in Germany. Historians have recorded only a single scandalous occurrence of a German emperor (Otto III) who, on one occasion, refused to sit *in medio*, as the Germanic custom demanded, and dined alone at a small table after the example of the Basileus of Constantinople.[68] It

---

[67] On the eve of the Battle of Bouvines Philippe Auguste is said to have invited his barons to dine with him, saying the words: 'Je prie a tous mes bons amis qu'ils mangent avec moi en souvenir des douze apotres qui, avec notre Seigneur, burent et mangerent ...' (*Chronique de Rheims*, thirteenth century, ed. Louis Pasis, quoted after de Page, *Le Roi très Chrétien*, Paris 1949, p. 369).

[68] Cf. Eberlein-Westhues 1979, p. 260.

[69] Cf. Dann 1980, p. 101: 'Solange das im naturrechtlichen Ansatz enhaltene Ideal von einer Gesellschaft, in der alle Menschen wirklich gleichgestellt sind

is therefore no wonder if the German philologists, who were familiar with their national Arthurian poetry, formed their view of the Table Ronde after the model of the *Tafelrunde*:

> es kam in disen siben tagen
> ein rîter geriten dar
> und nam des vil rehte war
> daz er zen selben stunden
> die von der tavelrunden
> umbe den künec sitzen sach.
>
> (Hartmann, *Iwein*, ed. Benecke/Lachmann/Wolff, vv.4530ff.)

> diu küneginne si nam
> vriundlichen bi ir hant
> und ginc do si den künec vant
> sitzen nach sinem rehte
> mit manegem guoten knehte
> da zuo der tavelrunde.
>
> (Hartmann, *Erec*, ed. Leitzmann/Cramer, vv.1611ff.)

> ir was nach der rehten zal
> vierzec und hundert über al   (vv.1696f.)

Another reason for the constant misunderstanding of the 'original' Round Table in our times can be found in the realm of collective psychology. The idea that a monarch might treat his nobility (whether their merit lay in *lignage* or *valour*) as his equals had great ideological impact in the minds of nineteenth century democrats. In an age where the concept of a constitutional monarchy and democratic parliaments in Europe were by no means a matter of course, but an ideal vision — especially in those bourgeois circles (who also brought forth the first great philologists) wishing to gain access to the political government of the nation — the reminiscence of King Arthur and his peers, of a King Arthur as *primus inter pares* constituted an *exemplum*, a symbol and model of democracy.[69] The

und gleiche Chancen im gesellschaftlich — ökonomischen Wettbewerb haben, gegen jene Wirklichkeit nicht offen durchzusetzen war, kam es innerhalb des europäischen Bürgertums zu charakterischen Ersatzreaktionen, zur partiellen Verwirklichung einer gleichheitlichen Gesellschaft im Rahmen unpolitischer und nicht-öffentlicher Vereinigungen. Die Intelligenz, die besondere Trägerschaft des naturrechtlichen Denkens, war hier als führende Gruppe des sich emanzipierenden Bürgertums in erster Linie aktiv.' The expression *primus inter pares* seems to be a phantom, untraceable in Roman antiquity. Professor Dann, the expert on matters of parity and equality, could not help in finding out the roots of this expression which might be of nineteenth century coinage.

whole conception was as tempting as it was revolutionary; nevertheless, it has had a certain effect, comparable to that of the Greek and Roman models of democracy. This romantic, idealizing vision, however, has prevented the conscious acceptance of the historical medieval reality as it is reflected in the literary opposition of Table Ronde and *dois*.

> Jadis au tens q'Artur regna,
> que il Bretaigne governa
> que Engleterre ert apelee. . .   (Tyolet, ed. Tobin, vv.1 ff.)

It was in the nineteenth century that collective memory forgot that Arthur was British; the awakening chauvinism dulled the view of those who believed that poetry in the French language must needs be an expression of France's grandeur. But the Round Table, symbol of Arthurian life and letters, is not a product of France's feudal nobility. It is primarily an ideological instrument of the Kings of Little and Great Britain.

It is to be found in the constitution of the City of Hamburg where the Bürgermeister has the rank of a *primus inter pares*.

LIST OF PUBLICATIONS ON THE ROUND TABLE

Binchy, D.A., 'Secular Institutions', in M.Dillon, ed., *Early Irish Society*, Cork 1954, pp.52-65.

Boussard, J., *Le Gouvernement d'Henri II Plantegenêt*, Paris 1957.

Brown, A.C.L., *The Round Table before Wace* (Harvard Studies and Notes VII), Harvard UP 1900.

Bruce, J.D., *Evolution of Arthurian Romance*, 2 vols, Göttingen 1923, repr. Gloucester, Mass. 1958, vol.I, pp.81-87 ('The Origin of the Round Table and Some Other Questions of Celtic Origin').

Dann, O., *Gleichheit und Gleichberechtigung. Das Gleichheitspostulat in der alteuropäischen Tradition und in Deutschland bis zum ausgehenden 19. Jh.*, (Histor. Forschungen 16), Berlin 1980.

Daube, D., 'King Arthur's Round Table', in *Gesellschaft, Kultur, Rezeption und Originalität. . .* , ed. K.Bosl (Monogr. z. Gesch. d. MA 11), Stuttgart 1975, pp.203-207.

Davis, R.H.C., 'What happened in Stephen's reign 1135-1154', *History* 49 (1964), pp.1-12.

Davis, R.H.C., *King Stephen, 1135-1154*, London 1967.

Delbouille, M., 'Le témoignage de Wace sur la légende arthurienne', *Romania* LXXIV (1953), pp.172-199.

Denomy, A.J., 'The Round Table and the Council of Rheims 1049', *Med. Studies* 4 (1951), pp.143-149.

Ditmas, E.M.R., 'The Round Table at Stirling', *BBSIA* 26 (1974), pp.186-196.

Eames, P., *Furniture in England, France and the Netherlands from the Twelfth to the Fifteenth Century*, London 1977.

Eberlein-Westhues, H., 'König Arthurs "Table Ronde". Studien zur Geschichte eines literarischen Herrschaftszeichens', in *Der afz. Prosaroman*, ed. E.Ruhe, München 1979, pp.184-263.

Emmel, H., *Probleme des Artusromans und der Graldichtung*, Bern 1951.

Field, P.J.C., 'The Winchester Round Table', in *Notes & Queries* XXV (1978), pp.204ff.

Fletcher, R.H., *Arthurian Material in the Chronicles*, Boston 1906, repr. 1973.

Flint, V.I.J., 'The Historia Regum Britanniae of Geoffrey of Monmouth: Parody and Its Purpose. A Suggestion', *Speculum* LIV (1979), pp.447-468.

Foulon, Ch., 'Wace', in *Arthurian Literature in the Middle Ages*, ed. R.S.Loomis, Oxford 1959, pp.94-103.

Göller, K.H., *König Arthur in der englischen Literatur des späten Mittelalters*, Göttingen 1963.

Hall, H., *Court Life Under the Plantagenets*, London 1890.

Hanoset, M., 'Des origines de la matière de Bretagne', *Marche Romane* X (1960), pp.25-38 and 67-78.

Hofer, St., 'Bemerkungen zu Galfrieds v. Monmouth Historia Regum Britanniae, I. Die Erwähnung des Rolandsliedes und die Frage der Tafelrunde', *Zeitschr. f. frz. Spr. u. Lit.* LIX (1935), pp.391-401.

Hofer, St., *Zeitschr. f. Rom. Phil.* LXII (1942). 'Wace und die höfische Kunst', and 'Die Tafelrunde im Roman de Brut', pp.87-91.

Houck, M., *Sources of the Roman de Brut*, Univ. of California Press 1941.

Kelly, S., 'A Note on Arthur's Round Table and the Welsh "Life of Saint Carantog",' *Folklore* 87 (1976), pp.223-225.

Köhler, E., *Ideal und Wirklichkeit in der höfischen Epik*, 2nd ed., Tübingen 1970, I. Kapitel: 'König Artus und sein Reich — Geschichtliche Wirklichkeit und ritterliches Wunschbild', pp.5-36.

Lecoy, F., '*Meain* et *forain* dans le "Roman de Brut",' *Romania* 86 (1956), pp.118-122.

Legge, M.D., *Anglo-Norman Literature and its Background*, Oxford 1963.

Loomis, L.H., 'Arthur's Round Table', *PMLA* XLI (1926), pp.771-784.

Loomis, L.H., 'The Table of the Last Supper in Religious and Secular Iconography', *Art Studies* 5 (1927), pp.71-88.

Loomis, L.H., 'The Round Table Again', *Mod. Lang. Notes* XLIV (1929), pp. 511-519.

Loomis, R.S., and Loomis, L.H., *Arthurian legends in Medieval Art*, MLA Monograph Series, New York 1938.

Loomis, R.S., 'The Round Table', in *Arthurian Tradition and Chrétien de Troyes*, New York 1949, Chapter VI, pp.61-68.

Loomis, R.S., 'Edward I, Arthurian Enthusiast', *Speculum* 28 (1953), pp.114-127.

Marx, J., *Nouvelles recherches sur la littérature arthurienne*, Paris 1965.

Meneghetti, M.L., 'Ideologia cavalleresca e politica culturale nel "Roman de Brut",' *Studi di Lett. Francese* 3 (1974), pp.26-48.

Mergell, B., *Der Gral in Wolframs Parzival*, Halle 1952.

Micha, A., 'Sur trois vers du Joseph de Robert de Boron', *Romania* 75 (1954), pp.240-243.

Micha, A., *De la Chanson de Geste au roman* (Publ. Romanes et Françaises CXXXIX), Geneva 1976. 'La Table Ronde chez Robert de Boron et dans la Queste del Saint Graal', pp.183-200; 'L'origine de la Table du Graal et de la Table Ronde chez Robert de Boron', pp.201-205.

Paris, G., Review of H. Andresen ed., *Maistre Wace's Roman de Rou*, Heilbronn 1877-1879, *Romania* 9 (1880), pp.592-614.

Petit-Dutaillis, Ch., *La monarchie féodale en France et en Angleterre*, Paris 1933.

Petit-Dutaillis, Ch., *La France et l'Angleterre depuis la constitution de l'empire angevin jusqu' à la mort de Saint Louis (1270) et de Henri III (1272)*, Paris 1937.

Pickford, C.E., 'Antoine Vérard éditeur du Lancelot et du Tristan', in *Mél. Ch. Foulon*, Rennes 1980, vol. I, pp.277-285.

Poole, A.L., 'Henry Plantagenet's Early Visits to England', *Engl. Hist. Review* 47 (1932), pp.447-452.

Poole, A.L., *From Domesday Book to Magna Carta* (The Oxford History of England), 2nd ed., 1955.

Richardson, H.G., 'The Coronation in Mediaeval England: the Evolution of the Office and the Oath', *Traditio* 16 (1960), pp.111-202.

Schirmer, W.F., and Broich, U., *Studien zum literarischen Patronat im England des 12 Jh.s*, Köln/Opladen 1962.

Schmolke-Hasselmann, B., *Der arthurische Versroman von Chrestien bis Froissart*, Tübingen 1980.

Schmolke-Hasselmann, B., 'Untersuchungen zur Typik des arthurischen Romananfangs', *German.-Roman. Monatss.* 31 (1981), pp.1-13.

Schramm, P.E., *Geschichte des englischen Königtums im Lichte der Krönung*, Weimar 1937.

Schultz, A., *Das höfische Leben zur Zeit der Minnesinger*, 2 vols, Leipzig 1879/80.

Schultz, J.A., 'The Shape of the Round Table: Structure and Genre in Middle High German Arthurian Romance', *DA* XXXVIII (1977/78), 5505 A – 5506 A (Diss. Princeton Univ.).

Stenton, F.M., *The First Century of English Feudalism 1066-1166*, 2nd ed., Oxford 1961.

Tatlock, J.S.P., *The Legendary History of Britain*, Berkeley 1950, pp.471-475.

Warren, W.L., *Henry II*, London 1973.

III

THE TRADITION OF THE TROUBADOURS AND THE TREATMENT OF THE LOVE THEME IN CHRETIEN DE TROYES' *CHEVALIER AU LION*

Fanni Bogdanow

To the unforgettable memory of my beloved Mother, Johanna Bogdanow, whose devotion and encouragement are for me a constant inspiration.

The interpretation of the *Chevalier au Lion*, the action of which is interwoven with that of the *Chevalier de la Charrette*, is no less controversial than that of Chrétien's other romances. Although most scholars would now agree that there is an element of ironical humour in nearly all of them, the traditional view since the days of Wendelin Foerster and Myrrha Lot-Borodine has been that Chrétien was both a psychologist and a committed moralist, anxious to convey a certain thesis and critical of the Provençal conception of *fin amor*.[1] Adduced as evidence of Chrétien's supposedly moral stance is the fact that in three out of the four romances that have love as their main theme the hero and heroine marry, and that, further, the poet apparently strove to reconcile the conflict between love and marriage: 'Au lieu d'accuser le contraste, Chrétien a cherché une conciliation.[2] ... Le conflit entre les obligations du mariage et de l'idéal chevaleresque de l'aventure est retracée en toute probité par un moraliste impartial, malgré les ironies du détail.'[3] To account for the *Chevalier de la Charrette*, which has adulterous love as its subject, it has been assumed that Chrétien disliked the theme and only wrote the work in compliance with the wishes of Marie de Champagne.[4] But it is doubtful whether Chrétien was motivated by doctrinal or moral considerations in any of his four love romances. What matters is not so much whether the plot involves marriage or extra-marital love, but Chrétien's

---

[1] W.Foerster, *Kristian von Troyes, Wörterbuch* (Halle, Niemeyer, 1914), pp. 43*, 89*; Myrrha Lot-Borodine, *La Femme et l'amour au XIIe siècle d'après les poèmes de Chrétien de Troyes* (Paris: Picard, 1919).
[2] J.Frappier, *Chrétien de Troyes* (Paris: Hatier, 1957), p.169.
[3] *Ibid.*, p.148.
[4] *Ibid.*, p.218.

underlying attitude, which in all his romances is one of detached amusement at the customs of the Arthurian world and the conventions of *fin amor* irrespective of whether displayed within the framework of lawful or unlawful love. Typical of his lighthearted approach are his comments when Laudine, welcoming Arthur and his knights, honours one and all. Some of them, he says, were fools, believing that such attentions are inspired by love. 'Indeed one can truly call *nice* anyone who thinks that a lady wishes to love the wretch whom she addresses kindly and treats courteously:'[5]

> fos est liez de bele parole,
> si l'a an molt tost amusé.   (*Chevalier au Lion*, 2466-67)

Chrétien is obviously playing off a common troubadour conceit that a *fin amant* is overjoyed if the lady deigns to greet him or give him a kindly look:

> C'ab sol lo bel semblan que·m fai
> can pot ni aizes lo·lh cossen,
> ai tan de joi que sol no·m sen,
> c'aissi·m torn e·m volv' e·m vire.
>   (Bernard de Ventadorn, 19, iv, 29-31)[6]

Each of Chrétien's romances is centred on a particular leitmotiv, which is at the basis of the *sen* or deeper meaning that, in the person of Calogrenant, Chrétien tells us will be lost to the listener unless the 'words heard are understood by the heart.'[7] But the 'theses' round which Chrétien builds his romances, far from being 'moral' problems, are themes inspired by the troubadour lyrics of his time. The attitude of the troubadours to love is far from uniform. Steeped as they were in the dialectical method, they enjoyed taking up in their songs many different stances, frequently expressing opposing sentiments. The changing leitmotives chosen by Chrétien in his successive works reflect something of this diversity and of his appreciation of the entertainment value of repeating themes in reverse and making his characters act out a variety of situations. In the *Chevalier au Lion*, the leitmotiv, introduced in the Prologue, is a transposition of the troubadour themes that only the genuine disciples of love enjoy its pleasures and that true love as result of which a man is courteous,

---

5 *Le Chevalier au Lion*, ed. Mario Roques (CFMA), 2456-2465. All references to the works of Chrétien de Troyes are to the editions in the CFMA; quotations from Bernard de Ventadorn are taken from M. Lazar's edition: *Bernard de Ventadour, Chansons d'Amour* (Paris: Klincksieck, 1966).

6 Cf. Bernard de Ventadorn, 21.iii, 26.ii, 42.vii.

7 'car parole est tote perdue / s'ele n'est de cuer entandue' (*Chevalier au Lion*, 151-152).

valiant and generous, is largely a thing of the past, for now people who appear to be *fin amant* are not: they claim they love but in reality they are lying:

> Li autre parloient d'Amors,
> des angoisses et des dolors
> et des granz biens qu'orent sovant
> li deciple de son covant,
> qui lors estoit molt dolz et buens;
> mes or i a molt po des suens
> qu'a bien pres l'ont ja tuit lessiee,
> s'an est Amors molt abessiee,
> car cil qui soloient amer
> se feisoient cortois clamer
> et preu et large et enorable;
> or est Amors tornee a fable
> por ce que cil qui rien n'en santent
> dïent qu'il aiment, mes il mantent,
> et cil fable et mançonge an font
> qui s'an vantent et droit n'i ont.
>
> (*Chevalier au Lion*, 13-28)

Individual details of this theme can be found in the poetry of various troubadours, but one of Bernard de Ventadorn's lyrics in particular has most of the points that Chrétien stresses in his Prologue. Combining William IX's observation that love gives joy only to those that observe its laws:

> Pero leumens
> Dona gran joy qui be·n mante
> Los aizimens   (ed. Jeanroy, 7, ii, 10-12)
>
> Ja no sera nuils hom ben fis
> Contr' Amor si non l'es aclis   (ed. Jeanroy, 7, v, 25-26)

with Marcabru's lament that while formerly love was upright, now it is twisted and broken:

> Amors soli' esser drecha,
> Mas er'es torta e brecha   (ed. Dejeanne, 18, v, 25-26)

Bernard de Ventadorn in lyric 11 says that 'he is grieved by what he sees, for while formerly man strove to gain worth, honour and glory, at present no one speaks of loyal love and so worth, courtesy and joy no longer exist.' 'The deceit,' he adds, 'starts with the barons, for none of them love in good faith. . . If their love comes to an end, it is because they do not conduct themselves in accordance with the precepts of love':

Ges de chantar no·m pren talans,
tan me peza de so que vei,
que metre·s soli' om en grans
com agues pretz, onor e lau,
mas era no vei ni non au
c'om parle de drudaria,
per que pretz e cortezia
e solatz torn' en no-chaler.

Dels baros comensa l'enjans,
c'us no·n ama per bona fei.
. . .
Ez amors no rema per au,
car be leu tals amaria
qui s'en te, car no·s sabria
a guiza d'amor chaptener.

(Bernard de Ventadorn, 11, i, 1-8, ii, 9-10, 12-16)

In Bernard's lyric the complaint serves to highlight the poet's own loyal love. Chrétien's comments, on the other hand, are meant to place the Arthurian world and the hero of the romance in their proper perspective. For while claiming that the past was the golden age of chivalrous love and assenting to the Bretons' belief that Arthur's renown would live on for ever, Chrétien with ironic humour introduces Arthur in a posture that does not at all live up to the courtly code, but deliberately recalls the nature of Erec's *recreantise*. Chrétien skilfully builds up a series of resonances from one romance to another, and more than hints that Arthur's love for the lady of his choice no more increased his worth than originally did Erec's.[8] The irony of the Prologue, however, bears not only on Arthur, but also on Yvain who will be presented precisely as one of those who super- ficially appear to be *fin amant*, who claim they love, but in reality fail to adhere to the rules of love. Chrétien himself slyly warns us that his hero is not all he seems. At the point where love has struck Yvain, the poet amplifies Bernard de Ventadorn's remark that 'Love descends where it pleases':

Pero Amors sap dissendre
lai on li ven a plazer   (27, iv, 25-26)

and comments that 'it is a great sorrow that Love lodges as readily in the meanest dwelling place as in the best ... It is awe-inspiring how Love dares shamefully to descend to such low estate. In this he behaves like one who spreads his balm upon the ashes and dust, who

8 Cf. *Chevalier au Lion*, 49-52 and *Erec*, 2442-44.

hates honour and loves blame, who mingles sugar with gall, and suet with honey. However, on this occasion love did not act so, but lodged in a noble place for which no one can reproach him':

> s'est granz diax quant Amors est tex
> et quant ele si mal se prueve
> qu'el plus despit leu qu'ele trueve
> se herberge ele autresi tost
> com an tot le meillor de l'ost.
> . . .
> . . . mervoille est comant ele ose
> de honte an malvés leu descendre.
> Celui sanble qui an la cendre
> et an la poudre espant son basme
> et het enor, et ainme blasme,
> et destranpre suie de miel,
> et mesle çucre avoeques fiel.
> Mes or n'a ele pas fet ceu,
> logiee s'est an franc aleu,
> dom nus ne li puet feire tort.   (1390-94, 1400-1409)

But this implied praise of Yvain is no less ironical than was the praise of Arthur, for, as subsequent events show, Yvain, when measured by the standards of those of Chrétien's characters who are true *fin amant*, falls far short of the qualities needed to provide a *franc aleu* for love.

The whole story of Yvain and his lady is explicable in terms of the theme that Yvain is one of those *qui dient qu'il aiment, mes il mantent*. Starting from Bernard de Ventadorn's complaint that it is so difficult to distinguish the false lovers from the sincere ones:

> Ai Deus! car se fosson trian
> d'entrols faus li fina amador   (1, v, 33-34)

Chrétien deliberately presents Yvain in the guise of a typical *fin amant* when first smitten by love. Not only does Chrétien make him act out in a general way Bernard de Ventadorn's favourite conceit that no one who is in love observes *mesure* and good sense, but he also makes him utter many of the sentiments expressed by the troubadours. Just as Bernard de Ventadorn on several occasions calls himself a fool for aspiring to the love of an unattainable lady:

> Fol nesci! ben as pauc de sen,
> qu'ela nonca t'amaria
> per nom que per drudaria,   (40, ii, 13-15)

80

> Amors, e que·us es veyaire?
> Trobatz mais fol mas can me?
> Cuidatz vos qu'eu si' amaire
> e que ja no trop merce?   (27, i, 1-4)

so Yvain judges himself a *fos* for desiring what he cannot hope to
obtain, the love of the lady whose husband he has slain:

> et dit: 'Por fos me puis tenir,
> quant je vuel ce que ja n'avrai.   (1432-3)

In fact, most of the arguments used by Yvain in his first monologue
to persuade himself that he will find mercy and that his enemy is
bound to become his *amie* can be traced to Bernard de Ventadorn.
Yvain begins by admitting that his lady rightfully hates him:

> Par foi, je ne cuit pas savoir
> qu'ele me het plus or en droit
> que nule rien, et si a droit   (1436-38)

an admission likewise made by Bernard de Ventadorn:

> per c'a dreih que·m ochaizo   (37, iv, 36)

But then his despair turns to hope, his optimism fired by the thought
that a lady frequently changes her mind:

> D'or en droit ai ge dit que sages,
> que fame a plus de cent corages.
> Celui corage qu'ele a ore,
> espoir, changera ele ancore.   (1439-1442)

another sentiment already expressed by Bernard de Ventadorn:

> qu'eu no·m vau ges chamjan
> si com las domnas fan.   (17, iii, 23-24)

And just as the latter is sure that love will yet make his lady change,
for love conquers all and forces him to love her:

> que nuls om no pot ni auza
> enves Amor contrastar;
> car Amors vens tota chauza
> e forsa·m de leis amar;
> atretal se pot leis far
> en una petita pauza!   (27, v, 35-40)

so Yvain expresses the hope that God may bring about a change in
his lady's disposition, since it is the will of love that he should be for
always in her power:

81

> molt sui fos quant je m'an despoir,
> et Dex li doint ancor changier,
> qu'estre m'estuet an son dongier
> tos jorz mes, des qu'Amors le vialt.   (1444-1447)

Yvain's further argument that he who refuses love commits treason and does not merit joy:

> Qui Amor en gré ne requialt
> des que ele an tor li l'atret
> felenie et traïson fet;
> et je di, qui se vialt si l'oie,
> que cil n'a droit en nule joie   (1448-1452)

may also be inspired by Bernhard de Ventadorn who in another lyric says that 'it does not seem to me that one can be of any worth if one does not desire love and joy':

> E no m'es vis c'om re poscha valer,
> s'eras no vol amor et joi aver.   (7, i, 5-6)

Certainly, this same lyric appears to have been in Chrétien's mind when he formulated Yvain's decision not to refrain from loving his enemy. Just as Bernard asserts: 'Do not think that I renounce joy or abstain from loving on account of the pains I am wont to suffer, for I have not got the power to tear myself away from love, since love takes me by assault, dominates me, and forces me to love whomsoever it pleases him':

> Ja no crezatz qu'eu de joi me recreya
> ni·m lais d'amar per dan c'aver en solha,
> qu'eu non ai ges en poder que m'en tolha,
> c'amors m'asalh, que·m sobresenhoreya
> e·m fai amar cal que·lh plass', e voler.   (7, ii, 8-12)

so Yvain declares that he must love whomsoever Love wishes him to love:

> toz jorz amerai m'anemie,
> que je ne la doi pas haïr
> se je ne voel Amor traïr.
> Ce qu'Amors vialt doi je amer.   (1454-1457)

When the hero is eventually brought face to face with Laudine, he continues to be presented in the posture of a *fin amant*. He is before the lady in the same attitude of speechless, humble adoration as Alexandre, Cligés and Lancelot, and Chrétien obviously delights in the irony that Yvain, unlike these other heroes, has real cause to fear

82

his lady, since he is quite literally her prisoner and not just a prisoner of love as in the lyrics. He is prompted by Lunete, into whose mouth Chrétien humorously places an argument similar to the one that Bernard de Ventadorn had used to persuade himself that he need not be afraid of his lady: 'You are hardly a bear or a lion to want to kill me if I give myself up to you':

> Ors ni leos non etz vos ges,
> que·m aucizatz, s'a vos me ren   (I, vii, 55-56)

> si li dit: 'En ça vos traiez,
> chevaliers, ne peor n'aiez
> de ma dame qu'el ne vos morde;
> mes querez la pes et l'acorde.   (1967-1970)

Yvain finally asserts, like Lancelot and Bernard de Ventadorn, that whatever it may please his lady to do could not displease him:

> Dame, voir, ja ne vos querrai
> merci, einz vos mercïerai
> de quan que vos me voldroiz feire,
> que riens ne me porroit despleire.
> (*Chevalier au Lion*, 1977-80)

> Ara·n fassa so que·s volha
> ma domna, al seu chauzit,
> qu'eu no m'en planh, si tot me dol.   (19, vi, 52-53)

And just as Bernard de Ventadorn remarks in another lyric that 'if it pleases her, let her kill me, I shall not complain of anything':

> En son plazer sia,
> qu'eu sui en sa merce.
> Si·lh platz, que m'aucia,
> qu'eu no m'en clam de re.   (38, v, 57-60)

so Yvain, in reply to Laudine's question: 'Et se je vos oci?' says:

> Dame, la vostre grant merci,
> que ja ne m'an orroiz dire el   (1982-3)

adding, in words that recall Bernard de Ventadorn's:

> Far me podetz e ben e mau;
> en la vostra merce sia;
> qu'eu sui garnitz tota via
> com fassa tot vostre plazer.   (11, vi, 45-48)

that Love commands him to consent completely to his lady's will and to do as it pleases her:

83

> . . . me comande a consantir
> vostre voloir del tot an tot.
> Rien nule a feire ne redot
> que moi vos pleise a comander. (1990-93)

But even before Yvain breaks his word, Chrétien hints that he will not be able to live up to his protestations of fidelity, for he lacks one of the essential virtues of a *verai ami*. Bernard de Ventadorn in more than one lyric tells us that love and pride are incompatible:

> pauc pot amors ab ergolh remaner,
> qu'ergolhs dechai e fin' amors capdolha. (7, iii, 20-21)

Lancelot, the perfect *fin amant*, will always subordinate his chivalric pride to his love and will not care if he suffers shame for his lady's sake:

> de la honte ne li chaut
> puisqu'Amors le comande et vialt
> (*Chevalier de la Charrette*, 375-377)

But Yvain will fail to do this, as in his heart love and pride coexist uneasily. At the point where Chrétien tells us that Yvain, even if he could have escaped from Laudine's prison, would not have done so, he adds, by way of explanation, that Love and Shame were holding him back:

> Amors et Honte le retienent
> qui de deus parz devant li vienent. (1535-36)

But this fear of shame was not a measure of Yvain's love. Rather, it stemmed from his pride, his wish not to return to court without some tangible proof of his successful exploit at the Fountain which will convince Kay.

It is because of such a preoccupation with his chivalric honour that Yvain will at the first opportunity display pride, and Laudine could have applied to him Berhard de Ventadorn's lament about his proud lady:

> E sembla·m trassios,
> can om par francs e bos
> e pois es orgolhos
> lai on es poderos. (17, viii, 61-63)

Unlike Lancelot, Yvain fails to realise that anything one does for love is honourable. And so when Gauvain, echoing Bernard de Ventadorn who had said:

> Ben a mauvais cor e mendic
> qui ama e no·s melhura (6, iii, 17-18)

reminds Yvain that

84

> Honiz soit de sainte Marie
> qui por anpirier se marie!
> Amander doit de bele dame
> qui l'a a amie ou a fame   (2489-92)

our hero readily defers to his friend's advice to seek leave of his lady *ou face folie ou savoir* (2546). Chrétien who relies in part for the interpretation of his heroes' actions on the parallels that can be drawn between situations in his successive romances, here would expect the listener to recall in particular the case of Erec and Maboagrain as well as that of Cligés. Maboagrain, who in contrast to both Erec and Yvain was a true *fin amant*, reacted quite differently when he found himself in a position similar to theirs. Although like Yvain, Maboagrain would have liked to have the freedom to leave his lady's domain, he would never let her know *que nule rien me despleust*, as he did not wish in any way to displease her or break the promise he had made. For, as he says:

> N'est pas amis qui antresait
> tot le boen s'amie ne fait,
> sanz rien leissier et sanz faintise.   (*Erec*, 6009-6011)

Yet, unlike Erec, Maboagrain never became guilty of *recreantise*. Rather, he earned himself the reputation of being the most redoutable knight by upholding the custom of the *Joie de la Cour*, just as Yvain, despite Gauvain's fears, could have done if only he had acted like Maboagrain and had kept his original promise to his lady to defend her Fountain. But the contrast between Yvain and Cligés is no less instructive. When the latter, anxious to obey his father's dying wish to test his valour in the company of Arthur's knights, sought leave of his lady to go to Great Britain, he did not do this by means of a trick as Yvain will do, but humbly, on his knees and with tears in his eyes. And whereas Cligés, who was *si leax / Que ja n'iert mançongniers ne fax* (4519-20) will, like the *fin amant* of the lyrics, find separation from his love unbearable and return to Fenice despite Gauvain's and Arthur's attempts to retain him, Yvain, notwithstanding his earlier protestations that a year will be too long a period to be separated from his lady, will forget the term that Laudine had set for his return. In predicting that Gauvain would succeed in keeping Yvain beyond the appointed date:

> Et je cuit qu'il le passera,
> que departir ne le leira
> mes sire Gauvains d'avoec lui.   (2669-71)

Chrétien deliberately and no doubt with sly humour recalls the reverse situation in *Cligés*:

> Mes molt pesa, si con je croi,
> Mon seignor Gauvain et le roi,
> Quant plus nel puent retenir. (5027-29)

Chrétien never denigrates his heroes, and though, as Yvain himself admits, *covant manti li avoit* (2702), he is nevertheless not one of the false lovers of the lyrics who deliberately sets out to deceive the lady. Nor, on the other hand, contrary to the view expressed by Myrrha Lot-Borodine and W.Foerster, is Yvain conveying his own (or Chrétien's) 'protestation sourde contre la tyrannie féminine, contre la toute-puissance du sentiment.'[9] Yvain is simply forgetful. He repents as soon as he realises his fault and becomes demented with grief on losing his lady's love. In many a lyric the troubadours express their regret at having lost their lady's favour through their own fault and Chrétien, far from expressing his disenchantment with the courtly ideal, delights in making Yvain act out this complaint. There is an almost exact parallel to Yvain's particular fault in Bernard de Ventadorn song 15 strophe 3 where he laments that he is no longer his lady's *privatz* as he had failed to return to her on account of his *foudat*:

> Per ma colpa m'esdeve
> que ja no·n sia privatz,
> car vas leis no sui tornatz
> per foudat que m'en rete. (15, iii, 17-20)

Yvain's explanation of his own unpardonable action is an echo of Bernhard de Ventadorn's:

> Folie me fist demorer,
> si m'an rent corpable et forfet (6774-5)

However, Chrétien cannot refrain from making lighthearted fun even of his repentant Yvain and in the second half of the romance, no less than in the first, there is an ironic discrepancy between Yvain's protestations and his actions. For some scholars the lion is a symbol of Yvain's rehabilitation: 'La rencontre du chevalier et du lion a été un événement spirituel.'[10] But Yvain is not one of those heroes 'qui se construisent et se dépassent.'[11] Despite his repentance, he remains what he is and the lion serves as a comic reminder of all that Yvain is not and never will be. Not only does Chrétien make the

---

9 Myrrha Lot-Borodine, *La Femme et l'amour au XIIe siècle*, pp. 281-2.
10 J.Frappier, *Étude sur Yvain ou le Chevalier au Lion de Chrétien de Troyes* (Paris: SEES, 1969), 216.
11 *Op. cit.*, p.158.

lion mimic the poses attributed to the perfect *fin amant* in the lyrics,[12] but some of his antics are meant to show up Yvain's deficiencies, and perhaps nowhere better than in the scene where he happens to find himself back for the first time at the Fountain and laments his lost joy. Like Raimbaut d'Orange who laments: 'Joy has fled from me! . . . If ever she loved me, now she holds me in disdain. Why don't I kill myself . . .?':[13]

> Jois m'es fugitz!
> . . .
> S'anc mi volc, er m'a en desdeing.
> Com no·m esteing . . .? (VIII, iv, 19-22)

so Yvain asks himself repeatedly why he does not kill himself since he has lost his joy:

> et dit: 'Que fet quant ne se tue
> cil las qui joie s'est tolue?
> Que fais je, las, qui ne m'oci? (3525-3527)

Finally, like Bernard de Ventadorn in one of his lyrics, Yvain admits that he who loses his joy through his own fault deserves to be deprived of it:

[12] Bernard de Ventadorn on more than one occasion presents himself as submitting to his lady hands joined, head bowed, kneeling or standing, humbly and weeping:

> Mas jonchas, ab col cle,
> vos m'autrei e.m coman (18, vi, 48-49)
>
> mas jonchas estau aclis,
> a genolhos et en pes (37, v, 39-40)
>
> Del cor sospir e dels olhs plor,
> car tan l'am eu . . . (1, iii, 19-20)
>
> francs e doutz et umilians (10, vi, 42)

The lion, on submitting to Ywain, is presented as doing all these things, to the point of first kneeling and then standing and then kneeling again and even weeping:

> . . . il li comança a feire
> sanblant que a lui se randoit,
> que ses piez joinz li estandoit
> et vers terre encline sa chiere;
> si s'estut sor ses piez derriere
> et puis si se ragenoilloit,
> et tote sa face moilloit
> de lermes, par humilité. (3390-97)

[13] Walter T. Pattison, *The Life and Works of the Troubadour Raimbaut d'Orange*, Minneapolis: The University of Minnesota Press, 1952), 94.

87

> Des joies fu la plus joieuse
> cele qui m'ert aseuree;
> mes molt ot petite duree.
> Et qui ce pert par son mesfet
> n'est droiz que boene aventure et.   (3552-56)

> Dreihz es que·m sofranha
> totz jois, qu'eus eis lo·m tolh.   (38, vi, 71-72)

But Yvain's protestations ring hollow when compared to the deeds of
the lion which attempts to kill itself when it thinks Yvain is dead.
And it is with ironic humour that Chrétien makes Yvain himself
point to the lion as an example, which he nonetheless does not
follow.[14]

Yvain's exploits subsequent to his recovery from his madness may
differ from those before, in the sense that he does not go aimlessly
from tournament to tournament, but goes to the aid of those in need
of his help. However, neither before nor after are his exploits motivated by love for his lady and he will never be a second Lancelot.
Chrétien could not have made this clearer than by an implied comparison with the latter whose adventures are deliberately interwoven
with those of Yvain. Lancelot, of whom Chrétien said as Bernard de
Ventadorn did of himself, that love made him rich:

> come cil cui Amors fet riche
> et puissant, et hardi par tot   (*Charrette*, 630-31)

> qu'eu sui d'aitan melhuratz
> c'ome de me no vei plus ric
>   (6, iii, 19-20; cf. 11, iii, 17-21)

was able to succeed in the most difficult combats where all others
before him had failed, just as Erec once he was again spurred on by
love triumphed in the most formidable of all battles, that of the Joie
de la Cour. But Yvain, of whom Chrétien significantly never says that
he undertook his deeds of chivalry for love of Laudine, is unable to
succeed without the aid of the lion, either against the giant Harpin or
the two upholders of the Pesme Aventure. And Yvain will need the
help of the lion even in his battle on behalf of Lunette who has been
accused of treason for recommending to her mistress a knight (i.e.
Yvain) who subsequently proved untrue to his word. Neither the
presence of Laudine at this battle nor yet the fact that Yvain had
claimed that 'God and right'[15] were on his side is able to give Yvain

---

14 *Chevalier au Lion*, 3542-47.
15 *Chevalier au Lion*, 4439.

the strength to overcome his opponents on his own and Chrétien underlines that it was only thanks to the lion's intervention that the hero was saved from defeat.[16] Our poet could not have chosen a better way of hinting that Lunette's accusers were perhaps not altogether so mistaken.

Chrétien delights right to the end in working up a contrast between Yvain's actions and his protestations. When our hero, after his combat for Lunette, was introduced incognito to Laudine, as the Chevalier au Lion, he had told her, in words that echo those of William IX, that he could not remain until his lady had pardoned him her ill will:

> Dame, ce n'iert hui
> que je me remaingne an cest point
> tant que ma dame me pardoint
> son mautalant et son corroz. (4582-85)

> Ni no m'aus traire adenan,
> Tro qe sacha ben de la fi
> S'el'es aissi com eu deman. (10, ii, 10-12)

And in reply to Laudine's comment that she does not consider *tres cortoise* the lady who bears the *Chevalier au Lion* ill will, Yvain had asserted equally humbly that 'however much it grieved him, whatever pleases his lady suits him':

> que qu'il me griet
> trestot me plest ce que li siet (4593-94)

words which recall both those of Lancelot and Bernard de Ventadorn:

> il n'est riens nule qui me griet
> a feire, des que il li siet
> (*Chevalier de la Charrette*, 5891-92)

> ni ja res no·m seri' afans,
> sol midons vengues a plazer
> (2, vii, 44-45; cf. 11, vi, 45-48)

But subsequently, in complete contrast to these affirmations of obedience, Yvain is determined like Erec to force his will upon his lady and returns to the Fountain,

> que par force et par estovoir
> li covanroit feire a lui pes (6512-13)

---

[16] *Chevalier au Lion*, 4550-4552.

89

an action which would have been inconceivable on the part of Lancelot who, like Bernard de Ventadorn, in lyric 15, iii, 21-24, would not have dared to return to his lady without being reassured of her good will:

Tan n'ai estat lonjamen
que de vergonha qu'eu n'ai,
non aus aver l'ardimen
que i an, s'ans no m'asegura.

But Chrétien is evenhanded in his treatment of the hero and the heroine. If he makes good-humoured fun of Yvain for his not-so-courtly behaviour, he does not present Laudine either as a paragon of *fin amor*. Quite apart from the fact that Chrétien had smiled at her for the rapid way in which she had forgotten her first husband, he implicitly makes us compare her unfavourably with Enide. The latter, who like Lancelot had acted out some of the troubadours' more idealistic sentiments, had refused to accept the love of any other man even after Erec was presumed dead.[17] But Laudine, so angered by Yvain's fault, immediately changed her love for him to hatred and twice was ready to exchange Yvain for the Chevalier au Lion. If she had loved Yvain *d'amor saintime*, with an affection *qui n'est fause ne fainte*,[18] her hatred of Yvain would have turned to love on recognizing him in the Chevalier au Lion, just as Yvain's and Gauvain's hatred of each other as they were pitted incognito in battle had turned again to love when they became aware of each other's identity. Laudine's first reaction, however, had been that she would rather suffer the storm for ever than be forced against her will to take back into her affection the man who in her view apparently neither loved nor esteemed her. Only her wish not to perjure herself makes her grudgingly pardon Yvain, whose final plea for mercy reflects the sentiment that had brought about the initial pardon and is an acting out of Bernard de Ventadorn's pleading for mercy in yet another lyric: 'My heart's tears which moisten my eyes are proof that I repent of my folly; and I know well that my lady will suffer for it if she continues to refuse to pardon me. Since I am in her power, she has more to lose than I have in my disgrace. It would therefore be good for her to negotiate an agreement with her liege-lord':

[17] Cf. F. Bogdanow, 'The tradition of the troubadour lyrics and the treatment of the love theme in Chrétien de Troyes *Erec et Enide*' (in *Court and Poet*, ed. Glyn S. Burgess, Liverpool: Francis Cairns, 1981), 79-92.
[18] *Chevalier au Lion*, 6044-45.

> L'aiga del cor, c'amdos los olhs me molha,
> m'es be guirens qu'eu penet mo folatge,
> e conosc be, midons en pren damnatge
> s'ela tan fai que perdonar no·m volha.
> Pois meus no sui et ilh m'a en poder,
> mais pert ilh qu'eu en lo meu dechazer;
> per so l'er gen s'ab son ome plaideya.   (7, vii, 43-49)

There can be no doubt that despite his inability to keep his word, Yvain loves Laudine, but Chrétien suggests with delightful humour that Yvain's love for his lady is not as great as that of the lion for Yvain. On some occasions Bernard de Ventadorn expresses the conviction that 'the love of two noble lovers lies in their reciprocal pleasure and desire and that no good can come of it if their desires are not identical':

> En agradar et en voler
> es l'amors de dos fis amans.
> Nula res no i pot pro tener,
> si·lh voluntatz non es egaus.   (2, v, 29-33)

In contrast to Yvain, who never took care to ascertain his lady's wishes, but constantly sought to impose his will on her, the lion, not unlike the perfect *fin amant*, would never do anything without first seeking Yvain's approval:

> que il le vialt servir an gré,
> car encontre sa volenté
> ne voloit aler nule part.   (3425-27)

And Yvain for his part says of the lion, but ironically never of Laudine:

> il est a moi, et je a lui;
> si somes compaignon andui.   (6461-62)

It is, indeed, not for nothing that Yvain calls himself the Chevalier au Lion. It is a name that symbolises the mutual attachment and perfect harmony between Yvain and the lion and ironically underlines the less than ideal relationship between Yvain and his lady. Part of the *sens* of both the *Chevalier de la Charrette* and the *Chevalier au Lion* is that without a total and self-abnegating love for his lady a knight cannot achieve complete success in all he undertakes. But while the one illustrates this in a positive way, the other does so in a negative way. Yvain fails where Lancelot succeeds, because only the latter realises that he who loves is *molt obeissanz* and *ja n'iert mançongniers*, a notion that not even the lion's example could bring home to Yvain.

91

IV

KAIRO-KŌ: A DIRGE

Toshiyuki Takamiya and Andrew Armour

Kairo-kō: A Dirge, written in 1905, is generally admitted to be the first and only serious Japanese adaptation in prose of any Arthurian theme. The author, Natsume Sōseki[1] (1867-1916), who even now ranks as the most popular novelist in Japan, as well as being a prominent man of letters, was also a renowned scholar of English literature. His deep interest in, and awareness of medieval romance can be traced back to his two years of study in London (October 1900 to December 1902), a traumatic period in his life.

While still an undergraduate at the University of Tokyo, Sōseki[2] already showed a good command of English in his translation of a Japanese literary classic, and a deep insight into English literature. Two articles which he wrote, 'On the Poetry of Walt Whitman the Egalitarian' (1892) and 'The Concept of Nature in English Poetry' (1893), were both highly regarded.

Soon after graduating in 1893, he took up a teaching career but was obviously unsettled, changing schools no less than three times within a short period. Things were to change, though, when he became the first recipient of a scholarship provided by the Ministry of Education for furthering his studies in England. Despite this wonderful opportunity, he was disturbed by the stipulation that he was to concentrate more on the study of the language than on that of the literature; he felt apprehensive about his aspirations towards the latter, considering it a thankless task for a Japanese to pursue research in English literature.

---

[1] An admirable literary assessment of Sōseki as a novelist, together with a useful list of his novels available in English translation, is found in 'The Agonies of Individualism: Natsume Sōseki' in Hisaaki Yamanouchi, *The Search for Authenticity in Modern Japanese Literature* (Cambridge: Cambridge University Press, 1978). See also Jun Etō, 'Natsume Sōseki: A Japanese Meiji Intellectual' *American Scholar*, 34 (1965), 603-19.

[2] It is customary to refer to Natsume Sōseki by his pen name, Sōseki, rather than by his surname, Natsume. His given name was Kinnosuke.

After settling in London, Sōseki went to see Professor W.P.Ker (1855-1923) of University College, perhaps the greatest medievalist of the time. His lectures presumably acted as an initiation for the Japanese scholar, an introduction to the world of medieval Europe. Alas, they also bored him, in part because he lacked a basic knowledge of medieval languages, and in part because of the low, soporific voice in which they were delivered.[3] After two months, Sōseki began instead to receive private tuition from Professor W.J.Craig (1843-1906), who was to become in the following year the editor of the Arden Shakespeare, and to whom he had been introduced by Professor Ker. How well he got on with his new tutor is evident in his short reminiscences of this old Irish scholar.[4]

'It was his professional duty,' Dr Yamanouchi rightly asserts, 'to improve his understanding of English literature, while such efforts at improvement made him increasingly aware of its difficulty and of the insecurity of his own cultural identity. Thus he experienced a split in his personality, or a cultural schizophrenia.'[5] The longer he stayed in London, the more neurotic he became. In fact the only time he left London during the two years of his stay were two short visits, one to Cambridge, the other to Pitlochry.[6] In later months, his landlady related that he would often confine himself to his room for days on end. These periods were evidently not wasted, however, for it seems that he devoted himself to reading extensively in English literature, despite the mental anguish which he was suffering. This laborious study was to bear fruit after his return to Japan, in *A Theory of Literature*, which will be touched on later.

It is true that, in London, Sōseki could not have avoided being influenced by the pervasive Victorian cult of the Arthurian legend, especially by its manifestation in poetry and the visual arts, such as the paintings and book illustrations of the Pre-Raphaelites. However, his keen interest in this particular field may have also been stimulated

---

3 Professor Ker's manner of delivery is described by Professor B.I.Evans in W.P.Ker, *Form and Style in Poetry*, ed. R.W.Chambers (London: Macmillan, 1928), p.viii.

4 Cf. Sukehiro Hirakawa, *Natsume Sōseki: Hiseiyō no Kutō* (*Natsume Sōseki: The Struggle of a Non-European*) (Tokyo: Shinchōsha, 1976), pp.12-80.

5 Yamanouchi, *op. cit.*, p.50.

6 Dr Neil Ker who lived at Pitlochry and was a cousin of W.P.Ker, kindly informed us that there is a reference to a man who may be Sōseki in *Pitlochry, Past & Present* (Pitlochry, 1925) written by John H.Dixon. It was recently discovered that it was this Mr Dixon who invited Sōseki to visit the Highlands in October of 1902, just before he left England for good.

from a hitherto unrecognized source; namely, his encounters with Professor J.W.Hales (1836-1914) of King's College, London, and Dr F.J.Furnivall (1825-1910), a veritable dynamo of medieval English scholarship, which took place in June and September 1901, respectively. How much they talked about medieval literature we do not know, but it is interesting to note that Professor Hales had written an introduction to a popular text of Malory's *Morte Darthur*, published in 1900, and that Dr Furnivall, founder of the Early English Text Society, was one of the pioneers who made critical editions of several Arthurian romances available. Notable among these was *Bishop Percy's Folio Manuscript*, containing a number of Arthurian ballads, which he and Professor Hales edited jointly.[7]

On returning to Japan, Sōseki took up a teaching post at the First National College. At the same time, he was appointed to a lectureship at the University of Tokyo.

Kairo-kō: A Dirge was one of Sōseki's earliest literary undertakings. It was composed in the autumn of 1905, when he was still a lecturer at the university, and published in the November issue of the journal *Chuō-Kōron*, which was celebrating its two-hundredth edition. At the same time, Sōseki was also engaged in writing a serial novel, *Wagahai wa Neko de aru* (*I am a Cat*, 1905-6), a satirical masterpiece of whimsical nature. This work, which achieved great popularity, is written in a plain, colloquial style that had little in common with the deliberately archaistic language adopted in *Kairo-kō*.

The editor of *Chuō-Kōron*, adding his own preface to *Kairo-kō*, reported that the author had devoted himself for a whole week to its composition, refusing all other engagements. Later Sōseki was to write to his friend, the celebrated haiku poet Takahama Kyoshi, that a single page of *Kairo-kō* took as much out of him as five pages of *I am a Cat*.[8] It is apparent that he worked very hard on this project

7 Sōseki was obviously impressed by the character of Dr Furnivall, who had celebrated his seventy-fifth birthday six months previously. In his diary of 13 September, 1901, he wrote: 'Met Dr Furnivall; he is elderly, but quite well and flourishing.' Nine years later, in his diary of 15 October, 1910, we find the following entry: 'Learnt in the *Athenæum* of 9 July that Dr Furnivall died that Saturday.' For an account of the exciting life of this characteristically prolific Victorian, who was actively involved both in publication and in the organization of literary societies, see *Frederick James Furnivall: A Volume of Personal Record* (London: Oxford University Press, 1911) and William Benzie, *Dr F.J.Furnivall: Victorian Scholar-Adventurer* (Norman, Oklahoma: Pilgrim Books, 1982).

8 Despite the single-mindedness which Sōseki showed in writing *Kairo-kō*, the work does contain some logical inconsistencies. The colour of Lancelot's

and had a proportionate measure of confidence in its success. He was, however, to be disappointed. Although it was received quite favourably by the critics, *Kairo-kō* failed to gain public popularity, probably because of its subject matter, which was somewhat obscure for the Japanese reader at that time.

Kairo-kō was subsequently included, together with *Maboroshi no Tate* (*A Phantom Shield*, 1905),[9] also set in the times of King Arthur, in a collection of his previously published short stories entitled *Yōkyo-shū* (*Fugitive Pieces*, May 1906). This first edition in book form was littered with typographical errors, none of which were corrected in a so-called second edition, which appeared only four days later. It was not until the publishing of the third edition in March 1907 that the author at last realized and corrected both printing mistakes and punctuation. No attempt was made to produce a critical edition of *Kairo-kō* until 1975, when Professor Etō published his doctoral dissertation, *Sōseki and the Arthurian Legend — A Comparative Study of Kairo-kō*.[10] Since no holograph, either in draft or fair copy, remains, the present translation is based on the text of the third edition, which Professor Etō also considers to be of primary importance in establishing what Sōseki meant to say.

Any reader of *Kairo-kō* will no doubt find himself somewhat bewildered from the beginning by the multi-layered enigma which he encounters. First, there is the problem of the title, which was no less puzzling seventy-five years ago than it is now. For the precise meaning of 'kairo-kō', one has to turn to a Chinese dictionary; Sōseki was versed not only in Japanese and English literature, but also in the Chinese classics. 'Kairo' literally means 'dew drops on a shallot leaf', and is derived from a line in an ancient Chinese dirge, originally composed for a nobleman who had committed suicide: 'Human life is as evanescent as the dew drops on a shallot leaf.' Still extant are two letters in which Sōseki explains the meaning of his title and its origin; unexplained is the pun on Shalott, which can have hardly been

horse changes in the course of events, as does the colour of Elaine's hair. Also inconsistent is the timing of the opening of the floodgates at the end of part four and part five. Dramatic effect could be cited as the reason for the third example, but there is no evidence to suggest that they were deliberate.

9   A recent discovery is that Sōseki, in writing *Maboroshi no Tate*, used as a source John Rutherford, *The Troubadours: their Loves and their Lyrics* (London, 1873). See Saburō Oka, 'Source Studies of *Maboroshi no Tate*' in his *Studies in Natsume Sōseki*, vol. I (Tokyo: Kokubunsha, 1981), pp. 487-519.

10 *Sōseki to Āsā-ō Densetsu* (Tokyo: University of Tokyo Press, 1975). For an abstract in French see *Bulletin Bibliographique de la Société Internationale Arthurienne*, 28 (1976), 159-160.

accidental, though there is no concrete evidence to support such an assertion. As for the 'kō', this refers to a song or poem characterized by a slow but steady rhythm. Thus, pedantic though it sounds, the title of *Kairo-kō* is meant to refer to a lament or dirge for one of noble birth.

Sōseki's Arthurian romance is divided into five parts,[11] following a preface which, though untitled, should be regarded as the author's apologia. In the latter he reveals that his intention is to make a modern rendering of an Arthurian romance; however, here too the reader may find it difficult to grasp exactly what the author is trying to say. It should be pointed out that, in disparaging Malory's treatment of Lancelot and Guinevere because the former resembles a rickshaw man and the latter his light-o'-love, Sōseki is suggesting that they have something in common with such simple-minded, uncouth characters.

We know that Sōseki thought highly of the simple, natural style of *Le Morte Darthur* from two series of lectures which he gave at the University of Tokyo between April and June of 1903, and between that September and June of the following year. These were later published under the titles, *Eibungaku Keishikiron* (*Form and Style in English Literature*, 1924) and *Bungakuron* (*A Theory of Literature*, 1907). Despite his admiration, however, he felt that neither Malory nor Chaucer had sufficient power of analytical observation for their character portrayals to answer to the demands of the modern reader. Like most of his fellow Victorians, Sōseki preferred Tennyson's approach to the characterization of Lancelot and Guinevere. However, there is evidence indicating that, in writing *Kairo-kō*, he actually turned to Malory; he follows, for example, Malory's spelling for Lavaine's brother, Tirre rather than Tennyson's Torre. Merlin's prophecy concerning Guinevere's illicit love, mentioned in part three, is also taken from Malory (Book III, Chapter 1).

Perhaps what is most puzzling about Sōseki's preface is the total absence of any mention of Tennyson's *The Lady of Shalott*, despite its prominent position in the construction of part two, entitled 'The Mirror', and in the denouement of the story. Both Elaine of Astolat

11 Sōseki's major sources for *Kairo-kō* are as follows: part one, 'The Dream' (Malory, Book XVIII, Chapters 8-9; Tennyson, *Lancelot and Elaine*, ll.73-159), part two, 'The Mirror' (Tennyson, *The Lady of Shalott*, Parts 1-3), part three, 'The Sleeve' (Malory, Book XVIII, Chapter 9; *Lancelot and Elaine*, ll.241-396), part four, 'The Transgression' (Malory, Book XVIII, Chapter 15; Book XX, Chapter 3; *Lancelot and Elaine*, ll.568-610), and part five, 'The Boat' (Malory, Book XVIII, Chapters 19-20; *Lancelot and Elaine*, ll.1-33, 899-1154 & 1233-1274; *The Lady of Shalott*, Part 4).

and the Lady of Shalott feature in *Kairo-kō*, but it should be noted that only a novelist's sixth sense can have hinted to Sōseki that Astolat and Shalott shared a common origin, Escalot or Ascalot in the Old French *Mort Artu*.[12] It is certainly to the author's credit that he incorporated, instinctively perhaps, the supernatural tale of the Lady of Shalott into the story of the Lily Maid of Astolat, which he read in Tennyson's *Lancelot and Elaine* as well as in Book XVIII of Caxton's Malory.[13] On the other hand, the inclusion of the Lady of Shalott undoubtedly makes the structure of *Kairo-kō* all the more intricate and enigmatic.

As well as playing an important part in the plot and imagery of *Kairo-kō*, mirrors had a special significance for Sōseki, who was a victim of smallpox at an early age.[14] The scars on his face served to feed an inferiority complex, so much so that he was virtually obsessed with his own reflection in mirrors and windows. It seems that his stay in London only exacerbated this condition, as can be seen by the following account of his experiences there:

> Everyone I see in the street is tall and good-looking. That, first of all, intimidates me, embarrasses me. Sometimes I see an unusually short man, but he is still two inches taller than I am, as I compare his height with mine when we pass each other. Then I see a dwarf coming, a man with an unpleasant complexion — and he happens to be my own reflection in the shop window. I don't know how many times I have laughed at my own ugly appearance right in front of myself. Sometimes, I even watched my reflection that laughed as I laughed.[15]

The mirror in *Kairo-kō* which 'was said to be the work of Merlin, the famous sorcerer,' is taken from neither Tennyson nor Malory. What seems possible is that both Tennyson and Sōseki independently found the description in *Faerie Queene* of Merlin's mirror, connected

[12] See Appendix for the transmission of Shalott and Astolat.
[13] The Sōseki Library, now in the University of Tōhoku Library, contains three editions of Malory and a number of Tennyson's texts, including *The Poetical Works of Alfred Lord Tennyson*, 23 vols (London: Macmillan) and *The Works of Alfred Lord Tennyson*, 10 vols (Macmillan). The following are the relevant books which have notes and underlinings in Sōseki's hand: *Le Morte Darthur: Sir Thomas Malory's Book of King Arthur and of his Noble Knights of the Round Table*, ed. A.W. Pollard, 2 vols (London: Macmillan, 1900), and *Lancelot and Elaine* by Alfred Lord Tennyson, with introductions and notes by F.J. Rowe (London: Macmillan, 1895).
[14] Professor Sneeze, a self-caricature of Sōseki, suffers from the same problem in *I am a Cat*, Chapter 9.
[15] Translated by Yamanouchi (*op. cit.*, pp.48-49) from 'London Shōsoku' ('A Letter from London', published in April–May, 1901).

with a folk motif called 'death from unrequited love',[16] though there is no curse attached to the mirror in Spenser's poem.[17]

Regarding one of the more involved pieces of imagery found in *Kairo-kō*, it is interesting to note that a close parallel to the description of Elaine in the beginning of part three can be found in the cherished lines of one of Wordsworth's Lucy Poems, the one that begins 'She dwelt among the untrodden ways'. Sōseki was evidently familiar with this poem, for he made reference to its second stanza in *A Theory of Literature* to illustrate the notion of a visual image of brilliance.

To conclude this brief introduction, it should be emphasized that what Sōseki did in writing *Kairo-kō* was no different to what was done by a medieval writer of Arthurian romance; that is, rely heavily on traditional Arthurian sources for the core, at the same time adding bits and pieces taken from various minor sources, and developing his own personal manner of presentation, or *sententia*. Sōseki's story differs from those of Malory and Tennyson in putting far greater stress on the sinfulness of adulterous love between Lancelot and Guinevere. Professor Etō suggests that this is because *Kairo-kō* is a preliminary attempt to express his guilty obsession with the illicit relationship which he had formed with his sister-in-law, Tose,[18] a theme which was developed in later novels. This hypothesis, though interesting and certainly possible, is based on circumstantial evidence alone; it has caused fierce controversy among critics, and Sōseki's intent remains a mystery.

16 Stith Thompson, *Motif-Index of Folk Literature* (London: Indiana University Press, 1966), T 81.2.
17 *Faerie Queene*, Book III, Canto II, xvii-xviii. The Sōseki Library holds no less than five editions of the poem, of which the following is marked and under-lined by Sōseki: *The Canterbury Tales and Faerie Queene, etc. etc.*, edited for popular perusal with current illustrations and explanatory notes by D. Laing Purves (Edinburgh: W.P. Nimmo, Hay & Mitchell, 1897).
18 Etō, *op. cit.*, pp.312-332.

APPENDIX

With regard to Alclud, the Old Gaelic name for Dumbarton, Geoffrey Ashe asserts that 'there seems to be no basis for the notion that Alclud was Astolat, except that they begin with "A".'[19] With the aid of Arthurian onomastics, however, one can reasonably assume that both Astolat and Shalott were originally Alclud or Atlclut, its older spelling, adopted in Nennius' *Historia Britonum*. As is shown in Table I below, one could also argue that, as far as the transmission of Astolat and Shalott is concerned, Sōseki's *Kairo-kō* occupies the terminal position in the long stream of Arthurian literature covering eleven centuries. However, the eternal triangle formed by Lancelot, Guinevere and Elaine can only be traced back as far as the *Mort Artu*.

Table I: The Transmission of Astolat[20]

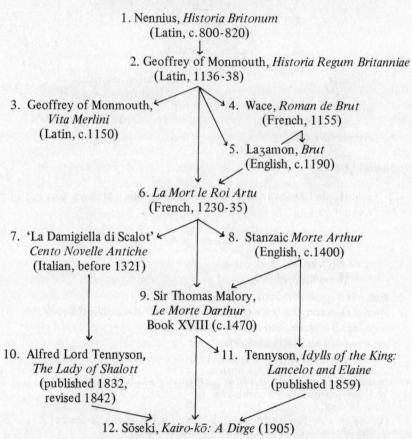

1. Nennius, *Historia Britonum*
   (Latin, c.800-820)

2. Geoffrey of Monmouth, *Historia Regum Britanniae*
   (Latin, 1136-38)

3. Geoffrey of Monmouth, *Vita Merlini* (Latin, c.1150)

4. Wace, *Roman de Brut* (French, 1155)

5. Laȝamon, *Brut* (English, c.1190)

6. *La Mort le Roi Artu* (French, 1230-35)

7. 'La Damigiella di Scalot' *Cento Novelle Antiche* (Italian, before 1321)

8. Stanzaic *Morte Arthur* (English, c.1400)

9. Sir Thomas Malory, *Le Morte Darthur* Book XVIII (c.1470)

10. Alfred Lord Tennyson, *The Lady of Shalott* (published 1832, revised 1842)

11. Tennyson, *Idylls of the King: Lancelot and Elaine* (published 1859)

12. Sōseki, *Kairo-kō: A Dirge* (1905)

99

Table II shows that these place names were subject to change at various stages of transmission, due to philological changes or scribal confusions. It should be noted that the figures in round brackets in Table II coincide with those in Table I and that *Asclut indicates the hypothetical, reconstructed form.

Table II

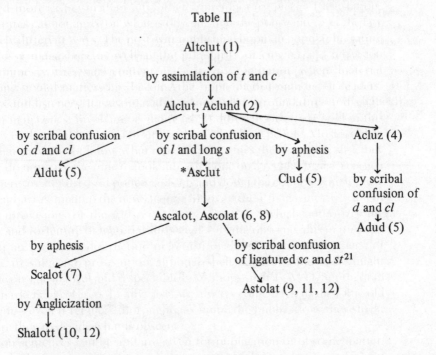

In Table III are found variant forms of Astolat with references to manuscripts and critical editions.

Table III: Variant Forms of Astolat

1. *Historia Britonum*: Ed. E. Faral.
   Altclut (BL Harley 3859)

2. *Historia Regum Britanniae*: Ed. E. Faral.
   Alclud (Leyden, Bibliothèque de la Ville, 20: Paris, Bibliothèque nationale, 6233; Berne, Bibliothèque de la Ville, 568)
   Alclut, Alchud, Alsclud (Berne)
   Aldclud (Paris, Berne)
   Acluhd (Trinity College Cambridge, 1125)
   Ascelud, Asclud, Acelud (see Louis-Fernand Flutre, *Table des Noms Propres*)

3. *Vita Merlini*:
   Alclud (BL Cotton Vespasian E. IV Ed. J.J. Parry; Ed. B. Clarke)
   Acelud (BL Cotton Vespasian E. IV Ed. E. Faral)

4. *Roman de Brut*: Ed. I.D.O. Arnold & M.M.Pelan.
   Acluz (Paris, Bibliothèque nationale, fr. 794)

5. *Brut*: Ed. F.Madden; Ed. G.L.Brook & R.F.Leslie.
   Clud (BL Cotton Caligula A. IX: Cotton Otho C. XIII)
   Adud (Caligula)
   Aldut (Otho)

6. *Mort Artu*:
   Escalot (BL Additional 10294 Ed. H.O.Sommer)
   Ascalot, Escalot (Paris, Bibliothèque nationale, fr. 342 Ed. J.D.Bruce)
   Escalot (other extant MSS Ed. J.Frappier)

7. 'La Damigiella di Scalot':
   Scalot (Ed. G.Ferrario)

7a. *Lancialotto Panciantichiano*:
   Scalliotto (Florence, Biblioteca Nazionale, Codice Panciatichiano 33
      Ed. E.G.Gardner)

8. Stanzaic *Morte Arthur*: Ed. J.D.Bruce; Ed. P.F.Hissiger.
   Ascolot, Ascalot, Ascolote, Ascalote (BL Harley 2252)

9. *Le Morte Darthur*:
   Astolot, Astolott, Astolat, Astolate (BL Additional 59768 Ed. E.Vinaver)
   Astolot, Astolat (Caxton's edition of 1485 Ed. H.O.Sommer)

10. *The Lady of Shalott*:
    Shalott

11. *Idylls of the King*:
    Astolat

12. *Kairo-kō*:
    Shalott (Part 2, 5)
    Astolat (Part 3, 5)

[19] Geoffrey Ashe, *A Guidebook to Arthurian Britain* (London: Longman, 1980), p.102.
[20] This is an expanded version of the table originally included in Toshiyuki Takamiya, 'Kairo-kō no Keifu' ('Tradition of *Kairo-kō*'), *The Rising Generation*, 120 (1975), 514-518.
[21] For the discussion that the Winchester MS (BL Additional MS 59678) reads Ascolat rather than Astolat, see Toshiyuki Takamiya, '"Ascolat" in the Winchester Malory', in *Aspects of Malory*, ed. Toshiyuki Takamiya and Derek Brewer (Cambridge: D.S.Brewer, 1981), pp.125-126.

A Note to the Translation

Although a work of the twentieth century, *Kairo-kō* was written in a language that is highly elaborate, somewhat antiquated and liberally spiced with terms taken from Chinese literature, with which Sōseki was familiar. As a result, it poses several problems for the translator, not the least of which is the rendering of certain passages of extemely cryptic Japanese into English, which generally demands greater lucidity. In this connection, we would like to express our gratitude for the invaluable assistance provided by Dr Hisaaki Yamanouchi and his wife Reiko, who were also kind enough to point out the parallel with Wordsworth in part three, and also to Dr Derek Brewer, Mr Takami Matsuda, Mr Peter Evans and Ms Yaeko Utagawa.

Turning to more technical aspects of the translation, the spelling of names has been aligned with those used by Tennyson, the one exception being Tirre, for reasons which have been explained in the introduction. Also, due to differences between the English and Japanese concepts of tenses, it was thought desirable to put the narrative sections in the past. Finally, some examples of Buddhist terminology have been transposed to more familiar equivalents in order to avoid creating an alien and unnatural impression that was not intended in the original. This is, after all, no more than what Sōseki was doing when he set an Arthurian romance in his native idiom. The result is, we believe, close to what is conveyed to the Japanese reader of this elegant, but at times enigmatic, work.

Kairo-kō: A Dirge

From the point of view of its simple, unsophisticated charm, Malory's famous Arthurian romance is without doubt a work of great value. However, because it is a product of the Middle Ages, when viewed as a novel it is open to the criticism of being desultory. For this reason, if one is interested in extracting and condensing part of the whole, it becomes virtually impossible to remain faithful to the original. Accordingly, in writing this piece I have taken the liberty of sometimes inverting the sequence of events, inventing new situations and remoulding the personalities of certain characters. The result is something which comes close to being a novel. However, I must say that I have done this merely because it seemed interesting, and not because I wanted to provide the reader with an introduction to Malory. I hope that he will bear this in mind.

To tell the truth, I have often thought that the Lancelot depicted by Malory resembled a rickshaw man, Guinevere being his light-o'-love. Were it for this alone, I think there would be sufficient reason to warrant a revision. Also, I need hardly say that, in composing this short story, I made frequent reference to Tennyson's 'Idylls of the King'. This epic is invaluable not only as a classic masterpiece of grace and beauty, but also because the character portrayal succeeds in making nineteenth-century men and women act out their parts on the medieval stage. I had originally intended to read it through again in order to refresh my memory, but I realized that in doing so I would be unconsciously tempted to imitate it, and so gave up the idea.

1. The Dream

Five, ten score in number, all the knights mustered and made ready to hasten northwards to the tournament. All that remained behind among the ancient stones of the castle of Camelot was the rustling of Queen Guinevere's long robes.

The pale crimson cloth swept heedlessly off one shoulder, exposing the whiteness of her arm. Falling gently over her lightly tripping jewelled slippers, the hem of her dress trailed down behind as she climbed the flight of stone steps. At the top a dark grey portière, on which was embroidered a large flower, hung immobile, as if sad to be alone. Guinevere pressed her ear to the cloth, listening. Then, turning away, she darted a searching glance at the foot of the stairs. Here and there on the deeply stained marble, white roses released their soft fragrance into the gloom: all that remained of the garland she had given him that evening. For a while, she appeared intent on even the rustle of the silk that hung about her feet. And then, on some sudden impulse, she straightened up, reaching out with her arm. Her slender hand described an arc as it pulled back the deep folds of the curtain. Like an arrow finding its target, a dazzling shaft of light spilled out from the room to splash upon Guinevere's crown. Gleaming in the centre of her forehead was a diamond.

'Lancelot!' she called, still pressing the curtain aside. Though in fear of heaven and earth, her voice contained an inner strength, powerful enough to free her from any constraint. Her crown was no barrier, for Love has no enemy.

'Guinevere!' answered a voice, almost too soft to belong to the man who stood before her. His tousled black hair, falling over his brow, was swept proudly back. His cheeks, ill-matched, were pale.

Guinevere quickly withdrew her hand from the curtain and entered. The shaft of light which had spilled out across the marble steps vanished abruptly. All that could be made out in the gathered gloom was the flower on the portière. To left and right, the shadows of the tall pillars fell about the passages, but, being shadows, they were silent. It appeared that the only living things present were the man and woman in the room.

'So you do not join the other knights and go north to the tourney? May it be that more than just unruly locks disturb the calm of your brow?' ventured Guinevere. She smiled gently, anxiously; a cloud lingering in the clear sky of her face.

' I am drugged with the perfume of your roses,' was his only reply, as he gazed out from the high window that overlooked the entrance to the castle. It was May. A thousand willows dipped their clear shadows into the languid waters of the river that meandered past. Even the crumbling cloud peaks could be seen carried down in the current. White sails, standing immobile, spoke of bargemen enjoying a merry tune as they made their way down to the sea. Drawing away from the river, and just visible through the trees, was a thin, white, powdery thread — the main road along which thundered the horses of Arthur and his knights of the Round Table on their way north, their hooves raising dust in the shadows of the early morning sun.

'If there be any sin in happiness, then I am a wretch who prays that sin may endure. Yet if it were to endure but one day, this day that you alone remain in the castle, it would be too cruel.' Her coral-red lips winced with the anguish that seethed in her breast.

'If it were to endure but one day? Even beyond the grave, it shall never fade.' His dark eyes stared back at her.

'So be it!' She raised up her right arm, turning her open palm toward Lancelot. Unthinkingly, his eyes followed the glittering gold bracelets adorning her wrist. 'So be it!' she repeated, 'Other than the two of us, there is none who would allow a malady born of the intoxicating perfume of a rose. Countless are the knights of Camelot, but there is not one who does not doubt the malady that keeps Lancelot from the tourney. If we grasp too firmly this bud of joy, it may wither for eternity. . .' She suddenly dropped her arm. The chime of sparkling gold echoed off the walls.

'Life is a long gift, but Love is longer still. Take heart!' The knight showed no trace of fear.

Guinevere reached up and took hold of her crown with both hands, 'This crown! This crown! How it burns into my head!' Were she able, she would surely have torn off the band of gold and gems, casting it down from the window. As she wrestled with it, the silk slipped down her white arms and, finding release, her curling tresses tumbled down over her cheek. The pale crimson sleeve gathered on her shoulder fell gently forward on her breast. Below, even the stiff folds of her dress swept softly along the floor. Lancelot merely gazed on at her graceful beauty. Cut off from both past and future, oblivious to anything but the present, Guinevere alone remained vivid in his eyes. The mirror which senses the subtle depths of the heart is said to be, of all things possessed by a woman, by far the clearest. As Guinevere struggled within herself, almost unable to bear the agony, her brave knight's heart went out to her like the swift shadow of a bird on the wing. In an instant, the pain vanished, brushed away like old cob-webs, leaving only happy contentment. 'If it be true. . .' she hoped, praying that that perilous spark of joy might last for eternity. She smiled radiantly.

'It is,' he reassured her, steadfast in his resolve.

'But. . .' she began again after pausing in thought, 'To make it come true. . . you must make haste to the tourney in the north! Follow the trail of those who departed at dawn, and tell them your malady is cured. Scatter the clouds of suspicion, these rumours that gather about us!'

'Can love endure where courage does not?' Brushing away the hair that tumbled over his broad forehead, he laughed aloud, though the mirth rang hollow. A strange and unsettling echo reverberated through the stillness of the high-ceilinged room. The laugh died as suddenly as it had begun. ''Tis no breeze that moves yonder curtain,' he said, as he strode over to the portière and shook the thick folds to left and right. The strange echo evaporated into silence.

'Echoes from a dream. . . the dream I had this morning,' she said, as the colour drained from her face. The sparkling gems in her crown trembled. Lancelot too appeared unsettled as he listened to Guinevere relate the dream she had had before waking.

'It was on a day when all the roses were in bloom. There were just the two of us, lying together among the roses — white, red and yellow. We watched the sun set on that happy day; the endless twilight was filled with joy. I was wearing this crown,' she explained, raising a finger to her forehead. Twice coiled around its base was a golden serpent, with finely etched scales and two sapphire eyes set in its upraised head.

'This crown began to burn into my flesh and around my head I heard a strange sound, like that of cloth being rubbed. This golden snake wound in my hair had begun to uncoil itself. Its head slithered towards you, leaving its tail on my breast. I watched it stretch like a curling wave, and then we were both entrapped in its slimy coils, bound so tight that there was no hope of release. You lay at arm's length, but I had no strength to draw nearer, no means to draw away. Yet loathsome though it was, that bond became a solace for my anguished heart, for to sever it would have been to separate us. But how cruel that we had to endure its bites and stings till the day the flesh rotted from its bones. Assailed thus by pleasure and pain, I looked on as the red roses burst into flame and engulfed the snake that bound us. Soon, the golden scales about its middle began to change colour, giving out a bluish smoke and an evil odour. It suddenly snapped in two. "With this, may both body and soul vanish for eternity," I prayed, when I heard someone beside me laugh mockingly, and I awoke. But, waking too, the voice continued to echo in my ears. The memory of it filled me with cold dread when I heard the echo of your laughter in this room.' The long lashes of her eyes could not conceal their anxiety, as she studied Lancelot's face. Having fought in battle more than seventy-five times, never unhorsed or even slipped from his stirrups, Lancelot was the bravest of knights. Yet this dream perturbed him. His worried brow was knitted in a frown, his teeth firmly clenched.

'So be it. Tardy though I may be, I will hasten northwards,' he said at last, unfolding his arms and stretching to his full height of over six feet.

106

'You will go, then?' questioned Guinevere, still doubting. But in the midst of her doubt, the hope that he would not leave her still glimmered faintly.

'I will,' he vowed, and swept back the curtain that barred his exit. He paused. Then, turning on his heel, he faced Guinevere, took her white hand in his and laid two burning lips on its cool softness. He felt as if he were inhaling lily petals, still moist with the morning dew. Turning, he hastened down the stone steps without looking back.

Presently, Guinevere heard a horse neigh thrice and the sound of steel-shod hooves striking the flags of the courtyard. Descending from the high chamber, she found a window directly overlooking the gate through which the knight must pass, and there she awaited his departure. At last the head of the black horse appeared below, whereupon she leaned out to wave her farewell with a long veil of white silk, causing her gold crown to slip from her beautiful hair. Grazing the horse's head, it almost shattered as it fell ringing on the flagstones. Lancelot lifted it up on the point of his lance to the window, offering it back to Guinevere. Their eyes suddenly met; 'O cursèd crown!' she swore as she took it.

'Fare thee well!' Lancelot shouted back, spurring the soft belly of his mount. With a wave of his white panache he was gone, leaving behind only a cloud of dust.

2. The Mirror

Never looking at the world of reality, but only at the world reflected in her mirror, the Lady of Shalott lived all alone in a tall tower. For someone who knows only the world that inhabits a mirror, what hope is there of finding a companion?

Sometimes the faint chirping of birds that pined for the coming of spring would filter up to her lonely chamber. But, eager to see their gaily-coloured plumage amidst the green leaves, she turned not to the window, but to the mirror which was set into the wall. The bright colours of their feathers and everything else outside her tower, even the setting sun, could be seen only in their reflection.

Hearing the whispering echoes of voices — the singing of men reaping barley and women threshing in the fields of Shalott, far away across the water — the Lady of Shalott would cover her eager ears and again turn to her mirror. It was but a sad melody that floated up

107

from somewhere along the hazy border where the line of billowing willows on the far bank of the river met the fields and sky.

Everyone who passed along the road that ran through Shalott was also reflected in her mirror. Sometimes she would see a man driving a horse, his red cap bobbing as he walked. Or a white-bearded pilgrim, clad in loose-fitting robes and plodding along with a staff, tied with a small gourd. And sometimes she saw a strange figure pass by, ringing a bell and draped in a long white habit which hid his limbs and features. Of course, the Lady of Shalott could not know that this was the sad lot of the leper, forced to advertise his dreadful fate.

The fardel on the back of a passing pedlar might be filled with red ribbons, white linen, coral, agate, quartz or pearls. But while it goes unopened, the contents will never be reflected in the mirror. And what is unseen by the mirror is also unseen by the Lady of Shalott.

From time immemorial, everything under the sky had been reflected in the infinitely varied kaleidoscope of the Lady of Shalott's mirror. But they were only flitting shadows — appearing, vanishing, and then appearing again. The very sun itself never tarried for long in her mirror. From time to time, she would wonder whether the shadows were fleeting because they were only shadows of reality, or whether the world of reality itself was composed of nothing but shadows. If that world is never viewed directly, it is impossible to decide between shadows and reality. If, in truth, they are only shadows that flit outside her window, then there is no loss for her who must see only their reflection. But if they are more than mere shadows. . .? There were times when she was seized by a sudden desire to rush to her window and look out freely over the world that existed outside her mirror. But the moment that she looks out from her high window is also the moment that a curse will fall on the Lady of Shalott. The world reflected in her mirror forms the walls of her prison. Just to turn from the distant scene framed therein would be to invite her instant doom.

She had heard it said, however, that the real world was a mire of sin, and that those who wearied of it found refuge high in the mountains. Confined though she was to the narrow cosmos of her mirror, the Lady of Shalott was spared from knowing pain and anguish, the bitterness of him who stands at the crossways, swept by the rains of sorrow, minding the comings and goings of his fellows. When a man causes a wave in the sea of destiny, it spreads out endlessly across the water, sweeping up all those in its path into the swirling maelstrom. Whither the currents will take us, we know not. If to suffer this fate is to be called wise, then in truth it is the height of folly to fritter away one's years alone in a tall tower, never setting foot to earth, and with the whole evanescent world shrunk to a white silver glare which confuses appearance and reality. What is seen is not the animate world, but something which creates its own reality in silent reflections. The Lady of Shalott's fate was as much to be envied as pitied, but sometimes she would become restless with a yearning to turn from the mirror and look down at the wide world spread beneath her window.

The mirror stood as high as the Lady herself. Made from dark iron burnished to its natural silvery white, it was said to be the work of Merlin, the famous sorcerer. If ever its surface were to mist over to a hazy gloom which not even the rising autumn sun could brighten, one should beware, for it portended ill. But if the mirror became clouded with dew, the drops of which one could hear dripping onto lotus petals, then peril threatened whoever stood before it. And when a web of white gossamer sprung up across the mirror, accompanied by an unholy tearing sound, then one must prepare to meet one's end. The Lady of Shalott no longer remembered how many months and years had passed by, reflected in her mirror. Looking into it morning after evening, evening after morning, she had even forgotten whether she had wearied of it. She had never seen the surface dulled by mist or beads of dew. She never even dreamt that it might one day crack. To her, it was like gazing into the silent depths of an autumn river, over whose limpid surface skittered shadows, countless and chaotic, forming a timeless continuum. This limitless cosmos had been compressed and forged into a plate of solid metal, the mirror before which the Lady of Shalott stood every evening and every morning.

Evening and morning she faced the mirror. Evening and morning she sat beside it. Evening and morning she wove a web at her loom. Sometimes the web was woven bright, sometimes it was dark.

Whenever a passer-by heard the sound of the shuttle plied by the Lady of Shalott, he would look up in dread at the window in the tall tower atop that lonely hill. It had the expression of an old man who had long outlived kith and kin, and who cursed the fate that condemned him to live on so long. The rhythmic sound of the shuttle that filtered from that ivy-hung window marked the passing of the days and months, like a pendulum that never rests. It was a lively rhythm, yet it echoed from another world. The still air rested heavily over silent Shalott, but seduced by the sound of her shuttle, it shivered imperceptibly. The numbing sense of desolation it produced was more unbearable than even the creeping silence that usually enveloped the tall tower of Shalott. Looking up at it, wide-eyed with terror, the passer-by would hurry on, his hands over his ears.

The Lady of Shalott worked at her loom without pause. If the pattern were one of bell flowers springing from the thick luxuriance of a fresh green meadow, she would choose such heavy shades that each blossom appeared almost to emerge from the fabric. If she were floating snow-like froth on the cresting waves of an angry sea, in one thin layer she described the fathomless depths below. Sometimes, she would weave a cross of flaming crimson on a sable field; the storms of sin rampaged throughout the four corners of the world and appeared to blow even into the pores of the woven cross, inciting the dancing flames to leap from the web. So bright did it shine in the heavy gloom of her chamber, that it seemed it would reduce everything to ashes.

With love and truth her warp and weft, she would weave the figure of Mary, arms crossed over her breast, gazing up to heaven. But choosing folly as her weft and wrath as her warp, she would weave a wintery night, swept by wind and hail: alone in the wilderness, his white beard flying in the face of the tempest, appeared the likeness of King Lear. Entwining the crimson thread of shyness with the bitter grey of steel, one could divine the heart of a lost lover. Blending modest yellow with conceited purple, a maiden appears: already one of the devil's own, her face is twisted in an arrogant sneer, her long sleeves gathered about by the tangled skein of secret desire.

Beauty had not graced the Lady of Shalott: her face lacked delicacy, her eyes were sunk deep and her lips overfull. Nine times had the sand run through the hourglass since the summer dawn, signalling that it was already past noon. Although the window was bathed in dazzling sunlight, the interior of her chamber was as dark as a cavern. The only things which shone in that gloom were the mirror of burnished iron and the loose strands of hair that floated about her shoulders. Passing the shuttle from right to left, she suddenly looked up at the mirror; a light still colder than that of the sharpest sword shone on every fine downy hair. . . Alas! What could this be? Without a sound, the surface of her mirror had suddenly misted over, robbed of its light as if blasted by the breath of a giant. The willows that had been visible along the banks of the river were hidden in the instant, and the river vanished. Gone too were the tiny figures of people who passed to and fro along the banks. The shuttle froze in her hands. Her black eyelashes quivered faintly. 'What omen is this?' she cried, and moved closer to the empty mirror. Then, just as swiftly as it had formed, the mist cleared: river, willows and people all reappeared, as if nothing had happened. The rhythm of the shuttle could be heard again.

After a while, the Lady of Shalott began to sing, in a voice too sad to belong to this world:

110

Lost in dreams and shadows,
In a world of sorrow.
But empty my life grows,
For ever and a morrow.

How beautiful Love shines,
In the mirror bright!
Alas, this flower pines,
Every morn and night.

From between the breeze-blown branches of the far-off willows reflected in the mirror, came a sudden flash of silver, and a thin veil of hot dust arose. Straight as an arrow, the silvery light approached Shalott from the south. Though she knew it was only a shadow, the Lady of Shalott followed the light in her mirror, totally absorbed in it, like an eagle stalking a young lamb. At last it emerged from behind the long avenue of willows, rushing like the wind; she saw the full armour of finely-tempered steel bathed in bright sunlight, the long white panache waving at the helm. The powerful bay was clad in leather trappers on head and chest; their countless studs glittered like a constellation of stars on an autumn night. With bated breath, the Lady of Shalott gazed on.

Following the curving river bank, the horse was brought around to the left, so she could now see the rider clearly as he made straight towards her mirror. A long lance was fitted to his rest and a shield hung over his bridle arm. She strained forward to try to discern the bearing on the shield. The knight, with neither sign nor greeting, rode closer and closer, until it seemed that he must burst straight through the mirror. At last, when he appeared larger than life before her eyes, the Lady of Shalott, as if lost in a dream, threw down the shuttle. Facing the mirror, she cried out aloud the name of Lancelot. The knight's eyes flashed from beneath his visor, as he looked up at the tall tower of Shalott. Somewhere in the recesses of the mirror, their eyes met — his fiery, hers piercing. She cried out once more, 'Sir Lancelot!' She rushed to the forbidden window and looked down at the world, her face as pale as death. Horse and rider galloped past below the tall tower with an earth-shaking sound like thunder disappearing into the distance.

With a sharp crack, the shining mirror split in twain; each half shattering into fragments with a noise like splintering ice. A cloud of fine debris filled every corner of the room. The whirlwind of chaos tore the many-coloured web on the loom into shreds, which joined the metal shivers in their dance of destruction. Inside the room was not a breath of wind, yet the threads — crimson, green, yellow and

111

purple — unravelled, twisted and tangled in mid-air, winding around her face, hands, sleeves and hair, like the viscid web of the earth-spider. With her last strength, she raised both arms above her and called out, 'Lancelot has killed the Lady of Shalott, but she shall kill Lancelot! You bear my dying curse, knight, as you ride north!' Then, like a rotted tree giving way before an autumn storm, she fell with a crash, amidst the havoc of threads and crystal splinters.

3. The Sleeve

Like a lonely violet, dyed with the deep purple dew of a falling star on a spring night, the lovely Elaine passed the days and months in the old castle of Astolat. No suitor had ever come to ask for her hand. She lived alone with her two brothers and her father, so old that even his eyebrows were frosted white.

'Whither are you bound, knight?' the old man asked in a gentle voice.

'I have been driving my mount hard that I may join the tourney in the north. Though it be summer, dusk came swift upon me, and in the darkness I lost my way at a fork in the road. I know well my horse was as glad as I to find your gate. I am only ashamed that I have nothing with which to repay your kindness and hospitality for this night.' Stripped of his armour, the knight now wore a yellow tunic. For what reason he knew not, but when coming through Shalott he had suddenly felt a chill, like ice-cold water, run through his body. Now, as he begged for a night's lodging, the pallor of his cheeks was more apparent.

Elaine, who was hiding her small frame behind her father, wondered what wind of fortune could have blown such a gallant hero to the shores of Astolat. From time to time, she would peer around the thin, almost birdlike, shoulders of her father, stealing a glance at Lancelot from below shy lashes. Perhaps she might dally among the flowers of the field, but the gnarled and twisted branches of the old pine in the valley afford no such opportunity; the little butterfly folds her frail white wings and rests immobile.

'I have a further request,' ventured Lancelot after a pause, 'It will not profit me to appear late at the tourney tomorrow and be recognized by all. Wherefore I pray thee, if there be any shield, old or new, whose device is not known to people, lend it to me that I may joust disguised.'

The old man clapped his hands together. 'Just as you wish, I shall lend you such a shield. Many months past, my elder son, Tirre, suffered a wound in his leg while tilting. His life was spared, but even now he lies abed, unable to rise. His shield bears silver with a cross gules, but tested only the once, it hangs even now upon his wall, gathering dust. If it is your wish, you may bear it at the tourney tomorrow, and alarm all those that set their eyes on it.'

'It is a great honour that you do me,' replied Lancelot, his fist held clenched at his chest. The old man continued.

'My younger son, Lavaine, is a brave youth. Though still young in years, it would be to his shame if he were not to attend King Arthur's pageant. I ask only that you let him follow you to the tourney. With your leave, I will go and tell him to hasten the morrow.'

'As you desire,' Lancelot replied without hesitating. For a brief moment, the old man's furrowed features wrinkled in a smile. Behind him, Elaine thought that if only she were a man, she too would follow the brave knight.

For generation after generation, the ivy clings to the tree in an eternal embrace. But for Elaine, there were but a few hours till the dawn that would bring parting. Were she to reach out and grasp happiness with all the strength in her frail body, the tempest that blows about the tree stem would surely lash her mercilessly to the ground. And yet, if she were to forgo this chance and remain apart, he would surely shake quietly free of her secretly coiling tendrils of love and leave her, lonelier than ever. Love melted, filling her eyes with sweet sparkling dew. The castle of Astolat was old indeed, but the fair Elaine who called it her home had seen the passing of no more than eighteen springs. She was filled with an indescribable feeling of melancholy love as the brooding clouds suddenly parted, allowing the glorious rays of the sun to bathe the vast earth. Over-flowing field and valley, the warm sunbeams were drawn across more than a thousand leagues. For Elaine, this sudden meeting with such a handsome knight as Lancelot was like emerging from some dark pit into the world above, caressed by the balmy breeze of spring. To part on the morrow, without exchanging a word, would be a cruel awakening.

One by one the candles died, lamenting the night. At midnight, the guest retired. But, alone, the sleepless Elaine struggled in vain to banish the memory of his face as it floated before her. Closing her eyes, she tried to drive away the flitting shadow; but closed eyelids are no barrier to such persistence, for there he was again, haunting her. Sometimes she would be racked by dreams so terrible that the world about her inspired only fear. Sometimes she would lie shivering with dread that the spirits of the night would come to take her soul, and then sit up with joy and relief at the cock's crow. Yet the fright and terror were no more than empty echoes of her repeated prayers for calm. The spectres of her dreams sprang from her own sweet innocence, but the anguish which she felt that night was of a different breed. Her soul was lost, and all her searching in vain. Frightened and bewildered, she knew not how to calm her fevered breast. No longer the mistress of her own heart, she was strangely, anxiously, sadly absorbed by the memory of Lancelot. Within the short passage of an evening, her soul had been replaced by that of the knight; her own self had vanished. She who answers the call 'Elaine!' is no longer Elaine; she is the knight who looks up at the tall tower from the deep shade of his visor as he dismounts in the yard. Again, to the call 'Elaine!', she answers that Elaine is Lancelot. 'Is Elaine dead?' the voice questions. 'She lives,' comes the answer. 'Whither is she gone?' it asks. 'I know not,' she replies. Elaine was trying to return to her own past, taking refuge in the countless millions of invisible pores that covered her body. However many pots of fragrant oil she might rub into her skin to make it as smooth as silk, Elaine refused to appear again.

At last she stirred. Opening the curtain that concealed the entrance to her chamber, she reached up to the long robe that hung on her wall. Taking it down, she held it before the flame of her candle. The thin cloth glowed with a crimson so bright that it seemed as if the midday sun were shining in the dark gloaming of her room. She held it for a while, draped from her right arm, gazing at its brilliance. In her left hand was a small dagger, still in its sheath, which suddenly flashed back and forth. There was the sound of metal ringing on the stone floor. The deed was done too swiftly for the eye to follow, but there in Elaine's hand lay a crimson sleeve, severed from the beautiful robe that drifted down to join the empty sheath on the floor. At that very moment, the flame of her candle faltered and died. Outside, the night deepened under a crescent moon.

Guided by the faint glow of the sleeve held up in her right hand, Elaine slipped from the clutches of the dark room. To the right lay the rooms of her brothers. To the left, at the end of the passage, lay the room of their guest. As if her feet never touched the floor, the slender Elaine glided along, quieter than a shadow in a dream. She paused outside the room where Lancelot slept. But Lancelot slept not.

It was known that the great King Arthur, when deliberating whether to make Guinevere his Queen, had asked the advice of Merlin, yet he, who was gifted with the knowledge of events yet to come, shook his head and refused to give his consent. With harsh words he warned the King that he would live to regret the match, for the woman would later love another. Lancelot, with clear conscience, knew of no such man, nor whom it might be. But with the passing days and months, he came to realize that it had been he who Merlin had spoken of. Both pain and pleasure assailed him: he cursed the sad fate that had chosen him, out of the countless souls that wandered the earth, to fulfil the prophecy of Merlin. Yet, at the same time, he rejoiced for the happy fortune that had brought him and Guinevere together. Pain and pleasure, pleasure and pain; they were braided together in a rope that held him fast. He struggled against his bonds, but he never cut them, for he knew that his freedom would be but unending sorrow. He drew the sweet honey of happiness from the forbidden flower of guilt: there were even times when he felt compelled to extract every last drop of the nectar to provide a balm for his heavy heart. This was the reason why, despite the whispered doubts of the other knights who sat at the Round Table, he had never forsaken the Queen. But if the whispers were to turn to shouts, the suspicion into proof? If Guinevere were taken and burned at the stake . . . ? Lancelot slept not.

Something seemed to brush against the door of his room. Lancelot raised his head to look in the direction of the sound; he listened awhile and then lay down again. No pulse beat through the lifeless shell of the old castle. All was quiet.

Again, the sound. This time it was almost like a tap on the wood. No longer doubting that someone stood outside, Lancelot rose from his bed and drew the door ajar. 'Who is there?' he asked. The flame of the candle held out before him bowed before the first gust of wind from the hall, but then revived to flicker towards the young girl who stood on the threshold. Her face was hidden in the shadow of the crimson sleeve which she held aloft. It was not only the candle flame that hesitated shyly.

'The hour is late . . . perhaps you have lost your way?' The words came out fitfully in his surprise.

'Paths untrod lead one astray, but not even the mice could lose their way in these old familiar halls.' She spoke softly, but with determination.

Lancelot merely gazed on, as if she were some wonderful vision, but her face — more lovely than a flower — was concealed by the veil of crimson silk. Whether from the silk, or from a swifter heartbeat, the colour of her cheeks was heightened. He could see the stray locks that lay on her shoulders and the three white roses that crowned her head.

Lancelot could sense the heavy perfume of the flowers, and even

115

count them as they lay in the shadow of the sleeve. Then, like a sudden chill, he remembered Guinevere's dream; some strange force drained the strength from his body. He almost dropped the candle which he held, but then recovered with a start. For the young girl there was nothing to hint of the anguish that raged within the breast of the man who stood before her.

'In crimson lies truth. Unbeckoned, I bring you my unworthy sleeve, that you might wear it at the tourney, tied to your helm,' she said at last, almost thrusting out the sleeve in front of her. Lancelot remained silent.

'Are you a knight that you would not accept a lady's favour?' pleaded Elaine, looking up at his face inquiringly.

His thin lips pursed, his brow knitted in a pensive frown, Lancelot took the burning sleeve in his right hand. At last, he broke the silence, 'I have fought in battle over three score times, and countless are the men felled by my lance at tourney. Yet not once have I ever worn a lady's favour. Though to refuse the generosity of the daughter of my kind host would be a discourtesy . . .'

'Speak neither of courtesy nor discourtesy! It was not for courtesy that I braved the dark. I have come to give this sleeve, symbol of my heart, to the bravest of all knights. I entreat you to accept it.' To refuse the young girl's earnest plea was no easier a task than to accept it, but Lancelot hesitated.

Of all the knights at Camelot, both young and old, there was not one who would fail to recognize the bearing on Lancelot's shield. And there was not one who had ever seen him wear a lady's favour on his arm or helm. To arrive late for a tourney which he had at first declined would be seen by all as a change of heart. To ride into the tilt-yard on the morrow and be greeted by his comrades as the late-comer Lancelot would cause the whispers of scandal to evaporate into thin air. But if they reasoned that, since he had come to the tourney, his malady had been none other than that of the malingerer, he would have no answer to their accusations. Now, by good fortune, he was to borrow a shield that was unknown to them. If, then, he wore the favour of this young girl and took care not to lift his visor, none should recognize him. And if, after felling some two dozen knights with his lance, he were to proudly announce that he was Lancelot, he would surely be greeted by their admiration rather than their contumely. Some among them might even think his malady a commendable ruse. Such was Lancelot's conclusion.

Gleaming in the darkness on the far side of the room lay Lancelot's armour, and leaning up against his breast plate stood his shield, which he picked up lightly in one hand and placed in front of Elaine.

116

'It is a great honour for any knight to wear the symbol of such a noble heart tied to his helm. I thank you,' he said, accepting the crimson sleeve.

'You will accept it?' she asked, half smiling with relief. It was as if the first rays of the morning sun had lit up a lily of the valley, drying every drop of dew.

'This shield will be of no use to me at the tourney. I shall leave it here. Please keep it by you until my return.'

'I will guard it with my body and soul,' replied Elaine, kneeling to embrace the shield. 'Crimson, crimson,' whispered Lancelot, admiring the long sleeve held up to his brow.

Below, a raven cawed as it flew past the tower. The sky began to glimmer with the first steaks of dawn.

4. The Transgression

While she loved Lancelot, Guinevere bore no ill-will against King Arthur. Her love was a secret which she shared only with herself.

All of the knights had returned from the tournament in the north; all save Lancelot, of whom there was no sign. She waited eagerly, but as the days passed, even her hopes of hearing some news of him waned. No longer did she look up expectantly at the sound of men riding into the castle courtyard. One day became two, two became three; she counted them off on her fingers. Ten days had passed, and yet she still prayed that he would return to Camelot.

'Our latecomer is biding his time,' remarked Arthur, who had, until then, shown no concern over Lancelot's absence.

Two steps lead up to the regal dais which lay at the far end of a high-vaulted hall. Built of solid stone, it was half-covered with a thick rug. There stood the large throne in which King Arthur now reclined.

'Though little is the time we are allotted to bide,' murmured Guinevere, half in answer. She sat on a tabouret to the King's left, just an arm's length away. Her delicate hands lay clasped in her lap, among the voluminous folds of the long dress which concealed even her feet.

Her reply had been purposely distant, but, in truth, her heart leapt at the mere mention of Lancelot. However, since the conversation had taken such a fortunate turn, she would regret having withered the opportunity with the icy breath of indifference. She spoke again.

117

'Perchance there is a rule that he who departs late must return late,' she added with a gentle smile. Beware the smile of a woman.

''Tis not a rule of tardiness, but a rule of love,' jested Arthur, laughing. The King's laugh too has hidden meaning.

With the word 'love' echoing in her ears, Guinevere felt a sharp pain, as if she had been stabbed in the breast. She sprang to her feet, with a warm flush spreading over her face and a faint singing in her ears. Arthur remained unperturbed.

'The owner of that sleeve is surely a rare beauty . . .'

'What sleeve? What owner? Who is a rare beauty?' she cried out, with hardly a pause for breath.

'A crimson mantle for his white plume. A parting gift, no doubt. In faith, it is no wonder that he bides his time so,' answered the King, again convulsed with laughter.

'And what is her name?'

'Her name I know not. However, on account of her great beauty, I hear they call her "the fair maid". He who bides these last ten days and more with her is a fortunate fellow indeed! I'll wager that he's in no hurry to return to Camelot.'

'Fair maid! Fair maid!' cried the Queen repeatedly, stamping the floor with her slippered foot. With each blow, the hair that rested on her shoulders shook in ripples.

From ancient times the Church has taught that one should be devoted to one's spouse, faithful until the final parting that death brings. To follow this teaching is to know great peace, a peace of mind which Guinevere herself had savoured. But, for the sake of Lancelot, she had freely renounced that peace, and happily embraced the anguish that replaced it. The spring breeze blows, but the flowers blossom of their own accord; the accusation that the blossom has transgressed is nothing more than the empty words of later generations. The clear reflection of love in a mirror is proof of the mirror's own purity, and to gaze on such a reflection is a solace for the troubled heart when beset by ill fortune. But, just as Guinevere searches the empty mirror in vain, the ground under her gives way, leaving not one speck of dust to provide support. To be drawn through life as iron is by lodestone is to fear no censure: if one can just cross the fragile boundary of fear, a life of peace and tranquility awaits beyond. But the lodestone has been transformed into flint, and the iron tumbles like a falling meteor into the bottomless abyss of Hades. The tabouret collapses, the dais crumbles and the very earth splits open. It was as if everything supporting her had suddenly vanished. She remained motionless, her hands clasped together over her breast, pressing them together with enough force to crack the

118

bones; the torrent of her anguish thus finding invisible release in the precarious balance.

'What is it?' questioned Arthur.

'I know not,' she replied, deceiving neither Arthur nor herself; she had been suddenly propelled into the realm of the unknown. It was as if another person were talking, for the words were out before she was even aware of the truth herself.

The same wave that but a moment before receded so meekly, now turns and forgets its former nature as it comes tumbling back, biting angrily into the shore. The transformation is so startling that even the wave itself would deny it. Guinevere, having sustained a terrible blow from an unexpected direction, had lost her composure. Yet, after teetering on the edge of distraction, she had receded into her familiar quiet melancholy, perhaps even more subdued than before. Arthur gazed fixedly at her with an expression of total perplexity, his eyebrows arched in surprise. And to Guinevere too, remembering that he was her husband, Arthur appeared subtly changed.

The remorse that stems from having harmed another who knows that he has been harmed, is not so painful to bear as the remorse which comes from harming a victim who is unaware of it. Even if there be no retribution, the man who scourges the saint will be sure to feel the horror of his deed if he repents. In the same way, the shame that Guinevere felt in front of a husband who displayed his suspicions openly, was less painful to bear than if Arthur were still unaware of the sin secreted in her breast. The shock of this realization pierced her to the quick with a dagger of ice-cold fear.

'You must put yourself in the place of others. The past, before we knew each other, was different; but it is now many years since we were wedded. The owner of the crimson sleeve thinks of Sir Lancelot as you think of me. Were I to have received such a favour, I too would tarry ten, nay, twenty days. To speak ill of him thus is ignoble of you,' accused Arthur, looking askance at Guinevere.

'Fair maid!' she repeated for a third time. Her voice was no longer shrill with anger, but there was little compassion in it.

Turning towards his Queen, Arthur again spoke. 'Do you remember the time when we first met? A tall stone cross, ten feet high and overgrown with ivy, stood beside the road. It was spring. I had lost my way and, seeking a rest, I set foot inside the wayside chapel. Who was it then that knelt before the silver altar, golden hair cascading over the deep blue of her robes?'

Guinevere acknowledged the memory with a tremulous sigh. Just as she was seeking the solace of Lethe, this sudden reminiscing of a past already stale was painful for her to bear.

119

'Until I heard your tearful confession that you languished for the return of one who had forsaken you, I thought that you were the Virgin Mary descended from heaven to stand before the holy altar of that shrine.'

One may chase the fleeting days, but what is past is not gone; it cannot be buried in eternal darkness, for there will always be some spark to kindle the heart that is pledged to forget.

'That day, I offered to bring you to my castle, and in reply you waved your golden hair and said you would follow me wherever ...' Arthur fell silent. He stood up from his throne and approached Guinevere. Taking her head between his hands, he looked down into her eyes. Perhaps these memories had stirred fresh affection in his heart. But her cheeks were as cold as a corpse; his hands withdrew at the touch. Just then, the distant sound of people advancing down the passage could be heard; their voices, raised in debate, approached the hall.

Thick curtains hung across the doorway, concealing the passage that opened beyond. The footsteps stopped outside and paused. Then suddenly, the curtains parted to reveal a tall knight with long, flowing hair. It was Mordred.

With neither salute nor word of greeting, Mordred strode into the hall and up to the dais on which the King stood. He was followed by Agravain, broad-shouldered and thickset; a man so stout that his ruddy neck was pinched white by the tight collar of his tunic. After them, a disorderly throng crowded into the hall and ranged themselves behind Mordred, their leader. In all, thirteen men stood facing the King. This was no trifling matter.

Mordred raised his head to Arthur in greeting. 'Is it not the duty of the King to punish transgression?' he began in a deep, resonant voice.

'You know it well,' replied Arthur, with an expression of uncomfortable surprise.

Again Mordred addressed the King, 'And are not all transgressors punished, even though they may be of the highest rank?'

Drawing himself up to his full height, Arthur struck his fist on his chest and proclaimed, 'The golden crown will not rest on the head of a sinner. The royal robes will not hide evil.' At these words, the hem of his scarlet cloak fell open, revealing the dazzling snow-white of its lining.

'If you swear that you grant pardon to none that have sinned, then the woman who sits at your side must also be denied it!' accused Mordred, pointing directly at Guinevere. The Queen rose to her feet.

As if he had been struck by lightning, King Arthur looked in mute

120

amazement at the man who stood before him, as awe-inspiring as a monolith newly sprung from the earth. It was Guinevere who spoke.

'You dare accuse me of transgression? Where is your proof, and what are the sins of which you count me guilty? Heaven witness your falsehood!' she cried, her slender arm pointing aloft.

'There is but one sin, and of that, ask Sir Lancelot. Therein lies our proof,' replied Mordred. With a glint in his hawk-like eyes, he turned to the twelve men mustered behind him. At the sign, they all raised their arms and chanted, 'God knows all. Evil will out!'

The strength drained from Guinevere's body as she fell back against the wall for support. 'Lancelot!' she cried out weakly. The King hesitated. His flowing scarlet cloak parted at his feet, and his right hand raised as if to calm the angry mob, he hesitated.

Suddenly cries of 'Black! Black!' echoed around the stones of the castle, like the distant moan of the winter wind. Then they heard the rasp of rusty chains and the thunderous knell of doom as the river floodgates grated open. They looked at each other in bewilderment, filled with a terrible foreboding.

5. The Boat

'The bright crimson of the silk sleeve bound to his helm must have dazzled his foes as they came tilting with their lances. That day at the tourney, Sir Lancelot felled more than twenty knights in the yard, but it was not until he finished that he eventually revealed himself, shouting out his name above the babble of the crowd. Then, before they could recover from their surprise, he rode out of the yard, with me fast behind. The two of us rode for Astolat.' So recounted the young Lavaine to his father and sister on his return, three days later.

'What then became of Lancelot?' queried his father with raised brows. The young girl only sighed, but the flowers in her hair trembled slightly.

'Alas, one of the men felled by Lancelot must have hit home with his lance, injuring him. I could see that he was hurt in his left thigh, just below his breast plate . . .'

'Was the wound deep?' his sister asked, her eyes wide with anxiety.

''Twas not so deep to prevent him from riding, for on and on we went until the summer's day had darkened into the deep blue of dusk over the fields. The hooves of our horses were wet with the early dew on the thick grass. Neither of us spoke. Of what thoughts filled Lancelot's mind I know not, but I was lost in memories of that day's tourney, pageantry so splendid I shall never see its like again. But for the wind soughing in the tops of the trees, the only sound was the soft tread of our mounts . . . Then we came to a fork in the path.'

'I know it well. To the left, a journey of ten miles leads to our gate,' interjected the old man, by way of explanation.

'Lancelot turned his horse to the right.'

'To the right? But that leads to the main road for Shalott. There must be at least fifteen miles.'

'Yes, to Shalott,' Lavaine confirmed. 'Despite my calls, he never looked back, but just rode off into the darkness with his bridle jangling. There was no choice for me but to follow on. Yet, by some strange chance, my horse reared up and whinnied with fright as I tried to turn him about. The echoes disappeared over the dark fields. By the time I had calmed my mount, Lancelot had vanished into the distant depths of the night. Striking my saddle, I galloped after him.'

'Did you catch him up?' father and daughter asked in unison.

'I did, but the night was by then far advanced. All I could see ahead of me was the white breath of my horse as it steamed into the gloom, but I spurred him all the more. Faster than the wind we sped along that empty road. At last I espied a dark shadow, about two hundred yards ahead. I shouted out Lancelot's name with all my might, but to no avail. The shadow moved on, almost silent but for the faint sound of a bridle jangling. Yet though he seemed to move slowly enough, I found it no easy task to catch up with him. And then, when I had closed to within a hundred yards, the shadow suddenly vanished, as if swallowed up by the night. What witchery this was I knew not, but I urged my mount on the more. We flew along at such a speed that I thought his hooves would surely splinter on the stones as we crossed the bridge that leads into Shalott. Then suddenly he seemed to trip. His legs collapsed under me and I tumbled forward, tearing vainly at his mane. My head struck hard against something, but it was not stone. There lying on the bridge was the steel gauntlet of one who had fallen before me.'

'Oh, peril!' cried the old man, as if the scene were unfolding before his eyes.

'It was not I who was in peril, but Sir Lancelot. For it was he that lay fallen on the bridge.'

'Then it was him?' asked Elaine, her voice faint with anxiety, gripping the edge of her chair as if she were afraid it would collapse.

Lavaine nodded. 'There was a grove of willows beside the bridge,

122

and there among the trees I found a small cottage. At first I thought it must be deserted, but an old hermit answered my knocking. He had a kind heart, and helped me to carry in the cold Lancelot. We laid him on a bed and removed his armour; as I lifted his helmet, I could see that his eyes were glazed with sickness.'

'Such recluses are often learned in the making of cures and salves from the roots and grasses of the forest. Could he heal Lancelot?' interrupted his father.

'The hermit did restore him, but he may as well have been in the other world. For it was not Lancelot that lay there, ranting like a man possessed. In his delirium he would sometimes rave about sin, or the Queen — Guinevere — or Shalott. His brow burned with a powerful fever that even the potions of the kindly hermit could not allay.'

'If I had only been at his side,' Elaine thought to herself.

'After passing the night, the fever gradually abated and Lancelot returned to his old self. Yet no sooner had he gathered his wits than he told me to leave him. Of course, the old hermit was worried for him and forbad me. Two days passed, and on the morning of the third, we awoke and looked over to the sickbed to see how our patient fared ... but he was gone! With the point of his sword he had scratched on the wall the words "Sin pursues me — I pursue Sin".'

'Fled?' asked the father. 'But whither?' asked the sister.

'If there had only been some sign to guide me ... but all I found was the wind, sweeping across a plain of waving summer grass, whose limits were drawn by the rising and setting of the sun. I returned alone to the hermit, who warned that Lancelot's sickness was not cured and that he was in grave danger, that he was surely running like a madman toward Camelot. The feverish words of Lancelot's delirium lead to this conclusion, but I am sure that the truth is elsewhere.' Finishing his tale, Lavaine drained his cup of bitter wine with a flourish. Elaine rose and quietly returned to her room.

The butterfly that dances among the flowers gives no hint of the sorrow that can be found in spring. But think of the chill that comes at sunset, on a night when even the moon is cloaked in darkness. Think of the fast-falling dew and those tender wings. Think of something no bigger than a thumbnail lost among the dark, towering grasses of the moor ... The dew that lies heavily on its folded wings must torment the butterfly's dreams. Curled up alone in the dark depths of the boundless moor, afraid of even the night breeze; nothing could be sadder. Elaine's days are numbered.

Every day Elaine would stare at the shield that Lancelot had left behind. It bore the design of a lady, tall and fair, before whom a knight knelt, pledging love and allegiance. The knight's armour was

123

silver, the lady's robes flaming crimson, and the field on which they stood a deep, deep blue. How could the poor Elaine have ever dreamt that the lady in red was Queen Guinevere?

There were times, even, when Elaine imagined that the lady on the shield was herself, and that the kneeling knight was Lancelot. From there, it was but a short step over the thin boundary that separates wishes from reality; in her mind she became the lady in red. Placing stone upon fanciful stone, she had built up a folly whose final shape was a mystery even to herself.

However, at one blow, the fantasy that she had constructed crumbled to dust. Her folly collapsed like a pebble tower kicked by a playful child. Amid the ruins, Elaine awoke to reality, only to realize that she was alone. Lancelot was running through the fields of Camelot, a madman. What reason was there for him to return to her side? What bond was there to draw him a thousand leagues to Astolat? For they had exchanged no vows. Indeed, what vows could they exchange? Her eyes filled with tears.

Suddenly her tears were interrupted. It was true that Lancelot had made no vow, but were vows only made between two? Her own pledge was in itself a vow. And she determined that there would be no undoing. The colour drained from her cheeks.

What Elaine feared was not death itself, but the separation which it brought. Yet she now realized that there was no separation greater than the present; it was only in the next world that she could hope to see Lancelot again. One should not mourn the fallen petals of the poppy: the flower fades that it may bloom again. Elaine began to fast.

Decay ravaged her delicate breast like fire consuming the spring grass. Little by little, grief ate away at her thin body. Until then, life had always seemed eternal. Though she had never prayed to live long, the face of death was unknown to her, even in her dreams. But now, she saw her eighteen years were no more than a fleeting spring. She saw that even within the bud that opens in the warm sunlight there lies the seed of bitterness. She became a prey to melancholy, uncertain whether the brightly shining moon outside her window would greet her again on the morrow. Her only business with this world was to depart from it.

When she thought the end was near, Elaine summoned her father and brother to her bedside. 'I pray you, write a letter to Lancelot for me,' she said, her voice thin as a reed. Her father brought paper and quill, and began to take down each word that left the lips of his dying daughter.

'Under heaven, you were the only man that I ever loved. Pity this poor maid that goes to her death for your sake. When the last lock of

Illustration for *Kairo-kō* (1906) by Nakamura Fusetsu

my shining black hair has turned to dust, the name of Lancelot, engraved on my heart, will still endure. Even until the stars themselves are reborn, it will endure. Fired in the furnace of love, neither earth nor water will fade it. I see your face reflected in a bead of dew, and then it is gone. If you have tears for me, shed them; for my life too hangs in a bead of dew. As Christ is my witness, I remain a virgin pure unto my death.'

The letter was written in an uncertain hand: the fault of either old age or fresh grief.

Again she spoke, 'When I have drawn my last breath, place this letter in my right hand, while there is still warmth in it. And when my limbs have grown cold, dress me in the best finery and lay me to rest in a small boat, decked from prow to stern in black. Then fill the boat with every white rose and lily that grows on the hills of Astolat, and set it free.' So saying, Elaine closed her eyes in sleep: a sleep from which there would be no awakening. Dutifully, father and son fulfilled her bidding, placing her body in a small black boat, moored on the river.

A light breeze rustled through the willows on the bank, but not a ripple showed on the mirror surface of the old river. Leaving the deep green shade of the trees, a lone man rowed the boat out into midstream. He was an old man, with flowing white hair and a white beard. At each slow stroke, the languid water glinted like lead. Without a sound, the boat glided through a bed of sleeping water-lilies. Brushed aside by the prow, each flower would wave in the gentle wake and then be still again. As each broad leaf rose again to the surface, it glistened with running tears of dew.

On and on, the boat drifted along, with no destination, only a cargo: a beautiful corpse surrounded by silks and flowers, and accompanied by a silent old man, as lifeless as a wooden doll. Apart from his arms, which moved rhythmically, dipping the long oar into the calm waters, he showed no sign of life.

From nowhere, there suddenly appeared a snow-white swan. With regal composure, it plied slowly through the river current, head held high and wings folded elegantly behind. It surveyed all and feared nothing. Cutting across the stream, it swam to the boat and took up position just ahead of the prow, as if to guide it. The black boat followed in its purling wake. Green were the willows that lined both banks.

As they passed by Shalott, the silence of the old river was broken by a melancholy voice, echoing over the still water from somewhere on the left bank. 'Lost in dreams and shadows . . . In a world of sorrow.' It was a haunting song, punctuated with silences. The dead

125

Elaine and the old man who sat in the stern were its only audience, but neither listened. The old man just dipped his oar, rhythmically: a deaf mute.

The sky was as heavy as thick, willowed cotton. The trees that lined both banks had become hazy clouds of verdure, like so many lost souls, hesitating at the gates of Hades. It was as if they had come to bid farewell to the beautiful girl as she floated down to another world.

The black boat came to rest alongside the floodgates of the castle of Camelot. The shadow-swan vanished into the waters, leaving only the awesome black reflection of the soaring castle towers. The floodgates opened to reveal a long flight of stone steps. There were gathered all the men and women of Camelot. In front stood King Arthur and Queen Guinevere.

Elaine's corpse was the most beautiful in the world. As she lay there, it almost seemed that she was smiling, her cool white face surrounded by soft billows of golden hair. She had been transformed into pure vibrant spirit, serene and eternal, washed clean of all earthly defilement. There was no trace of the fiery emotions that plague this world — pain, anguish, bitterness and rancour. To none did she appear a corpse destined for decay.

'Who is she?' asked the King, in a deep and dignified voice. But, like a mute, the old man who rested his oar spoke not a word. Suddenly Guinevere rushed down to the boat and, pulling Elaine's hand from the sea of white lilies, she took the letter and broke the seal.

Once more the same sad voice sang out across the water, 'How beautiful Love shines . . . Alas, this flower pines.' Its thin, plaintive thread haunted their ears.

When she had finished reading, Guinevere reached down and kissed Elaine's milky brow with quivering lips. 'Fair maid!' she whispered, and a hot tear fell onto an ice-cold cheek.

Behind her, thirteen knights turned and looked at one another.

V

TWENTIETH–CENTURY ARTHURIAN LITERATURE
an annotated bibliography

Mary Wildman

Introductory Note

The bibliography is arranged in two parts. The first contains primary twentieth-century Arthurian texts and the second secondary, critical works that I have consulted. The former section is regrettably incomplete, owing to delays in obtaining material through an inadequate Inter-library Loan system; items which I have not yet been able to see are marked with an asterisk. Modern translations of pre-twentieth-century works have been omitted but films and musical items with an Arthurian theme have been included. Each entry is preceded by a letter indicating whether the item is a play, a poem or a work of prose fiction and whether it is a work for children.

Annotations are omitted in the case of well-known primary texts and in the case of standard works of reference. The place of publication, unless otherwise stated, is London, except in the case of films, where only the production company is given. The order throughout is alphabetical.

Texts in languages other than English have not been included, though films and musical items from non-English speaking countries are listed.

Abbreviations

BBIAS   *Bibliographical Bulletin of the International Arthurian Society.*
BMC   *British Museum Catalogue.*
CUP   Cambridge University Press.
EETS   Early English Text Society.
Groves   *The New Grove Dictionary of Music and Musicians*, ed. Stanley Sadie, Macmillan, 1980.

JEGP	*Journal of English and Germanic Philology.*
JRIC	*Journal of the Royal Institute of Cornwall.*
O.E.D.	*Oxford English Dictionary* (1933).
OS	Orchestral score.
OUP	Oxford University Press.
Parry	Clark S. Northup and John J. Parry, 'The Arthurian Legends: Modern Retellings of the Old Stories: an Annotated Bibliography', *JEGP*, XLIII (April, 1944), 173-221.
PMLA	*Proceedings of the Modern Language Association of America.*
PSANHS	*Proceedings of the Somerset Archaeological and Natural History Society.*
Q.A.B.	Geoffrey Ashe, ed., *The Quest for Arthur's Britain* (1971).
RES	*Review of English Studies.*
RKP	Routledge and Kegan Paul.
RTS	Round Table Society.
TLS	*Times Literary Supplement.*
VS	Vocal score.

D	Drama.
F	Fiction/novel.
f	Film.
j	Junior.
M	Music.
m	Miscellaneous.
p	Poetry.
*	Not seen.
**	Editorial addition.

Twentieth-Century Arthurian Literature

I *Primary sources*

*f   *The Adventures of Sir Galahad*. Dir. Spencer A. Bennett. Columbia, 1949.
> Serial in fifteen episodes; non-traditional story.

*D   Ankenbrand, Frank. 'Tristram and Iseult: A Play in Five Acts'. In *Collected Poems*. Bodley Head, 1911.

*D   Anonymous. *Lancelot and Guinevere: A Study in Three Scenes*. Bell, 1919.

*D   Anspacher, L.K. *Tristan and Isolde: A Tragedy*. New York: Brentano's, 1904.

D   Arden, John and Margaretta D'Arcy. *The Island of the Mighty*. Methuen, 1974.
> Unsuccessful attempt to blend myth, history and modern political comment.

*jD *Arthur of the Britons*. Dir. Sidney Hayers. I.T.V. Series re-shown early 1982.
> First showing date unknown. Set in fifth century. Bears little resemblance to Arthurian legend.

F   Ashe, Geoffrey. *The Finger and the Moon*. Heinemann, 1973.
> Part science fiction, part occult novel set in Glastonbury; little else of Arthurian connection. Action of story said to be influenced by characters' Arthurian visions.

jF   Ashley, Dora. *King Arthur's Noble Knights*. Illus. Arthur A. Dixon. Raphael Tuck and Sons, [1922].
> Retelling of episodes from Malory.

*P   Austin, Martha W. *Tristram and Isoult*. Boston: Poet-Lore, 1905.

*P   Bacon, Leonard. 'Arthurian Interludes'. *University of California Chronicle*, XV (1915), 24-35.
> I 'Igraine to Arthur', II 'The Legend of Lamorak'. Inferior heroic couplets.

P   Badger, John D'Arcy. *The Arthuriad*. Toronto: Pendragon House, 1970.
> Fifty-six sonnets in seven cantos, with verse commentary; relates Arthurian myth to moral, religious, scientific and political aspects of present day.

*D   Bailey, C.W. (in collaboration with N.S.Millican and G.R.

Hammond). 'King Arthur and the Knights of the Round Table'. In *Quest of the Golden Fleece and Other Plays from Epic Poetry*. Nelson, 1929.

F   Baring, Maurice. 'The Camelot Jousts'. In *Dead Letters*. Constable, 1910.

> Humorous collection of letters between Guinevere, Arthur, Lancelot and Iseult.

jF   Barr, Ann. *King Arthur and the Knights of the Round Table: Adapted from Malory*. Illus. Jay Hyde Barnum. New York: Random House, 1954.

jF   Bateman, Elizabeth Yunge. *The Flowering Thorn*. Published by the author, 1961.

> A group of Welsh children interested in King Arthur and the Grail form a chivalric league and visit places connected with the Grail myth.

M   Bax, Arnold. *Tintagel: a Symphonic Poem*. OS. Chappell, n.d.

> 'Intended to evoke a tone picture of the castle-crowned cliff of Tintagel' (Preface). First performed 1917.

P   Bell, Harold Idris. From 'Tristan and Iseult'. In *Poems from the Welsh*. Carnarvon: Welsh Publishing Co., 1913.

> Translation of part of *Trystan ac Esyllt* by W.J.Gruffydd, Bangor Eisteddfod, 1902.

F   Berger, Thomas. *Arthur Rex*. Magnum, 1979.

> Bawdier version of Malory. Includes *Gawain and the Green Knight* story.

*P   Berry, Charles W. *King Arthur: a Poem*. Merritt and Hatcher, 1923.

> 'Poetic Drama'. Selections are reprinted in *The Round Table: Arthur*; 'Giant of St Michael's Mount' in *Arthurian Reverie* (q.v.).

m   Berry, Charles W. *The Round Table: Arthur: a Conversation between Two Knights of the Round Table Club*. 2nd. ed. Methuen, 1936.

> First published 1930. *Vade-mecum* for club members and potted history of Arthur from various medieval sources.

m   Berry, Charles W. *Arthurian Reverie*. For the Round Table Club, 1939.

> Light-hearted Who's Who in Arthurian legend.

*P   Binyon, Laurence. 'The Death of Tristram'. In *Odes*. Unicorn Press, 1901.

> Reprinted as 'Tristram's End' in *Selected Poems* (pp.22-40), New York: Macmillan, 1922, and in *Collected Poems* (II, 57-70), New York: Macmillan, 1931.

D Binyon, Laurence. *Arthur: a Tragedy.* Heinemann, 1923.
   Verse drama. Reviewed in *TLS*, 5 April 1923, p. 229. See also Elgar, Sir Edward.

P Binyon, Laurence. *The Madness of Merlin.* Intro. Gordon Bottomley. Macmillan, 1947.
   Verse drama, probably never meant for performance. Conceived in three parts, Parts II and III were never written.

*jF Bishop, Farnham and Arthur Gilchrist Brodeur. *The Altar of the Legion.* Boston: Little, Brown and Co., 1926.

*f *The Black Knight.* Dir. Tay Garnett. Warwick, 1954.

*M Blackford, Richard. *Sir Gawain and the Green Knight.* 1978.
   Opera specially commissioned for amateurs. Recorded on Argo (ZK85).

jF Blyton, Enid. *King Arthur and his Knights.* Old Thatch Series. Edinburgh and London: W. and A. K. Johnston, n.d.
   Episodes from the legend retold for very young readers.

*jF Blyton, Enid. *Knights of the Round Table.* 1950.

*jF Blyton, Enid. *Tales of Brave Adventure.* Dean, 1963.
   Stories about Robin Hood and King Arthur.

P Bond, Frederick Bligh. *The Story of King Arthur and How He Saw the Sangreal: of his Institution of the Quest of the Holy Grail: and of the Promise of the Fulfilment of that Quest in the Latter Days.* Glastonbury Scripts, IX. Glastonbury, 1925.
   'Founded on scripts, partly metrical, received during 1924'. Forty-eight irregular blank-verse stanzas sermonising on reality and symbol of Grail.

F Borowsky, Marvin. *The Queen's Knight.* Chatto and Windus, 1956.
   Chiefly based on Malory, sees affiliations between fifth- and eleventh-century Britain and present day.

* Boss, Eleanor. *In Quest of the Holy Grail.* Edinburgh: Marshall, Morgan and Scott, 1930.
   'Based on Tennyson's Idyll of the Holy Grail' (*BMC*).

D Bottomley, Gordon. 'Merlin's Grave'. In *Scenes and Plays.* Constable, 1929.
   Yeatsian verse drama.

*M Boughton, Rutland and Reginald R. Buckley. *Music-drama of the Future: Uther and Igraine, Choral Drama.* With essays by the collaborators. Reeves, 1911.
   Later reprinted as *The Birth of Arthur.* See under Buckley, Reginald R. According to *Groves* (vol. 3, pp. 97-99)

Boughton also wrote the following in his Arthurian cycle: *The Queen of Cornwall* (1923-4) based on Hardy's play (q.v.); *The Lily Maid* (1933-4); *Galahad* (1943-4); *Avalon* (1944-5). The last two were never performed. According to the previous edition of Grove he also wrote in 1905 *Chapel in Lyonesse* for three male voices, piano and strings, and *King Arthur had Three Sons*, choral variations on an English Folk Song.

jF   Bradburne, E.S. *Long Ago and Yesterday*. Illus. Trevor Stubley. Gold Book 6. Huddersfield: Schofield and Sims, 1968.
Pages 18-23 retell story of Arthur's birth and sword in anvil episode; for very young readers.

*   Bradley, Will. *Launcelot and the Ladies*. New York: Harper, 1927.

D   Bridie, James. 'Lancelot' and 'The Holy Isle'. In *Plays for Plain People*. Constable, 1944.
'Lancelot' gives a version of Lancelot's tragedy; 'The Holy Isle' is a non-Arthurian, Utopian satire featuring Morgan and Lot.

jF   Briggs, Phillis. *King Arthur and the Knights of the Round Table*. Dean, [1954].
Malory retold for 'modern boys and girls'.

*P   Brooks, Benjamin G. *Camelot*. Oxford: Blackwell, 1919.

F   Broun, Heywood. 'The Fifty-first Dragon'. In *Collected Edition*. Comp. Heywood Hale Broun. (pp.27-35). New York: Harcourt Brace, 1941.
Short story of Gawaine at Knight School. First printed in Christopher Morley's *Modern Essays*, 1st Series, Harcourt Brace, 1921; reprinted with drawings by Richard Decker in *The Golden Book*, XIII (May 1931), 60-63.

D   Buckley, Reginald R. *Arthur of Britain: A Poem of Festival Choral Drama in Four Parts*. Williams and Norgate, 1914.
I 'The Birth of Arthur'; II 'The Round Table'; III 'The Holy Grail'; IV 'The Death of Arthur'. Dramatic oratorio with music by Rutland Boughton to 'contain a dream of life'. See also Boughton, Rutland.

m   Burns, James. *Sir Galahad: A Call to the Heroic*. Clarke and Co., [1915].
Jingoistic recruitment piece of World War I based on G.F. Watts' portrait of Galahad; dedicated to Sir John French.

jF   Buxton, E.M.Wilmot-. *Old Celtic Tales*. Harrap, [1909].
Retelling of tales from different sources, including 'Kil-

hugh and Olwen'. 'Selected from *Britain Long Ago.* Harrap, 1906'. (*BMC*).

jF   Buxton, E.M.Wilmot-. *Tales of Early England.* Harrap, 1909.
Includes 'The Tale of Sir Cleges' and 'Sir Gawayne and the Green Knight'.

jF   Buxton, R.M.Wilmot-. *Kilhugh and Olwen: and Other Stories from the Mabinogion.* Nelson, [1913].

F   Cabell, James Branch. *Jurgen: A Comedy of Justice.* Bodley Head, 1923.
Non-Arthurian satire; some Arthurian characters appear. First published in a limited edn., 1921.

F   Cabell, James Branch. 'To Sir Galahad of the Siege Perilous'. In *Ladies and Gentlemen: A Parcel of Reconsiderations.* Freeport, New York: Books for Libraries Press, 1968.
Rather sardonic letter to Galahad referring to his story and the background of Arthur's court. First published by New York: MacBride, 1934.

f   *Camelot.* Dir. Joshua Logan. Warner, 1967.
Film version of musical by Lerner and Loewe (q.v.).

P   Cammell, Charles Richard. 'The Return of Arthur: Ballad written under the Threat of Invasion, 1941'. In *XXI Poems.* Edinburgh: Poseidon Press, 1944.
Morale-booster of World War II. See also *TLS*, 19 February 1944, p.96.

F   Canning, Victor. *The Crimson Chalice.* Heinemann, 1976.
Part I of a trilogy. Interesting variant on the usual legend; drawn from author's own imagination rather than from written sources.

F   Canning, Victor. *Circle of the Gods.* Heinemann, 1977.
Part II of trilogy.

F   Canning, Victor. *The Immortal Wound.* Heinemann, 1978.
Part III of trilogy. Follows more closely the usual accounts of the historical Arthur, though with variations.

P   Carpenter, Rhys. *The Tragedy of Etarre: a Poem.* OUP, 1914.
Based on Malory Book IV; in dialogue form and four acts. First published by New York: Sturgis and Walton, 1912.

D   Carr, J.W.Comyns. *Tristram and Iseult: A Drama in Four Acts.* Duckworth, 1906.
In 'Shakespearean' verse. Interesting use of the myth: Iseult White Hands appears as a kind of *doppelgänger*.

jP   Chant, A.G. *The Legend of Glastonbury.* Illus. Horace J. Knowles. Epworth Press, 1948.

Seventeen ballad poems on the legend of Joseph of Arimathea's journeys to Britain.

m   Chapman, Graham *et al. Monty Python and the Holy Grail (Book)*. Eyre Methuen, 1977.

Drafts and screenplay from the film (q.v.).

P   Chapman, Raymond. 'The Fisher King'. *Wales*, VI (Winter, 1946), 17.

Scarcely Arthurian sonnet.

*jF   Chapman, Vera. *The Green Knight.* Rex Collings, 1975.

*jF   Chapman, Vera. *King Arthur's Daughter.* Rex Collings, 1976.

*jF   Chapman, Vera. *The King's Damosel.* Rex Collings, 1976.

Three novels which view the Arthurian period through the eyes of three ladies: Vivien, Ursulet and Lynette respectively.

jF   Chaundler, Christine. *Arthur and his Knights.* Illus. Mackenzie. Nisbet, [1920].

Remarkable for its fine illustrations, retells episodes from Malory and Geoffrey of Monmouth.

*M   Chausson, Ernest. *Le Roi Artus.* Op. 23. Posthumous lyric drama (1903). ['Private' records, Paris 1981 (MRF 179 S (4)) *Ed.*]. Earlier works include symphonic poem *Viviane*, Op. 5 (1882), of which there are several recordings.

jF   Chester, Norley, *pseud.* (Emily Underdown). *Knights of the Grail: Lohengrin: Galahad.* Nelson, [1907].

Pages 111-154 retell the story of Galahad from the Siege Perilous episode to his death.

jD   Chesterton, Frances. 'Sir Cleges'. In *Three Plays for Children.* French, 1924.

Delightful version of moral tale against contempt and pride.

P   Chesterton, G.K. *The Grave of Arthur.* Illus, Celia Fiennes. No. 25 of *The Ariel Poems.* Faber, [1930].

Twelve stanzas on Arthur's grave discovered at Glastonbury.

F   Christian, Catherine. *The Sword and the Flame.* Macmillan, 1978.

Republished as *The Pendragon.* Pan Books (paperback) 1979. Published again by Pan Books in paperback under the original title, 1981.

Set in fifth century; Arthurian legend retold by Bedivere.

jF   Clay, Beatrice. *Stories from King Arthur and his Round Table.* Illus. Dora Curtis. Dent, 1913.

Chiefly based on Malory but includes the story of Geraint and Enid.

jF Clay, Beatrice. *Stories from Le Morte D'Arthur and the Mabinogion.* Dent, 1920.

Expanded version of *Stories from King Arthur and his Round Table.* (1913).

F Closs, Hannah. *Tristan.* Andrew Dakers, 1940.

The Tristan legend seen through modern eyes.

*f *A Connecticut Yankee.* Starring Harry Myers. 1921.

Based on Mark Twain. No further details available.

*f *A Connecticut Yankee.* Dir. David Butler. Fox, 1931.

Based on Mark Twain, starring Will Rogers.

f *A Connecticut Yankee in King Arthur's Court.* (British title *A Yankee in King Arthur's Court*). Dir. Tay Garnett. Paramount, 1949.

Musical version of the 1931 film, starring Bing Crosby.

F Costain, Thomas. *The Silver Chalice.* Hodder, 1953.

The early history of the Grail, the cup used at the Last Supper. Its later Arthurian history is hinted at.

P/D Coutts, Francis. *The Romance of King Arthur.* Bodley Head, 1907.

Consists of two poems, 'Uther Pendragon' and 'Death of Launcelot', and two plays, 'Merlin' and 'Launcelot du Lake'. There is a French version of the 'Merlin' by Villiers Barnett, music by Albenez (Paris and Monte Carlo: *Continental Weekly*, 1913).

jF Cox, John Harrington. *Sir Gawain and the Green Knight.* Illus. George Barraud. Harrap, 1913.

Close retelling of the fourteenth-century poem, for children.

jF Cutler, U. Waldo. *Stories of King Arthur and his Knights: Retold from Malory's 'Morte Darthur'.* Harrap, 1905.

Retold in modern English.

D Dane, Clemence. *The Saviours: Seven Plays on One Theme.* Heinemann, 1942.

Produced for radio by Val Gielgud with music by Richard Addinsell. Arthur returns through the ages as Alfred, Robin Hood, Elizabeth I, Nelson and others. Plays are linked by Merlin as narrator or character.

jD Davies, Andrew. *Legend of King Arthur.* Dir. Rodney Bennett. BBC 1, 7.10.79ff.

Eight part serial set in fifth century.

*   Davis, Georgene. *The Round Table: A History Drawn from Unreliable Chronicles*. Rutland, Vermont: Tory Press, 1930.

F   Dawson, Coningsby. *The Road to Avalon*. Hodder, 1911.
Bunyanesque allegory on search for knowledge and for the Arthur in every Christian soul.

*P   De Beverley, Thomas G.N. *The Youth of Sir Arthour, The Quest of Sangreale, and Other Poems*. Erskine Macdonald, 1925.

F   Deeping, Warwick. *Love among the Ruins*. Cassell, 1911.
Non-Arthurian but some Arthurian characters appear.

F   Deeping, Warwick. *Uther and Igraine*. Cassell, 1927.
Interesting version of the Uther and Igraine story. Uther appears saintly, Gorlois vile and Merlin as not all-seeing.

F   Deeping, Warwick. *The Man on the White Horse*. Cassell, 1934.
Non-Arthurian, though some characters have Arthurian names.

F   Deeping, Warwick. *The Man Who Went Back*. Cassell, 1940.
Non-Arthurian though set in the Arthurian period; Gildas appears as a character.

*   Dillon, Arthur. *King Arthur Pendragon*. Elkin Mathews, 1906.

F   Ditmas, E.M.R. *Gareth of Orkney*. Faber, 1956.
Historical novel based on Beaumains story.

*   Donaldson, J.W., ed. *Arthur Pendragon of Britain*. New York: Putnam, 1911.

F   Doyle, Arthur Conan. 'The Last of the Legions'. In *The Last Galley: Tales and Impressions*. (pp.84-93). Nelson, n.d. (Preface dated 1911).
Only Arthurian reference is to Mordred as 'the wild chief of the Western Cymri'.

F   Duggan, Alfred. *Conscience of the King*. Faber, 1951.
Historical novel: the memoirs of Cerdic in which Arthur makes a brief appearance.

**jF   Dunkerley, Desmond. *Deeds of the Nameless Knight* (i.e. Libeaus Desconus). Ladybird, 1977.

**jF   Dunkerley, Desmond. *Sir Lancelot of the Lake*. Ladybird, 1977.

**jF   Dunkerley, Desmond. *Mysteries of Merlin*. Ladybird, 1977.

P   Edwards, Francis. 'The Song of Tristan'. *Welsh Outlook*, IV (1917), 274.
Six stanzas translating *Can Trystan*, by Silwyn Roberts. Tennysonian tone.

*P   Edwards, Zachary. *Avilion and other poems*. Chapman and Hall, 1907.

**M   Elgar, Sir Edward. *King Arthur.*
Incidental music to play by Laurence Binyon, 1923 [Recorded by Bournemouth Sinfonietta, C.George Hurst, Polydor 2383 224] (q.v.).

P   Eliot, T.S. 'The Waste Land'. *The Criterion*, I (October, 1922), 50-64.
Heavily influenced by Jessie Weston's *From Ritual to Romance* (1920).

D   Ellis, T.E. *Lanval: A Drama in Four Acts.* Privately printed by J.Davy and Sons, 1908.
Based on the legend of a fairy enamoured of a knight. He disobeys her by revealing her name, but is eventually reunited with her in the Middle world.

*   Emma, Cyril. *The Love Song of Tristram and Iseult.* Elliot Stock, 1905.

P   Erskine, John. 'Sir Graelent' and 'At the Front'. In *Collected Poems 1907-1922.* (pp.54-65; 118-122). New York: Duffield, 1922.
Former retells story of knight who loses his fairy lover through speaking of her; the latter contains Arthurian references in sonnet II.

F   Erskine, John. *Galahad: Enough of his Life to Explain his Reputation.* Nash and Grayson, 1926.
Ostensibly set in medieval period but really belongs to 1920s.

F   Erskine, John. *Tristan and Isolde: Restoring Palamede.* Indianapolis: Bobbs-Merrill, 1932.
Humorous version of the Tristan legend making Palamede the hero.

*   Erskine, John. '7 Tales from King Arthur's Court'. Paintings by Dulac. *American Weekly*, Feb.–Mar., 1940.
1. 'The Tale of Arthur's Sword "Excalibur"'. Feb. 4, 1940.
2. 'The Tale of Sir Tristram and the Love Potion'. Feb. 11.
3. 'The Tale of the Enchantress and the Magic Scabbard'. Feb. 18.
4. 'The Tale of Sir Galahad and the Quest of the Sangreal'. Feb. 25.
5. 'The Tale of Sir Launcelot and the Four Queens'. Mar. 3.
6. 'The Tale of Merlin and One of the Ladies of the Lake'. Mar. 10.
7. 'The Tale of How Sir Launcelot Slew Sir Agravaine'. Mar. 17.

f   *Excalibur.* Dir. John Borman. C.I.C., 1981. Starring Nicol Williamson as Merlin.

> Brilliant cinematic recreation of Malory's story.

jF   Fadiman, Clifton. *The Story of Young King Arthur.* Illus. Paul Liberovsky. Muller, 1962.

> Retells the legend from Arthur's birth to his wedding and institution of the Round Table.

F   Faraday, W. Barnard. *Pendragon.* Methuen, 1930.

> Set in A.D. 503, covers the events leading up to Badon and the battle itself.
> Reviewed in *TLS*, 16 October 1930, p.840.
> See also Faraday's reply *TLS*, 6 November 1930, p.917.

jD   Farrar, Stewart. *The Boy Merlin.* Dir. Joe Bayer. I.T.V. from 24.4.79.

> Six-part series set in fifth-century Wales.

*   Field, Michael, *pseud.* (Katherine Harris Bradley and Edith Emma Cooper). 'Tristan de Leonois'. In *The Accuser.* Sidgwick and Jackson, 1911.

D   Field, Michael. *The Tragedy of Pardon.* Sidgwick and Jackson, 1911.

> Inferior blank-verse version of the Tristan legend.

Fields, Herbert. See Rogers, Richard.

jF   Finkel, George. *Twilight Province.* White Lion, 1976.

> First published by Angus and Robertson, 1967. Loosely based on the Chronicles, attempts to tell story of a northern Arthur, rationalising later romantic accretions.

*jF   Finkel, George. *Watch-fires to the North.*

jF   Fraser, Antonia. *King Arthur and the Knights of the Round Table.* Sidgwick and Jackson, 1970.

> Free retelling, illustrated by author's twelve-year old daughter, Rebecca. Text first published under maiden name of Pakenham by Heirloom Library, 1954.

F   Frankland, Edward. *The Bear of Britain.* Foreword by Lloyd George. Macdonald, [1944].

> Plausible reconstruction of Arthurian history from Celtic sources.

F   Frankland, Edward. *England Growing.* Macdonald, 1946.

> Episodic novel of British History. Second Episode (pp.15-21) covers relationship between Medraut and Gwenhwyvar in October, 515. First published in 1944.

*F   French, Allen. *Sir Marrok: A Tale of the Days of King Arthur.* New York: Century Co., 1902.

jF   Frith, Henry. *King Arthur and his Knights.* Illus. Henry C. Pitz.

Garden City, New York: Junior Deluxe Edns., 1955.
Malory retold in archaic prose for older children.

D   Fry, Christopher. 'Thor with Angels'. In *Plays*. OUP, 1969.
First acting edn. published by H.J.Goulden, 1948. Merlin appears as a kind of Old Testament prophet long after Arthur's death; setting 596 A.D.

*P   Furst, Clyde Bowman. *Merlin*. Merrymount Press, 1930.
Three hundred copies printed by D.B.Updike. No locations in Britain.

*   Galloway, C.F.J. *Exploits of Lancelot: A Satire*. Stockwell, 1924.

*f   *Gawain and the Green Knight*. Dir. Stephen Weeks. 1972.
Based on the fourteenth-century poem and on Chrétien's *Yvain*.

jF   Gilbert, Henry. *King Arthur's Knights: the Tales Retold for Boys and Girls*. Illus. Walter Crane and T.H.Robinson. Nelson, [1911].
Retelling of Malory in archaic language, though author claims language is simplified.

F   Glasscock, F.T. *The Symbolic Meaning of the Story of King Arthur*. King Arthur's Hall, Tintagel, 1929.
Retells legends of Arthur, Galahad, Lancelot, Gawaine and Tristram.

m   Glasscock, F.T. *The Book of the Order of the Fellowship of the Knights of the Round Table of King Arthur*. King Arthur's Hall, Tintagel, 1929.
Companion volume to the above. Handbook for the Society.

D   Glasscock, F.T. *King Arthur: the Symbolic Story of King Arthur and the Knights of the Round Table and the Twofold Quest*. King Arthur's Hall, Tintagel, 1931.
Symbolic interpretation of Malory. Preface (p.x) says that it owes much to Caxton's Preface.

F   Gloag, J. *Artorius Rex*. Cassell, 1977.
Ordinary historical novel. Told by Cay (Caius Geladius).

*P   Graff, Irvine. *Return of Arthur*. Boston: Stratford Co., 1922.
Arthur returns as Kitchener.

jF   Gray, Phoebe. *Little Sir Galahad*. Stanley Paul, n.d.
(Also published Boston: Small, Maynard, 1914). Moral American story in Coolidge-Burnett vein. Title character is a crippled boy who belongs to the Galahad Knights and searches all his life for a moral ideal symbolised by the Grail.

jF   Green, Roger Lancelyn. *King Arthur and his Knights of the Round Table*. Illus. Lotte Reiniger. Faber, 1957. *(Penguin, 1953).

> Retold chiefly from Malory in pseudo-medieval style.

*   Greenslet, Ferris. *The Quest of the Holy Grail: an Interpretation and a Paraphrase of the Holy Legends . . . with Illustrations from the Frieze Decoration in the Boston Public Library by Edwin Austin Abbey, R.A.* Boston: Curtis and Cameron, 1902.

m   Guerber. H.A. *Myths and Legends of the Middle Ages: Their Origin and Influence on Literature and Art.* Harrap, 1909.

> Pages 241-326 deal with Arthurian material. Largely retellings with comment and copious quotations from Tennyson.

*F   Guthrie, Kenneth Sylvan. *Peronik the Innocent: or the Quest of the Golden Basin and the Diamond Lance.* Brooklyn: Comparative Literature Press, 1915.

jF   Haar, J.T. *King Arthur.* Illus. Rien Poortuliet; adapted from original trans. by Maria Powell. Lutterworth, 1973. *(Bussum, Holland: Van Distoek, Van Holkema and Warendorf N V, 1967).

> Superb retelling of the myth, not really for children although classified as such by the publishers.

*jF   Hadfield, M. *King Arthur and the Round Table.* Dent.

Hadley, Henry Kimball. See Watts, Ethel Mumford.

*D   Hagedorn, Hermann. *The Silver Blade*. Berlin: A.Unger, 1907.

*P   Hagedorn, Hermann. 'Song of the Grail Seekers'. In *A Troop of the Guard and Other Poems.* Boston and New York: Houghton Mifflin, 1909.

F   Hamilton, Ernest. *Launcelot: a Romance of the Court of King Arthur.* Methuen, 1926.

> Very loosely based on Malory with variations such as Launcelot's marriage to Elaine of Corbin before meeting Guinevere. Told in 'Malorian' English.

*   Hanemann, H.N. 'Excaliber, or a Square Peg in a Round Table. Dr Collins Takes a Good Look at King Arthur'. Section VIII in *The Facts of Life. A Book of Brighter Biography Executed in the Manner of Some of Our Best or Best-Known Writers, Scriveners, and Scribes.* New York: Farrar and Rinehart, 1930.

D   Hardy, Thomas. *The Famous Tragedy of the Queen of Cornwall.* Macmillan, 1924.

> Mummers' play.

*D   Hare, Amory. *Tristram and Iseult: a Play*. Gaylordsville, Conn.:
       Slide Mountain Press, 1930.
       Hart, Lorenz. See Rogers, Richard.
**jF   Hastings, Selina. *Sir Gawain and the Green Knight*. Methuen/
       Walker, 1981.
           Edition for young readers.
*P   Hayes, James Juvenal. *Sir Kay: a Poem in the Old Style*. Sioux
       City, Iowa: Dark Harp Press, 1923.
jD   Hayles, Brian. *The Moon Stallion*. BBC 1. 15.11.78ff.
           Six-part serial. Concerns a white horse with possible
           Arthurian connections.
P   Heard, John. 'The Marriage of Tristram'. *Poet-Lore*, XLVIII
       (1942), 72-83.
           Somewhat unlikely and sentimentalised version of the Tris-
           tan myth, viewed largely in retrospect from his marriage.
*D   Hearne, Isabel. *Queen Herzeleid, or Sorrow-of-Heart, an Epi-
       sode in the Boyhood of the Hero Parzival: Poetic Play in
       Three Acts*. Nutt, 1911.
P   Heath-Stubbs, John. *Artorius*. Enitharmon Press, 1974.
           Arthur in sixth-century setting, presented as a hero of
           universal myth.
P   Hill, Geoffrey. 'Merlin'. In *The New Poetry*, ed. A. Alvarez (p.
       201). Penguin, 1966.
           Merlin considers the dead Arthurian characters in two
           quatrains.
D   Hill, Graham. *Guinevere: a Tragedy in Three Acts*. Elkin
       Mathews, 1906.
           Melodramatic version of the Lancelot-Guinevere story in
           pseudo-Shakespearean dialogue.
m   Hodges, Margaret. *Knight Prisoner: the Tale of Sir Thomas
       Malory and his King Arthur*. New York: Farrar, Strauss and
       Giraux, 1976.
           Fanciful life of Malory linking his life with that of his
           characters. Junior level.
*M   Hooker, Brian. *Morven and the Grail*, mus. Horatio Parker (op.
       79). VS and Libretto. Boston Music Co., 1915.
           Oratorio.
*D   Horton, Douglas. *A Legend of the Grail: To be Played or Read
       in the Season of Easter or Christmas*. Boston and Chicago:
       Pilgrim Press, 1925.
F   Housman, Clemence. *The Life of Sir Aglovale de Galis*. Cape,
       1954.
           A romance. First published by Methuen, 1905.

P Hughes, Ian. 'Marchlyn'. In *Slate*. Deiniol Press, 1977.
    On the industrial exploitation of Wales. First published in the *Anglo-Welsh Review*.

jF Hulpach, Vladimír, Emanuel Frynta and Václav Cibula. *Heroes of Folk Tale and Legend*. Trans. George Theiner; illus. Miloslav Troup. Hamlyn, 1970. (Prague: Artia, 1970).
    Various legends retold including Gawain and the Green Knight and Kilwich [sic] and Olwen.

F Hunter, Jim. *Percival and the Presence of God*. Faber, 1978.
    Percival's own account of his relationship with Blanchflower and of his Grail quest, told starkly. Arthur does not appear.

P James, Edwin Stanley. 'Avalon'. In *A Celtic Anthology*, ed. Grace Rhys. (pp.312-13). Harrap, 1927.
    Lyric poem of five stanzas. First published in *The Statue and Other Poems*. Erskine Macdonald, [n.d.].

P Jones, David. *The Anathemata: Fragments of an Attempted Writing*. Faber, 1952.
    Arthurian references *passim*.

P Jones, David. *In Parenthesis*. Faber, 1963.
    Jones' war experiences illuminated by use of Arthurian allusion. First published 1937.

P Jones, David. 'The Hunt'. *Agenda: David Jones Special Issue*, V (Spring/Summer, 1967), 22-27.
    Fragment based on *Culhwch ac Olwen*.

jD Jones, F.H. *The Life and Death of King Arthur: a Play*. Macmillan, 1930.
    'In IV Scenes, the first III adapted from the Morte d'Arthur, the last from Tennyson's "Idylls of the King".' Originally written for the boys of Wellesley School, Croydon.

*P Jones, Thomas Samuel. *Shadow of the Perfect Rose*. New York: Farrar and Rinehart, 1937.
    Collected poems; contains a number of Arthurian poems.

F Keith, Chester. *Queen's Knight: A Prose Epic*. Allen and Unwin, 1920.
    Sentimentalised and simplified version of Lancelot's story, based on Malory.

P Kendon, Frank. *Tristram*. Dent, 1934.
    Narrative poem in nine sections.

*D Kennedy, Charles R. *Seventh Trumpet*. French, 1942.
    A play of World War II.

* King, Baraganath. 'The Coming of Arthur'. In *Arthur and Others in Cornwall.* Erskine Macdonald, 1925.

jF *King Arthur and his Knights.* Arnold's Junior Story Readers, No.5. Arnold, [?1905].
School reader for 'Standard II'.

jF *King Arthur and his Knights.* Blackie, [1910].
Based on Malory but includes Mont St Michel episode.

*f *King Arthur was a Gentleman.* Starring Arthur Askey. 1942.
No further details available.

D Kinross, Martha. *Tristram and Isoult.* Macmillan, 1913.
Verse drama.

*f *Knights of the Round Table.* Dir. Richard Thorpe. MGM, 1953.
Lancelot returns to defeat Mordred. Non-traditional.

jF *Knights of the Round Table.* Illus. Mixi-Berel. Ward Lock, 1964. (Illustrations Société Nouvelles des Editions Bias, 1957).
Free retelling for very young readers.

*f *Lancelot and Guinevere.* (U.S. Title *Sword of Lancelot*). Dir. Cornel Wilde. Emblem, 1962.

f *Lancelot du Lac.* Dir. Robert Bresson. 1974.
Bresson's disillusioned view of the end of the Middle Ages.

*P Lang, M.R. *Yseulte: a Dramatic Poem.* Digby: Long, 1905.

jF Le Cain, Errol. *King Arthur's Sword.* Faber, 1968.
Picture book beautifully illustrated by the author.

jF Lee, F.H. *The Children's King Arthur.* Illus. Honor C.Appleton; frontis. Rowland Wheelwright. Harrap, 1935.

*D Lee, Thomas Herbert. 'The Marriage of Iseult: a Tragedy in Two Scenes'. In *The Marriage of Iseult and Other Plays.* Elkin Mathews, 1909.

M Lerner, Alan Jay and Frederick Loewe. *Camelot.* VS and Libretto. Chappell, 1960.
Stage musical loosely based on T.H.White's *The Once and Future King* (q.v.). See also *Camelot.*

*D Leslie, Vera. *Guinevere.* Court Theatre, 1903.

*D Levey, Sivori. *Sir Gareth's Quest: Adapted from Tennyson's 'Idylls of the King', and Arranged for Costume Presentation.* Fountain Publ. Co., 1920.

*D Levey, Sivori. *Guinevere and Arthur: Adapted from Tennyson's 'Idylls of the King'.* Fountain Publ. Co., 1920.

P Lewis, Charlton Miner. *Gawayne and the Green Knight: a Fairy Tale.* Boston and New York: Houghton Mifflin, 1904.
Humorous retelling in four cantos of couplets. Introduces

143

Elfinhart, a fairy in love with Gawayne and responsible for the beheading test.

P Lewis, C.S. 'Launcelot'. In *Narrative Poems*. Ed. Walter Hooper. (pp.93-103). Geoffrey Bles, 1969.
'Probably written in the 1930s' (Hooper). Lancelot returns from the Grail Quest.

F Lewis, C.S. *That Hideous Strength*. Bodley Head, 1945.
Third part of science-fiction trilogy in which Merlin returns to aid Logres.

F Lindsay, Philip. *The Little Wench*. Nicholson and Watson, 1935.
Publishers claim an 'accurate scholarly picture of life in England in the reign of King Stephen or King Henry II'. The little wench is Guinevere.

P Lindsay, Vachel. 'Galahad, the Knight Who Perished' and 'King Arthur's Men Have Come Again'. In *Collected Poems*. Rev. edn. Illus. by author. New York: Macmillan, 1955.
Non-Arthurian; emotive use of name associations. First edition 1913.

jF Lively, Penelope. *The Whispering Knights*. Heinemann, 1971.
Three twentieth-century children encounter Morgan Le Fay.

* MacCormac, John. 'The Enchanted Weekend'. In *From Unknown Worlds*. New York: Street and Smith, 1948.

F Machen, Arthur. 'The Great Return'. In *The Terror*. Caerleon Ed. 7. Secker, 1923.
BMC has *The Great Return*. Faith Press, 1915. The Grail returns to a Welsh village.

F Machen, Arthur. *The Secret Glory*. Caerleon Ed. 4. Secker, 1923.
A story of the Holy Grail.

F Machen, Arthur. 'Guinevere and Lancelot'. In *Notes and Queries*. (pp.1-18). Spurr and Swift, 1926. (No.9 of signed limited edn.).
Short story. Volume also contains an essay, 'The Holy Grail' (pp.67-73).

jF MacGregor, Mary. *Stories of King Arthur's Knights: Told to the Children*. Illus. C. Walter Hodges. Edinburgh: Nelson, n.d.
Stories taken from Malory and 'Geraint and Enid' from the Mabinogion.

jF MacGregor, Mary. Another edn. Illus. Katherine Cameron. Edinburgh: T.C. and E.C. Jack, [1905].

jF   MacLeod, Mary. *The Book of King Arthur and his Noble Knights: Stories from Sir Thomas Malory's Morte Darthur.* Illus. from drawings by A.G.Walker. Wells Gardner, Darton, 1945.
       First edn., a Fine Art edn., 1908.

jF   MacLeod, Mary. *King Arthur: Stories from Sir Thomas Malory's Morte D'Arthur.* Illus. Herschel Levit; afterword by Clifton Fadiman. New York: Macmillan, 1963.
       Later edn. of *The Book of King Arthur . . .* (1945).

*D   MacLiesh, Archibald Fleming. *The Destroyers.* New York: John Day, 1942.

jF   Manning, Rosemary. *The Dragon's Quest.* Illus. Constance Marshall. Longman, 1961.
       The Green Dragon on his quest becomes involved in Beaumain's adventures. Third in a series about the dragon and his friend, Susan.

m   *The Manual of the Knights of the Round Table Club (A.D. 1720): (Confirmed in General Council 12 Dec., 1927).* 1927. (No. 191 of limited edn. of 500).
       Of most interest for its list of past members, including Henry Irving.

P   Marquis, Don. 'Lancelot and Guinevere' and 'Tristram and Isolt'. In *Sonnets to a Red-haired Lady (By a Gentleman with a Blue Beard) and Famous Love Affairs.* Illus. Stuart Hay (pp.122-5; 73-80). Garden City, New York: Doubleday, 1922.
       Burlesque poems, the former of fifteen quatrains, the latter of nine Spenserian stanzas.

F   Marshall, Edison. *The Pagan King.* Frederick Muller, 1960.
       Plausible reconstruction of the legend in sixth-century setting. Disfigured by boiling oil Arthur retires; the story spreads of his passing to be healed of his wound.

F   *The Marvellous History of King Arthur in Avalon and of the Lifting of Lyonesse: a Chronicle of the Round Table, Communicated by Geoffrey of Monmouth.* Ed. Geoffrey Junior. John Murray, 1904.
       Editor was 'visited' by Geoffrey who told him how Arthur and his knights spent their time in Avalon with Morgan La Faye. Satire.

P   Masefield, John. 'Ballad of Sir Bors'. In *Collected Poems.* Heinemann, 1932.
       First published in *Poems and plays*, New York: Macmillan, 1919. (pp.79-80).

*D   Masefield, John. *Tristan and Isolt*. Heinemann, 1927.
            Verse drama. Reveals author's interest in tale's Celtic origins.

P   Masefield, John. *Midsummer Night: a Verse Cycle*. Heinemann, 1928.
            Concerns the legend of Arthur's sleeping knights waking on Midsummer Night.

P   Masefield, John. 'The Love Gift' and 'Tristan's Singing'. In *Minnie Maylow's Story and other Tales and Scenes*. (pp.33-40; 43-54). Heinemann, 1931.
            Also in *Poems* (1946).

P   Masefield, John. 'An Art Worker'. In *Gautama the Enlightened and Other Verse*. (pp.37-62). Heinemann, 1941.
            Contains some Arthurian lines (p.43).

F   Masefield, John. *Badon Parchments*. Heinemann, 1947.
            Fictional accounts of the Battle and the background to it. Aurelian is King and Arthur a general.

P   Masefield, John. 'Tristan and Isolt'. In *On the Hill*. (pp.77-88). Heinemann, 1949.
            In plot borrowed from *Romeo and Juliet*, Isolt counterfeits death, but here she and Tristan successfully escape.

P   Masters, Edgar Lee. 'The Ballad of Launcelot and Elaine' and 'The Death of Sir Launcelot'. In *Songs and Satires*. (pp.140-8; 149-54). New York: Macmillan, 1916.
            Ballads based on Malory.

*D   Merington, Marguerite. 'The Testing of Sir Gawayne: All Hallowe'en Play on the Arthurian Legend'. In *Festival Plays*. New York: Duffield, 1913.

**M   Messiaen, Olivier (b.1908). *La Dame de Shalott* (Op.1). 1917.

P   Millay, Edna St Vincent. 'Elaine'. In *Second April*. (pp.44-45). New York: Harper, 1929.

P   Millay, Edna St Vincent. 'Sonnet'. In *Second April*. (p.77).
            Contains reference to Isolde and Guinevere.

P   Millay, Edna St Vincent. *Collected Poems*. New York: Harper, 1956.
            Contains 'Elaine' (from *Second April*. New York: Mitchell Kennerley, 1921), five quatrains addressed by Elaine of Astolat to Lancelot, and 'Tristan' (from *Mine the Harvest*. New York: Harper, 1954).
            Tristan's reminiscences in four parts.

*D   Mitchell, D.M. *Sir Tristram: a Tragedy in Four Acts*. Fowler Wright, 1929.

F   Mitchison, Naomi. *To the Chapel Perilous*. White Lion, 1976.
Satire on the Press and on the power of Church and State. First published by Allen and Unwin, 1955.

**F   Monaco, Richard. *Parsival, or a Knight's Tale*. Raven Books, 1977.
Little trace of the traditional Perceval story.

f   *Monty Python and the Holy Grail*. Dir. Terry Gilliam and Terry Jones. Python (Monty) Pictures Ltd., 1974.
Arthurian skit by the *Monty Python* team.
See also Chapman, Graham.

*F   Moore, George. *Héloïse and Abélard*. Cuman Sean-Eolais na h-Eiremann, 1921.
'Vol. II, Ch. 22 contains an Arthurian episode' (Parry).

F   Moore, George. *Peronnik the Fool*. Rev. edn. Chapelle-Réanville, Eure, France: Hours Press, 1928. (No. 24 of signed limited edn. of 200).
Delightful romance-allegory of Grail type. First published Mount Vernon: Rudge, 1926.

F   Morgan, Charles. *Sparkenbroke*. Macmillan, 1955.
The love story of Sparkenbroke and Mary Leward is supposed to reflect that of Tristan and Iseult, but the parallel is not close. First published 1936.

jF   Mozley, Juliet. *King Arthur and the Knights of the Round Table*. Franklin Watts, 1971.
Picture book. Malory for under-sevens.

jD   *Mr Merlin*. I.T.V. Spring 1982.
American series starring Bernard Hughes as Max Merlin who attempts to teach Zac, a young garage mechanic, to learn his magic arts. Present day setting.

P   Muir, Edwin. 'Tristram Crazed'. *New Adelphi* (1929), 100-101.
Ballad of Tristram's madness. Also printed in *Literary Digest*, C (2 February 1929).

P   Muir, Edwin. 'Merlin'. In *Collected Poems 1921-1951*. (p. 51). Faber, 1952.
Fourteen-line poem. Source of title of Mary Stewart's *The Crystal Cave* (q.v.).

*M   Mumford, Ethel Watts. *Merlin and Vivian: a Lyric Drama*. New York: Schirmer, 1907.
Reported no locations in Britain. National Union Catalogue enters VS under Hadley, Henry Kimball.

*P   Newell, William Wells. *Isolt's Return*. Publ. Wayland, Mass. by the Author, 1907.

jF   Newman, Robert. *Merlin's Mistake.* First British edn. Heine-
     mann, 1971. (© 1970).
         Medieval setting. Merlin's mistake was to give Tertius all
         future knowledge. Featured on BBC-TV's *Jackanory*
         March 6-10, 1978.
jF   Newman, Robert. *The Testing of Tertius.* Hutchinson, 1974.
     (© 1973).
         A sequel to *Merlin's Mistake.*
*P   Newson, Ranald. 'Balin and Balan: a Dramatic Poem'. In
     Poems. (pp.3-9). New Testament Press, 1930.
jF   Norton, Andre. *Steel Magic.* Illus. Robin Jacques. Hamish
     Hamilton, 1967.
         Three modern children set out for Avalon to retrieve
         three magic talismen − Excalibur, Merlin's Ring and
         Huon's silver horn.
P   Noyes, Alfred. 'Riddles of Merlin'. In *Collected Poems: in One
     Volume.* (pp.353-4). John Murray, 1950.
         Nature poems.
F   Nye, Robert. *Merlin.* Hamish Hamilton, 1978.
         Modern, Rabelaisian version of Geoffrey's *Historia.* Merlin
         watches his life and retells it from inside his crystal cave.
P   Ormerod, James. 'Tristram's Tomb'. In *Tristram's Tomb and
     Other Poems.* (pp.9-13). Elkin Mathews, 1928.
         Ballad dated 1902. Mark fetches the bodies of Tristram
         and Iseult from Brittany.
D   Ormerod, James. 'Meliagrance and Guinevere'. In *Tristram's
     Tomb and Other Poems.* Elkin Mathews, 1928.
         Four melodramatic scenes; based on Malory. Dated 1913.
P   Ormerod, James. 'Joseph of Arimathea'. In *Tristram's Tomb
     and Other Poems.* Elkin Mathews, 1928.
         Dialogue between Joseph and Arviragus at Glastonbury.
         Dated 1921.
P   Owen, Wilfred. 'Hospital Barge at Cérisy'. In *The Collected
     Poems*, ed. C.Day Lewis. (p.197). Chatto and Windus, 1963.
         Sonnet. Barge suggests Arthur's barge carrying him to
         Avalon.
D   Padmore, E.S. *The Death of Arthur: the Story of the Holy
     Grail.* Herbert Jenkins, 1936.
         Type of Morality Play.
*P   Pallen, Condé Benoist. 'The Death of Sir Launcelot'. In *The
     Death of Sir Launcelot and Other Poems.* (pp.1-26). Boston:
     Small, Maynard, 1902.
         Reprinted in *Collected Poems*, (1916).

*P   Parker, Dorothy. 'Guinevere at her Fireside'. In *Deaths and Taxes*. New York: Viking Press, 1931.
> Reprinted in *Not So Deep as a Well*, 1936.

P   Parker, Dorothy. 'Iseult of Brittany'.
> Both reprinted in *The Collected Dorothy Parker*. (pp. 304 and 306). Duckworth, 1973.

jF   Paton, John. *The Adventures of Sir Lancelot: Adapted from the Television Film Series Starring William Russell*. Sapphire Film Prods for Incorporated Television Programme Co., n.d.
> *BMC* has No. 2, adapted by Arthur Groom, Adprint, 1957-.

F   Paul, Evelyn. *The Romance of Tristram of Lyones and La Beale Isoude: Drawn out of the Celtic-French and Illuminated by Evelyn Paul*. Harrap, 1920.
> Part prose, part poetry; based on Robert de Borron.

F   Peters, Elizabeth. *The Camelot Caper*. Cassell, 1969.
> Thriller. Action revolves round Arthurian sites.

*P   Philibin, An, *pseud*. (John Hackett Pollock). *Tristram and Iseult: a Dramatic Poem*. Dublin: Talbot Press, 1924.

P   Phillips, Douglas. 'Merlin's Town'. In *Beyond the Frontier*. Christopher Davis, 1972.
> Poem about Carmarthen and the legend of Merlin's oak. I am indebted to the poet for a copy of his type-script.

jF   Picard, Barbara Leonie. *Stories of King Arthur and his Knights*. Illus. Roy Morgan. OUP, 1955.
> From various sources but chiefly Malory.

jF   Picard, Barbara Leonie. *Hero-Tales from the British Isles*. Illus. John G. Galsworthy. Edmund Ward, 1963.
> Episodes from the legend retold in 'Arthur, King of England' section, (pp. 11-29).

P   Pomeroy, Florence M. *Tristan and Iseult: an Epic Poem in Twelve Books*. Bodley Head, 1958.
> Somewhat affected style.

F   Ponsar, Y.R. *Gawain and the Green Knight, Adventure at Camelot*. Illus. Darrell Sweet. Macmillan, 1979.
> Modern prose adaptation of the fourteenth-century original.

P   Porteous, Frances. *Knight of the Grail*. Guild Press, 1962.
> Anthology of religious poetry. Title poem (pp. 7-8) rambling free verse addressed to Galahad.

P   Pound, Ezra. *Cantos*. Faber, 1975.
> No. XCI, first published 1955, contains some Middle English references to Merlin.

F   Powys, J.C. *A Glastonbury Romance*. John Lane, 1933.
Contains Arthurian objects and characters in reincarnation.

F   Powys, J.C. *Maiden Castle*. Cassell, 1937.
Contains some Arthurian associations.

F   Powys, J.C. *Porius*. Macdonald, 1951.
Novel about Merlin *wyllt*. [Substantially cut for publication — a full edition of the MS text is in preparation. *Ed.*]

F   Price, Anthony. *Our Man in Camelot*. Gollancz, 1975.
Thriller. Unlikely plot centres round strategic importance of site of Badon.

jF   Price, Eleanor C. *The Adventures of King Arthur: Arranged from the Morte Darthur of Sir Thomas Malory*. Illus. Rowland Wheelwright. J.Coker, 1933.
Archaic style.

F   Priestley, J.B. *The Thirty-first of June: a Tale of True Love, Enterprise and Progress in the Arthurian and Ad-Atomic Ages*. Heinemann, 1961.
Pseudo-medieval setting in the reign of Arthur, otherwise non-Arthurian.

*F   *Prince Valiant*. Dir. Henry Hathaway. Fox, 1954.
Based on the Hal Foster comic strip in which Arthurian characters appear from time to time.

*jf   Pyle, Howard. *The Story of King Arthur and his Knights*. Newnes, 1903. (© Charles Scribner's Sons, New York, 1903).
First of four volumes.

jF   Pyle, Howard. *The Story of the Champions of the Round Table*. Illus. by the author. Newnes, 1905. (© Charles Scribner's Sons, 1905).
Second of four companion volumes. Retells the stories of Launcelot, Tristram and Percival. Medieval pastiche.

jF   Pyle, Howard. *The Story of Sir Launcelot and his Companions*. Chapman and Hall, 1907. (© Charles Scribner's Sons, 1907).
Third of four companion volumes.

jF   Pyle, Howard. *The Story of the Grail and the Passing of Arthur*. Bickers and Son, 1910. (© Charles Scribner's Sons, 1910).
Fourth in the series. Includes the story of Geraint.

*   Reynolds, Ernest. *Tristram and Iseult*. Nottingham: John Clough, 1930.

P   Reynolds, Ernest. *Mephistopheles and the Golden Apples: a Fantastic Symphony in Seven Movements*. Cambridge: Heffer, 1943.

Series of pageants. Nos. VI, VII, VIII and IX are Arthur-
ian.
*   Reynolds, Marion Lee. *Geraint of Devon*. Boston: Sherman,
French, 1916.
*D   Rhys, Ernest. *Gwenevere: a Lyric Play*. Dent, 1905.
P   Rhys, Ernest. *Lays of the Round Table and Other Lyric
Romances*. Dent, 1905.
Series of ballads on Arthurian subjects or ascribed to
Arthurian characters.
*P   Rhys, Ernest. 'Broceliande'. *Harper's Magazine*, CXII (January,
1906), 265.
'Three ten-line stanzas' (Parry).
*D   Rhys, Ernest. *Enid: a Lyric Play*. Dent, 1908.
D   Rhys, Ernest. *The Masque of the Grail*. Elkin Mathews, 1908.
First performed at the Court Theatre, 1908, directed by
Enid Rhys and William Poel. Incidental music by Vincent
Thomas.
*D   Rhys, Ernest. *The Quest of the Grail: a Masque*. Music by Vin-
cent Thomas. Blyth, [1915].
Parry believes this is a later edition of the previous item.
P   Rhys, Ernest. *The Leaf-burners and Other Poems*. Dent, 1918.
Contains three short Arthurian Poems: 'Dagonet's Love
Song' (p.109), 'La Morte Sans Pité' (pp.110-112), 'The
Castle of Carbonek' (pp.113-114).
F   Roberts, Dorothy James. *The Enchanted Cup*. Hutchinson,
1954.
Story of Tristram and Isoud, loosely based on Malory.
F   Roberts, Dorothy James. *Lancelot my Brother*. Hutchinson,
1956.
The Story of Lancelot and Guinevere told by Bors. Based
on Malory.
P   Robinson, Edwin Arlington. 'Merlin'. In *Collected Poems*.
Macmillan, 1961.
Merlin returns from his enchantment to help Arthur just
before the fall of the Round Table. Dated 1917.
P   Robinson, Edwin Arlington. 'Lancelot'. In *Collected Poems*.
Macmillan, 1961.
Covers the events after Lancelot's return from the Grail
Quest. Dated 1920.
P   Robinson, Edwin Arlington. 'Tristram'. In *Collected Poems*.
Macmillan, 1961.
Chief character is Isolt of Brittany. Dated 1927.

*P   Robinson, Edwin Arlington. *Modred: a Fragment.* New York and New Haven: E.B.Hackett, 1929.
First publication of a deleted fragment from the 'Lancelot'.

M   Rogers, Richard and Lorenz Hart. *A Connecticut Yankee.* c.1927.
Based on Twain's *A Yankee at the Court of King Arthur.*

jF   *The Romance of Sir Percival: Retold from the Mabinogion and 'Morte D'Arthur'.*
Part I covers Percival's boyhood, Part II his quest for the Grail.

*D   Royle, Edwin M. *Launcelot and Elaine.* New York: French, 1929.

jF   Rutley, C.M. *Stories of King Arthur's Knights.* Lutterworth Press, 1955.
Based chiefly on Malory. Includes a chapter on sources and how they came to be written. First published R.T.S., 1929.

P   Ryan, W.P. *King Arthur in Avalon.* Andrew S.Curtis, [1934].
Dialogue form.

D   Saul, George Brandon. 'The Fair Eselt: a Play'. In *Hound and Unicorn: Collected Verse – Lyrical, Narrative and Dramatic.* (pp.217-259). Philadelphia: Walton Press, 1969.
Verse drama. Author remarks (p.219) that he 'tried to move the story back to pre-Ur Tristan, and pre-Christian, conditions appropriate to an elopement story'.

F   Senior, Dorothy. *The Clutch of Circumstance or the Gates of Dawn.* Black, 1908.
'Scottian' romance. Non-Malorian characters include heroine, Finola. Based on Malory.

jF   Senior, Dorothy. *Tales of King Arthur.* Illus. Frank Watkins. Black, 1930.
Morte Darthur retold.

*F   Sharpe, Ruth Collier. *Tristram of Lyonesse: the Story of an Immortal Love.* New York: Greenberg, 1949.
Discussed by B.J.Whiting in *Speculum,* XXV (1950), 114-117.

D   Sheriff, R.C. *The Long Sunset.* French, 1955.
Setting is 410 A.D. but atmosphere is twentieth-century.

*f   *Siege of the Saxons.* Dir. Nathan Juran. Columbia/Ameran, 1963.

P   Skinner, Martyn. *The Return of Arthur: a Poem of the Future.* 3 parts in 1. Chapman and Hall, 1966.
Set in 2000 A.D., burlesque epic. Previously published

separately: *Merlin, or the Return of Arthur.* Muller, 1951: *The Return of Arthur.* Chapman and Hall, 1955.

P   Smith, Arthur Saxon Dennett. *Trystan Hag Ysolt: Verse.* An Hef, 1953.

        Tristan and Iseult in Cornish verse.

*jD   Smith, Evelyn. 'The Kitchen Knight'. In *Form Room Plays.* Dent, 1926.

        Six scenes; adapted from Le Morte Darthur.

*   Southworth, Mary. *Galahad: Knight Errant.* Boston: Badger, 1907.

*jf   *The Spaceman and King Arthur.* Disney, 1979.

F   Steinbeck, John. *Tortilla Flat.* Heinemann, 1935.

        Reveals author's belief that myth is real and eternal.

F   Steinbeck, John. *The Acts of King Arthur and his Noble Knights.* Heinemann, 1977.

        Unfinished version of Malory for a modern audience.

jD   Stephens, G. Arbour. 'Christmas Interlude at the Court of King Arthur'. In *Cameo Plays*, Book 2. Arnold, 1939.

        Prose version of the tale dramatised by Frances Chesterton (q.v.).

*F   Sterling, Sara Hawks. *A Lady of King Arthur's Court: Being a Romance of the Holy Grail.* Chatto and Windus, 1909.

P   Stevenson, Francis Seymour. *Conflict and Quest.* Longman, 1926.

        Twelve cantos of Spenserian stanzas. Canto IX 'A Castle of the Grail', (pp.194-215).

F   Stewart, Mary. *The Crystal Cave.* Hodder, 1970.

        'Autobiography' of Merlin told in modern terms.

F   Stewart, Mary. *The Hollow Hills.* Hodder, 1973.

        Sequel to the above.

F   Stewart, Mary. *The Last Enchantment.* Hodder, 1979.

        Final part of trilogy.

D   Steynor, Morley. *Lancelot and Elaine: a Play in Five Acts.* Bell, 1909.

D   Steynor, Morley. *Lancelot and Guenevere: a Play in Prologue and Four Acts.* Bell, 1909.

        Verse dramas; both performed at the Bijou Theatre, April 8, 1904.

jF   Storer, Ronald D.K. *King Arthur and his Knights.* Illus. William Stobbs. OUP, 1906.

        For very young readers.

jF   *Stories from King Arthur.* OUP, 1935.

        Malory for young readers.

jF   Sutcliff, Rosemary. *The Lantern Bearers.* OUP, 1972.
        Part of the 'Roman' series. Arthur appears as a boy.
        For older children. First edition 1959.

*jF   Sutcliff, Rosemary. *The Light Beyond the Forest.* Bodley
        Head, 1979.
        The Quest for the Holy Grail. Second part of Arthurian
        trilogy; retelling 'the Premier British Myth'.

jF   Sutcliff, Rosemary. *The Road to Camlann.* Bodley Head, 1981.
        Last part of trilogy; deals with death of Arthur.

F   Sutcliff, Rosemary. *Sword at Sunset.* Hodder, 1963.
        Accurate but soulless historical reconstruction.

*jF   Sutcliff, Rosemary. *The Sword and the Circle.* Bodley Head,
        1981.
        First part of trilogy comprising also *The Light Beyond
        the Forest* and *The Road to Camlann.* Covers Arthur's
        birth, foundation of Round Table and adventures of most
        famous knights.

jF   Sutcliff, Rosemary. *Tristan and Iseult.* Bodley Head, 1971.
        For younger children.

f   *The Sword in the Stone.* Dir. Wolfgang Reitherman. Walt
        Disney, 1963.
        Animated version of T.H.White's novel.

D   Symons, Arthur. *Tristan and Iseult.* Heinemann, 1917.
        One of the best dramatisations of the period.

*   Symons, Arthur. 'Iseult of Brittany'. In *Cesare Borgia.* New
        York: Brentano's, 1920.

P   Symons, Arthur. 'Merlin and Mark'. In *Jezebel Mort and Other
        Poems.* (pp.35-37). Heinemann, 1931.
        Dated March 4, 1922. Five stanzas. Merlin in his cavern,
        symbol of sin and Hell, shows Mark the adultery of
        Tristan and Iseult in a vision.

*D   Taft, Linwood. *Galahad: a Pageant of the Holy Grail.* New
        York: A.S.Barnes, 1926.

*F   Tatum, Edith. 'The Awakening of Iseult'. *Neale's Monthly*, II
        (August, 1913), 177-85.

*P   Tax, Ervin H. *The Wraith of Gawain.* Prairie City, Ill.: Decker,
        1948.
        Long poem in eight books.

F   Taylor, Anna. *Drustan the Wanderer: a Historical Novel Based
        on the Legend of Tristan and Yseult.* Longman, 1971.
        Uses Malory's French sources and modern archaeological
        evidence.

*D   Taylor, R.H. *Parsifal: a Romantic Mystery Drama.* Sidney: Angus and Robertson, 1906.

*P   Teasdale, Sara. *Collected Poems.* Macmillan, 1937.
> Includes 'Guenevere' originally published in *Helen of Troy and Other Poems*, Putnam, 1911, and 'At Tintagil' originally published in *Dark of the Moon*, New York: Macmillan, 1926.

P   Thomas, D. Vaughan. 'Parsifal heard in Wales'. *Welsh Outlook*, VII (1920), 225.
> Sonnet.

m   Thomas, Edward. *Cloud Castle and Other Papers.* Duckworth, 1922.
> Chapter VI muses on Isoud.

*D   Todhunter, John. *Isolt of Ireland: a Legend in a Prologue and Three Acts.* Dent, 1927.

*F   Toynbee, Philip. *Prothalamium, A Cycle of the Holy Graal: A Novel.* Garden City, New York: 1947.

jF   Treece, Henry. *The Eagles Have Flown.* Illus. Christine Price. Bodley Head, 1954.
> Story of two boys' involvement with Artos, depicted as in *The Great Captains*, (1956).

F   Treece, Henry. *The Great Captains.* Bodley Head, 1956.
> Fifth-century setting; Arthur depicted as 'Ursus horribilis'.

*D   Trevelyan, Robert C. *The Birth of Parsifal: a Drama.* Longman, 1905.

*   Trevelyan, Robert C. *The New Parsifal: an Operatic Fable.* Chiswick for the Author, 1914.
> Both reprinted in *Collected Works*. Longman, 1939.

jF   Troughton, Joanna. *Sir Gawain and the Loathly Damsel.* Illus. by the author. Macmillan, 1972.
> Picture book. Retelling of *The wedding of Sir Gawain and Dame Ragnell* for under-sevens.

D   Turnbull, E. Lucia and H. Dalwey. *Through the Gates of Remembrance.* First Series. Nelson, 1933.
> Trilogy of plays centered round Glastonbury.

F   Turner, Roy. *King of the Lordless Country.* Dobson, 1971.
> Celtic setting. Bedwyr's story.

F   Turton, Godfrey. *The Emperor Arthur.* W.H. Allen, 1968.
> Set in Romanised Britain. Merlin appears as totally evil.

*F   Tyler, Therese. *In the Shadow of the Sangreal.* Philadelphia: Campion, 1911.

F   Vansittart, Peter. *Lancelot.* Peter Owen, 1978.
> The 'autobiography' of Ker Maxim, a Roman survivor,

later to be known as Lancelot. Set in fifth-century Britain. Ambrosius is given the usual attributes of Arthur while Arthur himself is a roughneck who fails to rescue Britain from decay.

*P   Vere, B.D. *King Arthur: his Symbolic Story in Verse.* Tintagel: King Arthur's Hall, 1930.

F   Viney, Jayne. *The Bright-helmed One.* Hale, 1975.
Historical reconstruction based on Celtic sources.

M   Wakeman, Rick. *The Myths and Legends of King Arthur and the Knights of the Round Table.* Condor Music, 1975.
Modern musical interpretation.

jF   Walsh, J.H. ed. *Tales of King Arthur.* Illus. Joan Kiddell-Monroe. Longman, 1952.
'After Malory' (p.viii); also includes Geraint and Enid.

*   Ward, Christopher. *Sir Galahad and Other Rimes: Pass Keys to the Classics.* New York: Simon and Schuster, 1936.

D   Weinberger, Mildred. 'Elaine: a Poetic Drama'. *Poet-Lore*, XXXIV (1923), 72-110.
In a modern setting at a masked ball, Elaine and Lancelot meet again. Their story is re-enacted but in this version Elaine and Lancelot are married and in love.

F   White, T.H. *The Sword in the Stone.* Collins, 1938.
The Ill-Made Knight. New York: Putnam, 1940.
The Witch in the Wood. New York: Putnam, 1939.
All three later revised and published with 'A Candle in the Wind' as *The Once and Future King.* Collins, 1958.

F   White, T.H. *The Book of Merlyn.* Collins, 1978.
Sequel to *The Once and Future King.* Reviewed by Colin Manlove in *TLS*, 21 April 1978, p.451.
Uneven, but not unsatisfactory ending to the cycle.

*M   Whitehead, Gillian. *Tristan and Isolt.* Opera in 13 short scenes, with libretto by Malcolm Crowthers and Michael Hill. First performed at New Zealand Autumn Festival, 1978.

P   Wilbur, Richard. 'Merlin Enthralled'. In *Poems 1943-1956.* (pp.103-4). Faber, 1957.
Nine quatrains on the effect on Arthur's court of the loss of Merlin.

*   Williams, Antonia. *Isolt: a New Telling.* Publ. by the author, 1900.

F   Williams, Charles. *War in Heaven.* Faber, 1947.
A modern Grail story: occult struggle of Good and Evil focussed on the Graal, the cup used at the Last Supper. First published by Gollancz, 1930.

P   Williams, Charles. *Three Plays.* OUP, 1931.
          Five Arthurian poems are interpolated between the plays.
P   Williams, Charles. *Taliessin through Logres.* OUP, 1938.
          The Region of the Summer Stars. Nicholson and Watson,
          1944.
          Two verse cycles republished in one volume, OUP, 1948.
          See also C.S. Lewis, *Arthurian Torso* (1948) and Charles
          Moorman, *Arthurian Triptych* (1960).
*P   Williams, J. Price. 'Sing a Song of Avalon' and 'Olwen'. In *A
          Bangor Book of Verse.* Bangor: Jarvis and Foster, 1924.
*   Williams, W.S.G. *Arthur is Arising.* Wrexham: Hughes and
          Son, 1924.
jF   Wilson, Barbara Ker. *Legends of the Round Table.* Illus. Maria
          Calati. Hamlyn, 1966.
          Based on the Vulgate *Lancelot.*
jF   Winder, Blanche. *Stories of King Arthur.* Illus. Harry G. Theaker.
          Ward Lock, [1925].
          Based on Geoffrey and Malory.
jF   Winder, Blanche. *King Arthur and his Knights.* Ward Lock,
          1935.
          Later edition of the above.
*   Wodehouse, P.G. 'Sir Agravaine: a Blithesome and Knightly
          Tale: Throwing New Light upon the Mystery of Affinities'.
          Chicago American, July 8, 1923.
*   Wright, S. Fowler. *Scenes from the Morte d'Arthur.* Merton
          Press, 1929.
*   Wright, S. Fowler. *The Ballad of Elaine.* Merton Press, 1929.
*   Wright, S. Fowler. *The Riding of Lancelot.* Fowler Wright,
          1929.
*   Yeames, James. *Sir Gawain and the Green Knight: a Play in
          Five Acts.* Detroit: Knights of King Arthur, 1911.
*   Young, Stark. *Guenevere: a Play in Five Acts.* New York:
          Grafton, 1906.

II *Some secondary works consulted while compiling section I*

*Ackerman, Robert W. Review of Richard Barber's *Arthur of Albion*
(1961) in *College English*, XXIII (1962), 512.
Agenda: *David Jones Special Issue*, V (Spring/Summer, 1967) .
    See esp. articles by David Blamires, pp.101-111 and 159-171.
Aquarius 10: In Honour of John Heath-Stubbs. Ed. Eddie S.Linden.
Martin Brian and O'Keeffe, 1978.
        To mark Heath-Stubbs' sixtieth birthday. Reviewed by
        Andrew Motion in the *TLS*, 2 May 1978, p.496.
Barber, Richard. *Arthur of Albion: an Introduction to the Arthurian
    Literature and Legends of England.* Foreword by David Jones.
    Barrie and Rockliff with Pall Mall Press, 1961.
        Chapters 8 and 9 contain critical material on twentieth-
        century Arthurian literature. For reviews see Ackerman,
        Robert W.; Davies, R.T.; and Starr, Nathan Comfort.
Barber, Richard. *King Arthur in Legend and History.* Sphere Books,
    1973.
        Parts of this work were originally published under title *Arthur
        of Albion*, (1961). Pages 159-168 contain critical comment
        on some twentieth-century Arthurian works.
Bibliographical Bulletin of the International Arthurian Society. See
    Bulletin Bibliographique de la Société Internationale Arthurienne.
*Review of Laurence Binyon, *Arthur: a Tragedy* in *TLS*, 5 April
    1923, p.229.
Blamires, David. 'The Ordered World: *The Anathemata*' and ' "King
    Arthur is nat dede".' *Agenda*, V (Spring/Summer, 1967), 101-
    111; 159-171.
Blamires, David. *David Jones: Artist and Writer.* Manchester: Univer-
    sity Press, 1971.
        See esp. Chapters 5 and 8.
Brooke-Rose, Christine. *A Z.B.C. of Ezra Pound.* Faber, 1971.
        On the allusive nature of Pound's poetry. Pages 188-203
        discuss the Arthurian material in Canto XCI.
Brown, Paul A. 'The Arthurian Legends: Supplement to Northup and
    Parry's Annotated Bibliography (with further Supplement by
    John J.Parry)'. *JEGP*, XLIX (April, 1950), 208-216.
*Bulletin Bibliographique de la Société Internationale Arthurienne:
    Bibliographical Bulletin of the International Arthurian Society.*
        Annual since 1949. Title reversed from No.19 (1967) on-
        wards. Nos 1-18 ed. Jean Frappier; 19- by Lewis Thorpe.
        Chiefly concerned with pre-seventeenth-century material.

Cavaliero, Glen. *J. C. Powys: Novelist.* OUP, 1973.
> Contains useful chapters on Powys' Arthurian material.

Clancy, Joseph. *Pendragon: Arthur and his Britain.* Macmillan, 1971.
> Non-scholarly account of the historical background to the Arthurian period and selective account of the literature. Pages 112-117 cover some twentieth-century items.

Crowder, Richard. 'E. A. Robinson's Camelot'. *College English*, IX (1947), 72-9.
> A reconsideration of earlier criticism.

Davies, R.T. Review of Richard Barber's *Arthur of Albion* (1961) in *RES*, NS. XIII (1962), 399-400.

Ditmas, E.M.R. 'King Arthur in Literature'. *Books*, No. 331 (1960), 159-64.
> Very brief summary of eight hundred years of Arthurian Literature, from Geoffrey to Charles Williams.

Eadie, John W. 'The Development of Roman Mailed Cavalry'. *Journal of Roman Studies*, LVII (1967), 161-73.
> Traces development of armed mounted fighter in Roman army from *sagittaria equitata* to fourth-century *clibanarius*.

Eliot, T.S. 'The Significance of Charles Williams'. *The Listener*, 19 December 1946, pp. 894-5.
> A kind of literary obituary.

Eisner, Sigmund. *The Tristan Legend: a Study in Sources.* Illinois: Northwestern University Press, 1969.
> Seeks to show how the Tristan legend has always been part of the Arthurian corpus.

Review of W. B. Faraday's *Pendragon* (1930) in *TLS*, 16 October 1930, p. 840. See also Faraday's reply in *TLS*, 6 November 1930, p. 917.

Golther, Wolfgang. *Tristan un Isolde in den Dictungen des Mittelalters und de neuen Zeit.* Leipzig: Hirzel, 1907.
> Pages 385-390 discuss the version by Comyns Carr and its relationship to Wagner and Swinburne.

Halliwell, Leslie. *Halliwell's Film Guide.* Hart-Davis, MacGibbon, 1977.
> Lists British and American films in alphabetical order of title.

Halliwell, Leslie. *Halliwell's Filmgoer's Companion.* 6th edn. Hart-Davis, MacGibbon, 1977.
> Companion volume to the above.

*Halpérin, Maurice. *Le roman de Tristan et Iseut dans la littérature anglo-americaine au XIXe et au XXe siècles.* Paris: Jouve et Cie, 1931.

Hooker, Jeremy. *David Jones: an Exploratory Study of the Writings.* Enitharmon Press, 1975.

Hurd, Michael. 'Rutland Boughton' in *Groves*, Vol.3, pp.97-99.

Jenkins, Elizabeth. *The Mystery of King Arthur.* Michael Joseph, 1975.
> Coffee-table history of Arthur.

Jones, David. *Epoch and Artist: Selected Writings.* Ed. Harman Grisewood. Faber, 1959.
> Contains two Arthurian essays: 'The Arthurian Legend (1948)' and 'The Myth of Arthur (1942)'; the former originally appeared as a review of C.S.Lewis, *Arthurian Torso* (1948) in *The Tablet*, 25 December 1948.

Knight, G.Wilson. *The Saturnian Quest: a Chart of the Prose Works of John Cowper Powys.* Methuen, 1964.
> Seeks to explore the deepest meaning of Powys' works and their relationship to each other.

Lewis, C.S. *Arthurian Torso.* OUP, 1948.
> Contains commentary on Charles Williams' Arthurian poems and his posthumous fragment 'The Figure of Arthur'.
> See also Jones, David *Epoch and Artist* (1959).

Lowell, Amy. *Tendencies in Modern American Poetry.* Oxford: Blackwell, n.d. (Preface dated 1917).
> Contains chapters on E.A.Robinson and Edgar Lee Masters.

Manlove, Colin. Review of T.H.White's *The Book of Merlyn* (1978) in *TLS*, 21 April 1978, p.451.

Mathias, Roland, ed. *David Jones: Eight Essays on his Work as Writer and Artist.* Gower Press, 1976.
> Contains an essay on *The Anathemata* (pp.50-72).

Merriman, James Douglas. *The Flower of Kings: a Study of the Arthurian Legend in England between 1485 and 1835.* Wichita: University Press of Kansas, 1973.
> Contains a useful and extensive bibliography.

Monroe, Harriet. 'Mr Robinson in Camelot'. *Poetry*, X (July, 1917), 211-13.
> Review of *Merlin* (1917).

Moore, Thomas Sturge. 'The Story of Tristram and Isolt in Modern Poetry'. *The Criterion*, I (1922-1923), 34-49; 171-187.
> Includes discussion on versions by Laurence Binyon and Michael Field.

Moorman, Charles. *Arthurian Triptych: Mythic Materials in Charles Williams, C.S.Lewis and T.S.Eliot.* Berkeley and Los Angeles, University of California Press, 1960.
> Compact and lucid discussion of subject.

Moorman, Charles. *A Knight There Was: the Evolution of the Knight in Literature.* Lexington: University of Kentucky Press, 1967.
> On the symbolic use of the knight in literature after the end of the age of knighthood.

Motion, Andrew. Review of *Aquarius 10: In Honour of John Heath-Stubbs* (1978) in *TLS*, 12 May 1978, p.496.

Nitze, William Albert. *Arthurian Romance and Modern Poetry and Music.* New York Haskell House, 1971. (1940).
> Series of lectures given at Chicago Art Institute. Mainly concerned with Wagner but some useful comment on E.A.Robinson.

Northup, Clarke S. and John J.Parry. 'The Arthurian Legends: Modern Retellings of the Old Stories: an Annotated Bibliography'. *JEGP*, XLIII (April, 1944), 173-221.

Reid, M.J.C. *The Arthurian Legend: Comparison of Treatment in Modern and Medieval Literature: a Study in the Literary Value of Myth and Legend.* Oliver and Boyd, 1938.
> See esp. Chapter XV. Reviewed by Eugene Vinaver in *Review of English Studies*, XVI (1940), 331-2.

Richards, Jeffrey. *Swordsmen of the Screen: from Douglas Fairbanks to Michael York.* RKP, 1977.
> Filmography in narrative form; pp.79-91 cover Arthurian films.

Starr, Nathan Comfort. *King Arthur Today: the Arthurian Legend in English and American Literature 1901-1953.* Gainsville: University of Florida Press, 1954.
> Invaluable critical work, arranged thematically.

Starr, Nathan Comfort. Review of Richard Barber's *Arthur of Albion* (1961) in *Modern Language Quarterly*, XXIII (1962), 401-2.

Steinbeck, John. *A Life in Letters.* Ed. Elaine Steinbeck and Robert Wallsten. Heinemann, 1975.
> Reveals Steinbeck's life-long obsession with the Arthurian myth and follows the progress of *The Acts of King Arthur...*

*Van Doren, Mark. *Edwin Arlington Robinson.* New York: Literary Guild of America, 1927.

Vinaver, Eugene. Review of M.J.C.Reid, *The Arthurian Legend* in *RES*, XVI (1940), 331-2.
> Terms Miss Reid's book as 'a beginner's thesis, not a work of research'.

Warner, Sylvia Townsend. *T.H.White: a Biography.* Cape with Chatto and Windus, 1967.

Whiting, B.J. 'Historical Novels 1948-1949'. *Speculum*, XXV (1950), 104-122.

Contains summaries of a number of historical novels; pp.114-7 discuss Ruth Collie Sharpe's *Tristram of Lyonesse.*

Wildman, S.G. *The Black Horseman: Some English Inns and King Arthur.* John Baker, 1971.

Explores Mr Wildman's theory that Black Horse Inns mark the extent of Arthur's kingdom.

Williamson, Hugh Ross. *The Arrow and the Sword.* Faber, 1947.

Pages 54-57 see a possible connection between Mithraic ritual and the Arthurian cycle: the Grail may correspond to the cup given to initiates.

VI

ADDITIONAL MANUSCRIPT EVIDENCE FOR THE
VERA HISTORIA DE MORTE ARTHURI

Michael Lapidge

In the first volume of this periodical I printed an edition of the anonymous *Vera Historia de Morte Arthuri* from the one complete surviving manuscript then known, namely London, Gray's Inn 7 (s. xiv in), with variant readings from an abbreviated version of the work preserved in London, British Library, Cotton Cleopatra D.III (Hailes, s. xiii/xiv).[1] Since that time Dr N.R.Ker has very kindly drawn my attention to another manuscript of the work.[2] Although this newly-discovered manuscript is at least a century later in date than the two manuscripts on which the edition was based, it is at many points a more accurate witness to the text. I give a full collation of its variant readings below.

London, British Library, Cotton Titus A.XIX[3] is a paper manuscript of fifteenth-century date and very various contents. Many of the contents pertain to the cathedral church of York (Symeon of Durham, *De pontificibus Eboracensis ecclesiae; Versus de statu regni Angliae et Eboracensis ecclesiae; Vita beati Thurstani Archiepiscopi Eboracensis*)[4] or to monasteries in the near vicinity of York.[5] The

---

1 'An Edition of the *Vera Historia de Morte Arthuri*', *Arthurian Literature* I (1981), 79-93.
2 I am extremely grateful to Dr Ker for notice of this manuscript and for much helpful advice on its construction during our consultation of it, as well as for reading this article in typescript and saving me from a number of errors.
3 There is no adequate published description of the manuscript. For certain of its contents see H.L.D.Ward and J.A.Herbert, *Catalogue of Romances in the Department of Manuscripts in the British Library*, 3 vols (London 1883-1910), I, 201, 290-2, 578-80 and 630-1; see also J.Hammer, 'Une version métrique de l'*Historia Regum Britanniae* de Geoffroy de Monmouth', *Latomus* II (1938), 131-51.
4 Most of the works pertaining to York are printed by J.Raine, *The Historians of the Church of York and its Archbishops*, 3 vols. RS (London 1879-94), II; on Cotton Titus A.XIX, see especially pp.xvi, xviii and xxvii.
5 In particular, there are several entries pertaining to Kirkstall Abbey, a Cis-

contents indicate, therefore, that the manuscript was written in York itself or its near vicinity. The manuscript itself is the work of several scribes. The scribe of the first fifteen folios (who copies *De pontificibus Eboracensis ecclesiae* and other materials) reappears later in the manuscript (ff.103r-114v) to copy a tract entitled *De origine gigantum in insula Albion*. A second scribe who copies ff.16r-43r (including materials *inter alia* pertaining to King Arthur) also reappears[6] later in the manuscript to copy Thomas Stubb's *Super statu Eboracensis ecclesiae*, a work of evident York interest.[7] It is the work of this second scribe which is important here, for it was he who copied the *Vera Historia de Morte Arthuri*. This text is found on ff.16v-17v in the company of other materials relevant to King Arthur. The collection of Arthurian material is contained on ff.16r-23r (23v is blank); its contents will be fully catalogued and studied by Richard Barber in *Arthurian Literature* III.[8] It is noteworthy that these contents include a number of items directly relevant to Glastonbury: several chapters excerpted from William of Malmesbury's *De Antiquitate Glastonie Ecclesie*, several from the fourteenth-century *Cronica* of John of Glastonbury, together with brief notices pertaining to the relics of Benignus, David and Dunstan, all of whom were venerated at Glastonbury. The local Glastonbury interest of these various items suggests that they were copied by the York scribe of Titus A.XIX from what may originally have been a single quire of Glastonbury

tercian house some 20 miles SW of York (e.g. *Notae quaedam electionis quorundam abbatum de Kyrkestall, Miscellanea de abbatia de Kyrckestall,* etc.). On the Kirkstall items in this manuscript, see J.Taylor, *The Kirkstall Abbey Chronicles*, Publications of the Thoresby Society XLII (1952), 32-5.

The connection with Kirkstall needs further exploration, for here, as in the case of the Hailes manuscript (BL, Cotton Cleopatra D.III), there may be some evidence for the circulation of the *Vera Historia* by the Cistercians.

6 The script of the two scribal stints (ff.16r-43r and 117v-143r) is similar enough to justify the assumption that the scribes are identical (the identification was kindly confirmed for me by Dr Ker). Note, however, that scribal practice varies in certain respects between the two stints (i.e. the practice of using catchwords and surrounding them with boxes found in the first stint is not employed in the later stint).

7 The point is worth stressing, for one might otherwise suspect that ff.16-43 were originally separate, given their pronounced Glastonbury interest. The point could not be proved or disproved on codicological grounds alone, for all the paper leaves of Titus A.XIX are mounted. Stubb's *Chronica Pontificum Ecclesiae Eboracensis* (which begins with the words 'Super statu Eboracensis ecclesiae') are printed by Raine, *Historians of the Church of York*, II, 312-421; Titus A.XIX is one of the best surviving manuscripts of this work.

8 'The Arthurian Materials in MS Cotton Titus A.XIX'.

origin.[9] This hypothesis need carry no implication that the *Vera Historia de Morte Arthuri* was composed at Glastonbury, only that it formed part of a collection of Arthurian materials that was assembled there. Nor is it possible to estimate when the collection was made: certainly not before 1342, the date when John of Glastonbury's *Cronica* were completed.

Titus A. XIX, therefore, offers no help in establishing the date or origin of the *Vera Historia de Morte Arthuri*, but it does provide a text which in most respects is more accurate than that contained in Gray's Inn 7, and allows us to restore some corrupt and damaged passages in that manuscript. In the following list of variants I give first the line number and lemma of my edition, followed by the corresponding reading in Titus A. XIX. I use the following sigla: G = Gray's Inn 7, H = Cleopatra D. III, T = Titus A. XIX and T[1] = a later corrector in Titus A. XIX.[10]

6   abcessit] *omitted by* T *but added in margin by* T[1]
9   reddidit acciones] acciones reddidit T
11   his] hiis T
13   residens] T[1] *adds* uero *after* residens
14-15   diligenter armis] armis diligenter T
16   quidem] igitur T
18   forma] formam T
19   equi] eque T
22   quauis] quamuis T

[9] The Glastonbury material ends on f. 23r; f. 23v is blank. The same scribe continues writing *Turpinus de gestis Karoli magni* on f. 24r. Although the paper leaves of Titus A. XIX are mounted, it would seem that ff. 16-23 may once have been a quire of 8; if so, it may be that the scribe had copied the contents of a separate quire (of Glastonbury origin) into this quire of 8, which would explain why he left a page blank before beginning a new work (with a separate exemplar) on f. 24r. Against this hypothesis one might argue that the fact that the *Vera Historia* does not state Arthur's burial to have taken place at Glastonbury makes it an unlikely choice for a Glastonbury compiler of Arthurian materials, and since there may have been a copy of the *Vera Historia* at York from the beginning of the thirteenth century (see below), the York scribe of Titus A. XIX may simply have inserted the *Vera Historia* into a collection of materials of various origin.

[10] It is not clear that the corrector was working from a copy of the *Vera Historia de Morte Arthuri*. He was able to restore one word omitted by the main scribe (6 *abcessit*), which would seem to imply collation rather than conjecture; but for the most part his corrections seem to have been made *ad libitum* with the intention of restoring what he supposed to be more elegant Latin. On several occasions he misunderstood the text and introduced errors (e.g. at line 31, where he mistakenly took *more* to be ablative of *mos* rather than genitive of *mora*).

165

24   studio] *after* studio T *adds* que
31   more] *after* more T[1] *adds* solito
31   impaciens] *after* impaciens T[1] *adds* uindicie
32   tergum] dorso T
34-5   itaque regis mortis auctore morte excepto summam] itaque regis
        mortis autore mortis excepto sentenciam T
35   oram] ora T
38   profluit] perfundit T
38   affigit] affligit T
40-1   raro bono succedit melior multo rarius optimo succedit optimus]
        raro bonus succedit melior multo rarius meliori succedit optimus T
43   uenodociam] uenedociam T
48   sollicitudinibus] sollicitudinis T
51   adiunctorum] adiuncto T
52   urien] uriam T
52   urbegenii] urgenu T
55   incommodio] incommodo T
58   largitus] largitas T
63   silicium] cilicium T
67   ista] illa T
68   raruit] tacuit T[1]
69   libertatis] libertas T[1]
70   nobilitas] *after* nobilitas T[1] *adds* subpeditata
76   ipsum] eum T
76   oratione] deuocione T
77   deuocione] oracione T
80   infuncti] defuncti T[1]
82-3   alia sua] alio loco suo T[1]
83   telluri] tellure T
85   quam] *after* quam T *adds* uiuens: T[1] *adds* adhuc *before* uiuens
92   latere premisso uno] uno latere premisso T
95   auctionum] a uiciorum T
95-6   tanto gustauit quiem suauissime domus] tanto gustauit quam
        suauis est dominus T
96   quam maiores] quid moror T
98   doctum] dictum T
98   defuncti] *after* defuncti T[1] *adds* inhumatus
101   demum] deinde T
106   celebris] crebris T
109   uero] .n. [= enim?] T
111-12 quousque] ideoque T
112   ista] illa T
114   tenebrae cernuntur] tenebris tenentur T
116   adhuc et sanus et] adhuc sanus et T
121   sublata] *after* sublata T *adds* que
124   et] *omitted by* T

127   inuencio] mensio T
129   uirtutis] uirtutum T
131   gubernauit] *after* gubernauit T¹ *adds* sine querela

These variant readings give rise to several observations. It is clear that T cannot have been copied from either G or H: not from G, because T preserves several readings omitted in G but confirmed by H; and not from H, because H offers a much-abbreviated version of the text. Furthermore, T and G often agree against H,[11] but T and H also occasionally agree against G.[12] At points where T and G preserve equally acceptable variant readings and H is not a witness, it is impossible to adjudicate between them.[13] However, T clearly preserves a text superior in most respects to that in G,[14] and nowhere more obviously so than in the passage beginning at line 94. In fact it is worth giving a revised version of this passage in the light of T:

> *Huius capelle incola fuit quidam heremita, qui, quanto fuerat a uiciorum sordibus alienus, tanto gustauit quam suauis est Dominus. Quid moror? Intrant episcopi; pro regis anima diuina misteria celebrantur; et foris, ut dictum est, manet corpus defuncti.*

> The inhabitant of this chapel was a certain hermit who, the more he had been remote from the squalor of sins, the more did he taste how sweet is the Lord. Why do I delay? The bishops enter; the holy services are performed for the soul of the king; and outside, as it is reported, the dead man's body remains.

A few other passages also require minor surgery in the light of T.[15] In sum, T is a very useful index to the amount of corruption in G; it also provides a salutary reminder that any editor working only from corrupt witnesses is unlikely to be able to restore a true reading by conjecture in every instance. In any case, a future editor of the *Vera*

---

11 The frequent agreements of T and G against H do not appear in the above list of variants, because the printed text is in effect based on G.

12 E.g. in lines 16 and 129.

13 E.g. the variants *ista / illa* (line 67), *ipsum / eum* (line 76), *ista / illa* (line 112), or the variant versions of the common proverb quoted in lines 40-1.

14 However, there are some few points where T's readings are evidently erroneous, such as the spellings of the names in line 52, and probably the readings *adiuncto* (line 51) and *mensio* (line 127) as well.

15 E.g. lines 34-5, which should now be emended to read *Itaque, regis mortis auctore mortis excepto sententiam, ilico pallor regis ora decolorat* ('Accordingly, when the author of the king's death had himself received the death sentence, pallor immediately discolours the king's visage' etc.); and lines 114-5 to read *necnon adhuc presenti tempore tenebris tenentur ignorancie* ('and even up to the present time they are held by shadows of ignorance as to where' etc.).

Historia de Morte Arthuri will necessarily have to rely on all three manuscript witnesses.

A final point may be mentioned. In Bernard's massive catalogue of the contents of English and Irish libraries published in 1697, there is a description of a manuscript in the library of York Minster which contained an item 'De morte et sepultura Arthuri regis'.[16] This manuscript survives as York, Minster Library, XVI. Q. 14. It consists of 114 folios and contains a number of twelfth-century Latin texts (Laurence of Durham, *Hypognosticon*; Hildebert of Lavardin, *Carmina de ueteri et nouo testamento*; Richard of Saint-Victor, *De tabernaculo foederis*; Alan of Lille, *Anticlaudianus*; Geoffrey of Monmouth, *Vita Merlini*, etc.); it may be dated on palaeographical grounds to s. xii/xiii and s. xiiiin.[17] Unfortunately, six items at the end of the manuscript (including the 'De morte et sepultura Arthuri regis') have been lost since the time of Bernard's catalogue. There is some possibility that 'De morte et sepultura Arthuri regis' was another copy of the *Vera Historia de Morte Arthuri*, but certainty in the matter is impossible unless the lost leaves of MS XVI.Q.14 can be recovered. But if it was indeed the *Vera Historia de Morte Arthuri*, then two copies of that work were available at York from the fifteenth century on.[18] In any case, we now have evidence of three (and possibly five) manuscripts of the *Vera Historia de Morte Arthuri* from various parts of the country: one (or two) from York, one from Chester, one from Hailes (Glos.), and perhaps one (later lost) from Glastonbury. This widespread geographical distribution indicates that the work had a far wider circulation than hitherto suspected,[19] and that there need be no difficulty in the assumption (say) that it could have been available to Malory. It now remains to be seen whether further manuscript evidence will come to light.

[16] E. Bernard, *Catalogi librorum manuscriptorum Angliae et Hiberniae*, 2 vols in 1 (Oxford 1697), II, pt.1, 4 (item no.42).

[17] A full description of this manuscript is forthcoming in vol.IV of Ker's *Medieval Manuscripts in British Libraries*.

[18] Given the later York provenance of the manuscript, there is some probability that it was written there as well. However, there is no certain evidence in the manuscript itself that it was at York before the fifteenth century, and two scribbles of sixteenth-century date on f.57r ('Assit principio sancta maria meo Ampthyll') and f.64v ('Iohannes Conyngesby') are unhelpful in tracing the manuscript's history, as Dr Ker points out to me.

[19] See the remarks of Richard Barber in *Arthurian Literature* I (1981), 70, who suggests that 'we are dealing with a text which evidently had a modest circulation'. The manuscript evidence presented here suggests wide circulation but perhaps infrequent copying.